LAWS AND LEGISLATION

A SELECTION OF FEDERAL ACTS

SUMMARIES AND ANALYSES

Laws and Legislation

Additional books in this series can be found on Nova's website
under the Series tab.

Additional e-books in this series can be found on Nova's website
under the e-books tab.

Government Procedures and Operations

Additional books in this series can be found on Nova's website
under the Series tab.

Additional e-books in this series can be found on Nova's website
under the e-books tab.

LAWS AND LEGISLATION

A SELECTION OF FEDERAL ACTS

SUMMARIES AND ANALYSES

PATRICIA BROWN
AND
KEVIN M. MITCHELL
EDITORS

nova publishers
New York

For permission to use material from this book please contact us:
Telephone 631-231-7269; Fax 631-231-8175
Web Site: http://www.novapublishers.com

Additional color graphics may be available in the e-book version of this book.

Library of Congress Cataloging-in-Publication Data

ISBN: 978-1-62417-047-8

Published by Nova Science Publishers, Inc. † New York

CONTENTS

PREFACE

This book present a selection of federal acts including the Posse Comitatus Act; the Foreign Corrupt Practices Act (FCPA); the Arsenal Act; the Emergency Planning and Community Right-to-Know Act (EPCRA); the Toxic Substances Control Act (TSCA); the Fair Credit Reporting Act and the Combating Autism Act.

Chapter 1 - The Constitution permits Congress to authorize the use of the militia "to execute the Laws of the Union, suppress Insurrections and repel Invasions." And it guarantees the states protection against invasion or usurpation of their "republican form of government," and, upon the request of the state legislature, against "domestic violence." These constitutional provisions are reflected in the Insurrection Acts, which have been invoked numerous times both before and after passage of the Posse Comitatus Act, 18 U.S.C. § 1385, in 1878. Congress has also enacted a number of statutes that authorize the use of the land and naval forces to execute their objective. The Posse Comitatus Act outlaws the willful use of any part of the Army or Air Force to execute the law unless expressly authorized by the Constitution or an act of Congress. History supplies the grist for an argument that the Constitution prohibits military involvement in civilian affairs subject to only limited alterations by Congress or the President, but the courts do not appear to have ever accepted the argument unless violation of more explicit constitutional command could also be shown. The express statutory exceptions include the legislation that allows the President to use military force to suppress insurrection or to enforce federal authority, 10 U.S.C. §§ 331-335, and laws that permit the Department of Defense to provide federal, state and local police with information, equipment, and personnel, 10 U.S.C. §§ 371-382.

Chapter 2 - The Foreign Corrupt Practices Act of 1977 (FCPA) was enacted principally to prevent corporate bribery of foreign officials. This act had three major parts: (1) it required the keeping by corporations of accurate books, records, and accounts; (2) it required issuers registered with the Securities and Exchange Commission to maintain a responsible internal accounting control system; and (3) it prohibited bribery by American corporations of foreign officials. For a number of years after passage of the act, Congress debated amending it in response to numerous criticisms. On August 23, 1988, the President signed into law the Omnibus Trade and Competitiveness Act of 1988, of which Title V is known as the Foreign Corrupt Practices Act Amendments of 1988.

Chapter 3 - The Arsenal Act (10 U.S.C. §4532) requires the Secretary of the Army to have all supplies needed by the Army to be made in government-owned factories or arsenals if this can be accomplished "on an economical basis." It also grants the Secretary the authority to "abolish any United States arsenal that he considers unnecessary." This broad mandate, and even broader authority, has lead some observers to question whether the Department of the Army is abiding by either the spirit or the letter of the law in awarding development and procurement contracts. Others have expressed concern that the seeming unilateral authority to abolish arsenals could place them at a disadvantage should the Department of Defense (DOD) seek to close military installations. Federal arsenals, those government-owned industrial sites that have produced the engines of war for the United States Army virtually since the birth of the nation, exist and operate under the jurisdiction of the Secretary of the Army. They, along with their naval counterparts in the form of federally owned shipyards, have sustained the military services for more than two centuries.

Chapter 4 - This report summarizes the Emergency Planning and Community Right-to-Know Act (EPCRA) and the major regulatory programs that mandate reporting by industrial facilities of releases of potentially hazardous chemicals to the environment, as well as local planning to respond in the event of significant, accidental releases. The Emergency Planning and Community Right-to-Know Act (42 U.S.C. 11001-11050) was enacted in 1986 as Title III of the Superfund Amendments and Reauthorization Act (P.L. 99-499). In Subtitle A, EPCRA established a national framework for the U.S. Environmental Protection Agency (EPA) to mobilize local government officials, businesses, and other citizens to plan ahead for chemical accidents in their communities. EPCRA required each state to create a State Emergency Response Commission (SERC), to designate emergency planning districts, and to establish local emergency planning committees (LEPCs) for each district. EPA is required to list extremely hazardous substances, and to establish threshold planning quantities for each substance. The law directs each facility to notify the LEPC for its district if it stores or uses any "extremely hazardous substance" in excess of its threshold planning quantity. LEPCs are to work with such facilities to develop response procedures, evacuation plans, and training programs for people who will be the first to respond in the event of an accident. EPCRA requires that facilities immediately report a sudden release of any hazardous substance that exceeds the reportable quantity to appropriate state, local, and federal officials.

Chapter 5 - This report summarizes the Toxic Substances Control Act (TSCA) and the major regulatory programs dealing with chemical production and distribution in U.S. commerce. The President's Council on Environmental Quality proposed comprehensive federal legislation in 1971 to identify and control potentially dangerous chemicals in U.S. commerce that were not adequately regulated under other environmental statutes. President Ford signed TSCA into law on October 11, 1976. Subsequently, five titles were added to address specific concerns—asbestos in 1986 (Title II, P.L. 99-519), radon in 1988 (Title III, P.L. 100-551), lead in 1992 (Title IV, P.L. 102-550), environmental and energy issues in schools in 2007 (Title V, P.L. 110-140), and formaldehyde emissions from composite wood products in 2010 (Title VI, P.L. 111-199). In 2008, Congress added provisions to Title I, Section 6 and Section 12, banning certain activities with respect to elemental mercury (P.L. 110-414).

Chapter 6 - The purpose of the Fair Credit Reporting Act (FCRA) is "to require that consumer reporting agencies adopt reasonable procedures for meeting the needs of commerce for consumer credit, personnel, insurance, and other information in a manner which is fair and equitable to the consumer, with regard to the confidentiality, accuracy, relevancy, and proper utilization of such information." The FCRA establishes consumers' rights in relation to their credit reports, as well as permissible uses of credit reports. It also imposes certain responsibilities on those who collect, furnish, and use the information contained in consumers' credit reports. The FCRA has been amended several times over the last decade. The Fair and Accurate Credit Transactions Act of 2003 (FACT Act, P.L. 108-159) amended the FCRA to include a number of provisions aimed at preventing identity theft and assisting victims. The Credit Card Accountability Responsibility and Disclosure Act of 2009 (Credit CARD Act, P.L. 111-24) strengthened protections for young consumers and advertising disclosures regarding free credit reports from consumer reporting agencies. More recently, the Consumer Financial Protection Act of 2010, part of the Dodd-Frank Wall Street Reform and Consumer Protection Act (P.L. 111-203), established the Consumer Financial Protection Bureau and transferred administrative functions, including most rulemaking and reporting, as well as certain enforcement functions, from other federal agencies, such as the Federal Trade Commission and the Federal Reserve Board, to the Bureau.

Chapter 7 - Autism spectrum disorder (ASD) and autism are general terms for a group of developmental disabilities that cause impairments in social skills and communication, and are often characterized by certain atypical behaviors. The federal government has a role in the financing (through Medicaid and State Children's Health Insurance Programs) and delivery (through funding of developmental disabilities programming in schools, Title V Maternal and Child Health funding, and other sources) of treatment for ASD. The number of autism cases and their appropriate diagnosis and treatment affect federal and state expenditures. As such, Congress has shown interest in financing research on ASD prevalence, causes, and optimal treatment for individuals with ASD. On September 26, 2011, the 112th Congress passed the Combating Autism Reauthorization Act (CARA, P.L. 112-32), which reauthorized funding for autism research authorized under the Combating Autism Act of 2006 (CAA, P.L. 109-416). The CAA was enacted to address public and congressional concern with growing rates of autism; to increase existing autism research funding authorizations; and to stimulate state-level coordination of health, education, and disability programs. The CAA authorizes funding for ASD surveillance, research, and education at the Department of Health and Human Services (HHS), at the Centers for Disease Control and Prevention (CDC), the Health Resources and Services Administration (HRSA), and the National Institutes of Health (NIH).

In: A Selection of Federal Acts
Editors: P. Brown and K. M. Mitchell
ISBN: 978-1-62417-047-8

Chapter 1

THE POSSE COMITATUS ACT AND RELATED MATTERS: THE USE OF THE MILITARY TO EXECUTE CIVILIAN LAW*

Charles Doyle and Jennifer K. Elsea

SUMMARY

The Constitution permits Congress to authorize the use of the militia "to execute the Laws of the Union, suppress Insurrections and repel Invasions." And it guarantees the states protection against invasion or usurpation of their "republican form of government," and, upon the request of the state legislature, against "domestic violence." These constitutional provisions are reflected in the Insurrection Acts, which have been invoked numerous times both before and after passage of the Posse Comitatus Act, 18 U.S.C. § 1385, in 1878. Congress has also enacted a number of statutes that authorize the use of the land and naval forces to execute their objective.

The Posse Comitatus Act outlaws the willful use of any part of the Army or Air Force to execute the law unless expressly authorized by the Constitution or an act of Congress. History supplies the grist for an argument that the Constitution prohibits military involvement in civilian affairs subject to only limited alterations by Congress or the President, but the courts do not appear to have ever accepted the argument unless violation of more explicit constitutional command could also be shown. The express statutory exceptions include the legislation that allows the President to use military force to suppress insurrection or to enforce federal authority, 10 U.S.C. §§ 331-335, and laws that permit the Department of Defense to provide federal, state and local police with information, equipment, and personnel, 10 U.S.C. §§ 371-382.

Case law indicates that "execution of the law" in violation of the Posse Comitatus Act occurs (a) when the Armed Forces perform tasks assigned to an organ of civil government, or (b) when the Armed Forces perform tasks assigned to them solely for purposes of civilian

* This is an edited, reformatted and augmented version of the Congressional Research Service Publication, CRS Report for Congress R42659, dated August 16, 2012.

government. Questions concerning the act's application arise most often in the context of assistance to civilian police. At least in this context, the courts have held that, absent a recognized exception, the Posse Comitatus Act is violated when (1) civilian law enforcement officials make "direct active use" of military investigators; or (2) the use of the military "pervades the activities" of the civilian officials; or (3) the military is used so as to subject "citizens to the exercise of military power which was regulatory, prescriptive, or compulsory in nature." The act is not violated when the Armed Forces conduct activities for a military purpose.

The language of the act mentions only the Army and the Air Force, but it is applicable to the Navy and Marines by virtue of administrative action and commands of other laws. The law enforcement functions of the Coast Guard have been expressly authorized by act of Congress and consequently cannot be said to be contrary to the act. The act has been applied to the National Guard when it is in federal service, to civilian employees of the Armed Forces, and to off-duty military personnel. The act probably only applies within the geographical confines of the United States, but the supplemental provisions of 10 U.S.C. §§ 371-382 appear to apply worldwide.

Finally, the act is a criminal statute under which there has been but a handful of known prosecutions. Although violations will on rare occasions result in the exclusion of evidence, the dismissal of criminal charges, or a civil cause of action, as a practical matter compliance is ordinarily the result of military self-restraint.

This report provides an historical analysis of the use of the Armed Forces to execute domestic law and of the Posse Comitatus Act, including their apparent theoretical and constitutional underpinnings. The report then outlines the current application of the act as well as its statutory exceptions, and reviews the consequences of its violation.

> Whoever, except in cases and under circumstances expressly authorized by the Constitution or Act of Congress, willfully uses any part of the Army or the Air Force as a posse comitatus or otherwise to execute the laws shall be fined under this title or imprisoned not more than two years, or both. 18 U.S.C. § 1385.

INTRODUCTION

Americans have a tradition, born in England and developed in the early years of our nation, that abhors military involvement in civilian affairs, at least under ordinary circumstances. It finds its most tangible expression in the 19th century Posse Comitatus Act, 18 U.S.C. § 1385, which forbids use of the Army and (as amended) the Air Force to execute civil law except where expressly authorized.

The exception documents a contrary component of the tradition. Congress has expressly approved the use of the Armed Forces in extraordinary circumstances or where federal manpower to enforce the law was seen as inadequate. Striking the balance between rule and exception has never been easy, but failure to do so has often proven unfortunate. If the rule is too unforgiving, a Shays's Rebellion may go unchecked. If exceptions are too generously granted, a Boston Massacre or Kent State tragedy may follow.

The terrorist attacks against the United States in September 2001 produced some calls for more generous exceptions to the rule.[1] The USA PATRIOT Act[2] broadened the permissible circumstances for the use of the military to assist law enforcement agencies in countering terrorism,[3] but Congress also reaffirmed its determination to maintain the principle of the posse comitatus law.[4] The perceived breakdown in civil law and order in Hurricane Katrina's wake evoked more calls to reevaluate the military's role in responding to disasters.[5] The possibility of using military surveillance equipment and resources, including unmanned aerial vehicles (drones), to assist civilian law enforcement has raised some objections based on the military role. This report provides an historical analysis of the use of the Armed Forces to execute domestic law and of the Posse Comitatus Act, including their apparent theoretical and constitutional underpinnings. The report then outlines the current application of the Posse Comitatus Act as well as its statutory exceptions, and reviews the consequences of its violation.

BACKGROUND

The Magna Carta provides the first recorded acknowledgment of the origins of the Anglo-American tradition against military involvement in civilian affairs with its declaration that "no free man shall be ... imprisoned ... or in any other way destroyed ... except by the legal judgment of his peers or by the law of the land."[6] Subsequent legislation in the reign of Edward III explained that this precluded punishment by the King except "in due Manner ... or by Process made by Writ ... [or] by Course of the Law,"[7] or as later more simply stated, except "by due Process of the Law."[8] Three hundred years after the passage of the Edwardian statutes, Lord Coke and other members of Parliament read these due process and law of the land requirements to include a broad prohibition against the use of martial law in peacetime, an interpretation they compelled King Charles I to acknowledge.[9]

King Charles I, preparing for a military expedition in France, had quartered his troops in homes along the southern English coastline.[10] Rioting resulted, and the participants, both military and civilian, were tried and punished by commissioners operating under the authority of martial law. Offended by this peacetime exercise of military judicial authority over civilians, Parliament sought and was granted the Petition of Right of 1628, which outlawed both quartering and martial law commissions.[11]

When, in the following century, the British responded to colonial unrest by quartering troops in Boston, the colonists saw it as a breach of this fundamental promise of English law. Their circumstances, however, were not exactly identical to those surrounding the Petition of Right. First, the question arose in the British colonies rather than England itself. England had stationed troops in the colonies to protect them against the French and Indians and had opted for military governorships in other territories. Second, there was no military usurpation of judicial functions. The colonists remained subject to civil rather than military justice, and soldiers who employed more force than civilian law permitted were themselves subject to civilian justice as the trial of the soldiers involved in the Boston Massacre demonstrates.

On the other hand, the troops involved in the Boston Massacre were stationed in Massachusetts not for protection against a marauding invader as they had been in the French and Indian Wars, nor to accomplish the transition between civil governments within a conquered territory as they had been after the French lost Canada to the British as a consequence of those conflicts, but as an independent military force quartered among a disgruntled civilian population to police it.[12] Public resentment of the use of the troops in such a manner sparked the incident, which led in turn to further heightened resentment.[13]

In any event, the experience was sufficiently vexing that the Declaration of Independence listed among our grievances against Great Britain that the King had "kept among us, in times of peace, Standing Armies without the consent of our legislatures," had "affected to render the Military independent of and superior to the civil power," and had "quarter[ed] large bodies of armed troops among us ... protecting them, by a mock trial, from punishment for any murders which they should commit on the inhabitants of these States."[14]

The Articles of Confederation for the newly established United States addressed the threat of military intrusion into civilian affairs by demanding that the Armed Forces assembled during peacetime be no more numerous than absolutely necessary for the common defense; by entrusting control to civil authorities within the states; and by a preference for the farmer in arms as a member of the militia over the standing professional army.[15]

The Constitution continued these themes, albeit with greater authority vested in the federal government. It provided that a civilian (the President) should be the Commander in Chief of the Army and Navy of the United States, and civilian authorities (Congress) should be solely empowered to raise and support Armies, provide and maintain a Navy, and make rules for their government and regulation.[16] The Bill of Rights limited the quartering of troops in private homes,[17] and noted that "a well regulated Militia, being necessary to the security of a free State, the right of the people to keep and bear Arms, shall not be infringed."[18] The Constitution, on the other hand, explicitly permitted Congress to provide for calling out the militia to execute the laws, suppress insurrection, and repel invasion.[19]

The Use of Federal Troops Prior to 1878

Notwithstanding the founders' aversion to the use of a standing army to control the civilian populace, the Constitution nowhere explicitly prohibits it, and Congress lost no time in authorizing the President to call out the militia for the purposes permitted under the Constitution. Despite the retention of most police powers by the several states, Congress quickly established a law enforcement capability in the federal government in order to effectuate its constitutional powers and provide a means to enforce the process of federal courts.[20] This authority was vested through the President in federal marshals, who were empowered to call upon the posse comitatus[21] to assist them, an authority similar to that enjoyed by the sheriff at common law,[22] and which was understood to include the authority to call for military assistance.

Thus, the militia under federal control (and later the Armed Forces) could operate either as an arm of the government or to support the federal marshal. These two roles of the military were similar in many respects, but, at least in theory, differed in one key aspect: troops serving as a posse comitatus remained subordinate to civil law enforcement authorities, while troops called up to suppress an insurrection or remove an obstruction to the execution of the laws supplanted civil authorities that had been rendered ineffective. In some cases, if the marshal feared he would be unable to control a disturbance even with the aid of a posse, or if local military commanders declined to give assistance, the marshal would try to persuade the President that an insurrection was underway. At other times, the President might order troops to quell what appeared to amount to an insurrection, yet limit the role of the Armed Forces to responding to the requests of the appropriate civil official, possibly dispensing with the need to issue the requisite proclamation under the Insurrection Act.

In addition, Congress has from time to time enacted statutes authorizing federal troops to enforce specific proscriptions, sometimes in aid of civil authorities and sometimes (apparently) in their stead, and Presidents have issued proclamations exhorting all federal officials, civilian or military, to assist in arresting a particular conspiracy or uprising.[23] It is not always easy to ascertain which statutory authority (if any) forms the basis for sending in federal troops.

Presidents have relied upon the militia and Armed Forces with some frequency for riot control or when in extreme cases they felt it necessary to ensure the execution of federal law.[24] The following sections provide an overview of the domestic employment of military forces and the statutes that govern such use.

The Insurrection Act and other Statutes

Soon after Congress was first assembled under the Constitution, it authorized the President to call out the militia, initially to protect the frontier against "hostile incursions of the Indians,"[25] and subsequently in cases of invasion, insurrection, or obstruction of the laws.[26] Soon thereafter, and echoing Article I, § 8, cl. 15 and Article IV, § 4 of the Constitution, Congress enacted the Calling Forth Act, authorizing the President to call out the militia in case of invasion or, at the request of a state legislature (or its governor, if the legislature could not be convened) in case of an insurrection within a state.[27] Congress also empowered the President to call forth the militia, for a period of 30 days,

> whenever the laws of the United States shall be opposed, or the execution thereof obstructed, in any state, by combinations too powerful to be suppressed by the ordinary course of judicial proceedings, or by the powers vested in the marshals by this act, the same being notified to the President of the United States, by an associate justice or the district judge.[28]

In any of these events, the President was first required to issue a proclamation commanding the "insurgents" to disperse.[29] President Washington used this authority to put down the Whiskey Rebellion in western Pennsylvania.[30] After the authority expired two years later, Congress reenacted virtually the same language, except that a court finding was no longer necessary, and the proclamation to disperse did not have to occur prior to calling up the militia.[31] It appears that the Calling Forth Act was understood to cover the use of the militia and Armed Forces as an aid to civilian power or, in rare cases, as a means of temporarily supplanting local civilian authority.[32]

Both provisions of the Calling Forth Act were extended in 1807 to allow for the employment of the Army and Navy in domestic circumstances where the militia could be employed.[33] Even before this change, President John Adams had used regular federal troops to put down, more by intimidation rather than the actual use of force,[34] the 1799 Fries Rebellion in eastern Pennsylvania.[35] The cavalry arrested the instigator of the resistance, John Fries, along with other participants, and turned them over to civil authorities to be tried for treason. Those convicted were eventually pardoned.[36]

Resistance to Taxes and Duties

As in the Whiskey and Fries Rebellions, resistance to the laws of the United States during the early years of the republic had mainly to do with citizens' objections to steadily increasing federal taxes, which were largely necessary to build up the military establishment,[37] and other laws that tended to make themselves felt in citizens' pocketbooks. In 1808, President Jefferson called out federal troops to suppress opposition to the Embargo Act[38] by groups of traders in Vermont whose livelihood depended on imports and exports with Canada.[39] Congress subsequently amended the Embargo Act specifically to authorize the use of troops to enforce the embargo.[40] Although President Jefferson followed the contemporary practice of turning to states' governors to supply militia in support of revenue collectors, resentment at the newly enacted authority to use federal military force to enforce ordinary laws in the absence of armed resistance led to a speedy demise of the embargo statute.[41]

In 1832, resistance to revenue laws again led to the prospect of using federal troops. Southerners objected to the system of protective tariffs that had been adopted in 1816 after the post-war resumption of trade threatened new domestic industries. Rather than gradually reducing the tariffs, as it had indicated was its intent, Congress steadily increased the tariff until by 1832 it became a policy fixture.[42] Southerners believed that the money was raised unfairly at their expense and was expended mainly for the benefit of Northerners. The legislature of South Carolina voted to nullify the tariff and declared the state ready to meet force with force in the event the federal government sought to collect the tax.[43] Congress passed a "Force Bill" to authorize the President to use the Army and Navy to collect duties,[44] but at the same time reduced the duties. South Carolina rescinded its nullification ordinance, bringing the confrontation to an end without the use of force (although, as a final defiant gesture, it issued a new ordinance to nullify the Force Bill).

Neutrality Act Enforcement

The early U.S. desire to avoid foreign entanglements of the sort that kept Europe in arms during the founders' era manifested itself in a policy of neutrality which tended, at times, to conflict with the economic interests or political views of some part of the citizenry.[45] Congress enacted a statute to prohibit the enlistment in or recruitment for foreign military service, the arming of foreign war vessels or privateers, and the dispatch of military expeditions against the territory of a state at peace with the United States.[46] The statute also empowered the President to call upon the Armed Forces to detain or take possession of illicitly armed vessels and to prevent expeditions from departing U.S. territory.[47] Even prior to its enactment, President Washington had called on state militias to deal with efforts of the French Ambassador to fit out privateers and military expeditions against British and Spanish interests.[48] President Jefferson relied on this authority to counter Aaron Burr's conspiracy in 1806[49] as well as other schemes to liberate Spain's South American colonies.[50] State militias employed for this purpose remained under the control of their respective governors.[51]

In 1836, at the time of Texas's struggle for independence from Mexico, the Armed Forces were employed in an effort to prevent armed American sympathizers from crossing the border to join the fight[52] in violation of the Neutrality Act of 1818,[53] which expressly authorized the employment of the militia and Armed Forces in its enforcement. The next year, the Army was employed in a similar vein to quiet militant activity along the Canadian border.[54] President Zachary Taylor issued a proclamation urging all officials, "civil and military," to halt a planned expedition to attack Cuba,[55] which resulted in the Navy dispatching vessels to New Orleans to prevent the expedition from departing.[56] To prevent American sympathizers from aiding Cuban separatists during the Ten Years' War and to halt Fenian expeditions against Canada, President Grant issued a proclamation in 1870 urging civil and military officers to take measures to prevent expeditions in violation of neutrality and bring violators to justice.[57]

Requests from States for Military Aid

Section 2 of the Calling Forth Act, authorizing the President to employ military force when the state made a proper application for assistance, lay dormant until the 1830s, when violence between contending groups of Irish laborers on the Chesapeake and Ohio Canal led Maryland's legislature to request federal aid in 1834. President Jackson promptly endorsed the request to the Secretary of War and ordered "at least two companies of regulars" be sent to aid state civil authorities, without, however, issuing a proclamation to the laborers to disperse.[58] The presence of federal troops helped to stabilize the situation without requiring any actual use of force.[59]

A second request was occasioned in 1838, when both parties to the Pennsylvania state election claimed victory and set about to establish majority control of the state House. When public reaction turned violent, the governor called out the militia and requested aid from the local military commander, who denied the request. The governor then appealed to President Van Buren for federal assistance under the Domestic Violence Clause of the Constitution. Despite that clause's guarantee of protection, President Van Buren took the position that his duty was discretionary, and believing the domestic violence was not of a character that the "State authorities, civil and military ... have proved inadequate to suppress it," he declined to authorize assistance.[60] In the meantime, however, the commanding general of the U.S. arsenal at Frankford brought men and ordnance in response to the governor's request. The "Buckshot War" ended without armed confrontation, but the general was reprimanded by the War Department for acting without authorization.[61]

A more serious state of affairs was reached in Rhode Island in 1842, where dissatisfaction with the government under the state's charter, still that granted by King Charles II in 1663, led to efforts to draft a new constitution. Two separate conventions were established, resulting in two separate sets of government officials claiming legitimate authority. The governor under the charter declared martial law and requested the President provide federal troops to stop the feared violence, but President Tyler declared he had no power to anticipate insurrections. Three more similar requests were similarly denied.

After the Civil War, federal troops were requested numerous times to suppress violence related to labor disputes. In 1877, in response to strikes and related violence that erupted after railroads cut the pay of their workers by 10%, federal troops were requested by the governors of Pennsylvania,[62] West Virginia,[63] Maryland,[64] Illinois,[65] and Missouri, Indiana,[66] Wisconsin, California, and Kentucky,[67] with varying degrees of conformity to the requirements of the Insurrection Act, as interpreted by President Hayes.[68] Although Ohio's governor did not request federal troops to quell strike-related violence in Toledo, Cincinnati, and other places, local officials appealed for assistance from nearby military commanders.[69] No direct help was given, although supplies of arms from Rock Island Arsenal were made available to the state. It has been suggested that federal authority might have been asserted on the basis of the protection of a federal function (i.e., the delivery of the mail), but either due to an understanding that federal assistance to enforce state law was constitutionally unavailable without the request of the state government, or due to the lack of available federal troops, the President made no effort to do so.[70]

Questions regarding the federal versus state control of troops arose during the 1877 riots.[71] In West Virginia and Maryland, federal troops were placed under the command of the governors to be employed alongside state troops. In Indiana, where the governor's request was initially turned down for lack of compliance under the Constitution and Insurrection Act,[72] federal troops were to be furnished on the request of the federal marshal as a posse comitatus and were not turned over to the governor. When disorder spread to Pennsylvania, federal troops were initially sent in to protect federal property, the governor's first request for assistance having apparently been deemed deficient.[73] After the deficiencies were corrected and a proclamation was issued, the general officer in charge of federal troops requested clarification as to the disposition of federal troops[74] and espoused the doctrine that whenever a state government asks for assistance under the Insurrection Act, federal military power should supplant local civil authority:

> When the governor of a State has declared his inability to suppress an insurrection and has called upon the President of the United States under the Constitution to do so, that from that time commences a state not of peace but of war, and that although civil local authority still exists, yet the only outcome is to resort to force through the Federal military authorities, and that can only be through a subordination of the State authorities for the time being and until lawful order is restored; otherwise there can be no complete exercise of power in a military way within the limits of the State by the Federal officers.[75]

The doctrine appears to have gained the approval of President Hayes, at least insofar as it had to do with command of state troops, although a telegram advising the commander to in effect federalize state troops arrived too late to be carried into effect.[76] The proposed equation of insurrection to war calling for the substitution of military force for ordinary methods of law enforcement seems to have found its way into later War Department manuals regarding the military role in civil disturbances.[77]

Trouble in the Western States and Territories

U.S. troops were sent to deal with disputes in western territories and new states on several occasions. In California, the failure of the governor to request assistance under the Insurrection Act led to a denial of military assistance. The California Gold Rush was marked by a heightened tendency toward lawlessness, which was for a time brought under relative control by vigilantes. The self-appointed Vigilance Committee of San Francisco, which had been allowed to operate separately from federal and local law enforcement authorities, refused to surrender a prisoner to the federal court under a writ of habeas corpus.[78] The governor called out the militia to put down the insurrection, and, having received a less than enthusiastic response, requested assistance from the Army, and when that was refused, from the President. The Attorney General advised the President that the situation was not sufficiently dire to require federal intervention,[79] and noted that during the month of turmoil said to require armed intervention, no effort had been made to convene the legislature. When the Vigilante Committee took another prisoner, a judge of the California Supreme Court, the state governor again requested assistance from the military, this time from the commander of a ship in the harbor. Again, the request was turned down. The senior naval commander in San

Francisco, stressing the constitutional requirements for requesting aid from the federal government to put down domestic violence, instructed the ship's captain that there was to be no interference in the domestic troubles of the state.

The territory of Utah was the site of considerable resistance to federal law after it was established in 1850 and Brigham Young, the head of the Mormon Church, appointed its governor.[80] Most inhabitants of Utah were also members of the Church and tended to regard laws not emanating from the governor to be invalid, eventually compelling nearly all federal officials to leave the territory for their own safety.[81] In 1857, the President appointed a new governor, and federal Armed Forces were sent in to ensure a peaceful transfer of power.[82] Governor Young responded by declaring martial law and forbidding any Armed Forces from entering the territory.[83] It was not until April 1858 that President Buchanan issued a proclamation offering amnesty to those who would obey the law and promising to prosecute those who did not.[84] The proclamation was not

Slavery, the Civil War, and Reconstruction

In 1831, federal troops were sent out on several occasions to respond to reports of slave insurrections, initially in New Orleans and later in Virginia, Maryland, Delaware, and the Carolinas. These actions appear to have been undertaken by the local military commandants in response to requests from local officials, and do not appear to have been justified by any statute or presidential proclamation.[85]

During troubles related to the slavery issue in Kansas in 1856, President Pierce issued a proclamation commanding persons involved in unlawful combinations to disperse.[86] In the following months, the new governor sent frequent requests to the commandants at Ft. Leavenworth and Ft. Riley for troops to disband a territorial militia that had formed in Lawrence.[87] When Kansas's pending entry into the Union in 1858 again brought tensions to a head, the governor called upon the commander of U.S. troops for troops to act "as a posse comitatus in aid of the civil authorities."[88] There does not appear to have been another proclamation under the Insurrection Act, and since only the federal marshal and his deputies were empowered to request the assistance of the military as a posse comitatus, there was no statutory basis for this action. Rather, it appears to have been an exercise of the newly emerging theory known as the Cushing Doctrine, explained below, under which the Armed Forces could act as a posse comitatus to enforce the law without invoking the Insurrection Act or other law that permitted the use of the Armed Forces.

At the dawn of the secessionist movement that led to the Civil War, President Buchanan declined to send troops into seceding states, apparently based on his misapprehension that any troops dispatched to execute the laws of the Union would necessarily be subordinate to civil authorities.[89] He informed Congress that because federal law enforcement and judicial machinery in those areas had already been demolished, his duty to execute the law could not be accomplished even with the aid of military troops.[90] On coming into office, President Lincoln took a very different view, at times using federal military power without subordination to civil authority even in loyal Union states.[91] Congress also enacted a new provision to replace Section 2 of the Calling Forth Act, adding "rebellions" to instances for which the use of the Armed Forces was envisioned and to change the standard from a situation in which a combination or obstruction to law enforcement was "too powerful to be suppressed by the ordinary course of judicial proceedings" to one in which the unlawful obstruction or assemblage "make[s] it impracticable to enforce the laws ... by the ordinary course of judicial proceedings."[92]

The successful suppression of the rebellion did not put an end to violence in the South. The Reconstruction period after the Civil War was characterized by constant political turbulence in the South.[93] Efforts to establish new governments in former Confederate states were particularly contentious during the decade following the Civil War, and Presidents received more requests for military aid from state governors during these years than all previous decades combined, sometimes receiving simultaneous requests from two rival governors claiming legitimacy in the same state after an election.[94]

Resistance to efforts to achieve equal status for newly freed blacks led Congress to pass the Civil Rights Act of 1871 (also called the "Ku Klux Klan Act"),[95] which among other things added a new insurrection provision permitting the President to employ the land and naval forces to enforce civil rights. This authority was used immediately after enactment when President Grant issued a proclamation calling attention to the new law and declaring himself ready to invoke it if necessary.[96] This was followed several months later by a proclamation under the new act commanding conspirators in nine counties in South Carolina to disperse within five days and turn in their firearms, ammunition, and disguises to the local marshals or military officers,[97] and shortly thereafter by a proclamation suspending habeas corpus, as permitted under Section 4 of the act.[98] Hundreds of suspected Klansmen were arrested over the following months and tried in district court.[99]

Use of Military Forces as a Posse Comitatus

Even though Congress had since 1792 empowered the President to call out the militia to overcome obstructions to law enforcement and it had also provided authority in a number of statutes for the President to employ the land and naval forces for certain law enforcement purposes, it was understood that federal law enforcement officials could themselves call on local military commanders for assistance without involving the President. Congress had vested the federal equivalent of the sheriff, the federal marshal, with the power to call forth the posse comitatus in performance of his duties.[100] The federal marshals and their deputies were thus implicitly empowered to request the assistance of the military when force became necessary to execute the process of federal courts, but the military units serving on a posse were to remain subordinate to the marshal and could not initiate legal proceedings.[101]

In some cases when it passed a particular statute, Congress specifically authorized recourse to the posse comitatus for its enforcement. The Fugitive Slave Act[102] was such a law, and its use led to the crystallization of the government's doctrine regarding the use of the military in the role of a posse.[103] Under that act, owners whose slaves had escaped to another state were entitled to an arrest warrant for the slaves and to have the warrant executed by the federal marshals. The marshals in turn might "summon and call to their aid the bystanders, or *posse comitatus* of the proper county ... [and] all good citizens [were] commanded to aid and assist in the prompt and efficient execution of this law, whenever their services may be required, as aforesaid, for that purpose."[104] The act did not specifically authorize the use of the military or militia in its execution, but when particularly fierce opposition arose in Boston in 1851, the President issued a proclamation requiring "all officers and persons, civil and military to aid and assist by all means in their power in quelling [such] combinations.... "[105]

The Secretary of War sent orders to Army units to be ready to respond to the call of a marshal or deputy, or the certification of a federal judge stating that military force would likely be necessary.[106] Troops in Boston Harbor were made ready to intervene in the event of a riot, but such intervention was unnecessary.

When asked by the Senate whether sufficient authority for vigorous enforcement of the Fugitive Slave Act was available, President Fillmore advanced the doctrine that his use of the Army and Navy to enforce federal law was an inherent power, suggesting that it ought not be construed as restricted by the Insurrection Act's requirements, in particular that of issuing a proclamation to disperse.[107] He also made the argument that all citizens, whether enrolled in any military service or not, may be summoned as a posse comitatus, while conceding doubt as to whether an organized military force acting under military command might be employed in such a manner.[108] The Senate Judiciary Committee declared that it saw no reason to consider military members exempt from duty to serve as a posse comitatus, whether as individuals or organized under their ordinary command structure.[109]

In June of 1851, a federal marshal in Chicago arrested a fugitive slave on a warrant issued under the act. He called for the assistance of members of the police force and of the state militia to prevent abolitionists from rescuing the prisoner before he could be returned to his owner. The marshal subsequently filed a claim with the Department of the Treasury for reimbursement of the funds he had paid the members of the police force and the militia who responded to his call. Attorney General Caleb Cushing was asked whether the United States was obligated to honor the claim. While this question remained pending, another incident in Boston arose in response to the arrest of fugitive slave Anthony Burns in 1854. Two batteries of artillery and a detachment of federal troops were sent into the city while the governor also called up the local militia,[110] but when additional forces were requested, military commanders considered further authorization from Washington to be necessary before complying with the requests.[111]

The Attorney General took the opportunity, ostensibly in response to the earlier request, to announce a new doctrine regarding the employment of the Armed Forces.[112] Cushing's response went well beyond the question of whether the "bystanders" contemplated by the Fugitive Slave Act might include members of a state militia when not in federal service, and announced a broader principle—members of the military by virtue of their duties as citizens were part of the posse comitatus. Apparently adopting the views expressed earlier by the Senate Judiciary Committee in reaction to the previous Administration's views on the matter, Cushing declared:

> The posse comitatus comprises every person in the district or county above the age of fifteen years, whatever may be their occupation, whether civilians or not; and including the military of all denominations, militia, soldiers, marines, all of whom are alike bound to obey the commands of the sheriff or marshal. The fact that they are organized as military bodies, under the immediate command of their own officers, does not in any wise affect their legal character. They are still the posse comitatus. (xxi Parl. Hist., p.672, 688, per Lord Mansfield).[113]

Two years later, Cushing's opinion supplied the justification for the use of federal troops at the call of civil law enforcement authorities in what some saw as partisan involvement in the conflict between pro- and anti-slavery forces in Kansas.[114] Congress reacted with a rider to an Army appropriations bill forbidding the use of any "part of the military forces of the United States to enforce territorial law in Kansas."[115] After some discussion of whether the amendment was germane, it was defeated.

PASSAGE OF THE POSSE COMITATUS ACT

Following the Civil War, the use of federal troops to execute the laws, particularly in the states that had been part of the Confederacy, continued even after all other political restrictions had been lifted. By 1877, there was evidence that Republican state governments in more than one southern state owed their continued political existence to the presence of the military and that the activities of federal troops may have influenced the outcome of the Hayes-Tilden presidential election.[116]

The House of Representatives, controlled by a Democratic majority, passed an Army appropriation bill which expressly prohibited use of the Army to shore up Republican state governments in the South, or more precisely, to shore up either side of the political dispute in Louisiana or anywhere else.[117] The Senate, controlled by a Republican majority, refused to accept the provision. No compromise could be reached, and the session ended without passage of an Army appropriation bill. Money to pay the Army was subsequently appropriated in a special session,[118] without reference to restrictions on use of the Army.[119] But when the issue of Army appropriations next arose, the House included a posse comitatus section.[120] The Senate accepted the House version with minor amendments.[121]

At least one contemporary military jurist viewed the new law as having less than momentous impact on the relationship between civil and military authorities. Colonel William Winthrop opined that, the occasion for its enactment having passed, the act remained "a mere impediment to the constitutional exercise of the executive power of the nation."[122] While federal marshals could no longer avail themselves of military assistance to arrest individuals charged with offenses against the United States, he stressed that wherever a combination existed to resist the enforcement of the laws, the President always could invoke the Insurrection Act.[123] He further made note of the already sizable list of exceptions to the prohibition.

Others have viewed the act as having a deleterious effect on the nation's commitment to civilian law enforcement. While soldiers serving on a posse remained subordinate to civilian rules and law enforcement officers, troops called out under the Insurrection Act came to be viewed as an independent military force enforcing something like martial law, if not engaging in all-out war.[124] Today, however, the act is widely regarded as the embodiment of the American tradition of anti-militarism.[125]

Despite early efforts on the part of the executive branch to get the provision repealed or amended,[126] the Posse Comitatus Act has remained essentially unchanged since its passage.[127] Congress has, however, authorized a substantial number of exceptions and has buttressed the act with an additional proscription against use of the Armed Forces to make arrests or conduct searches and seizures.[128]

Constitutional Considerations

The Posse Comitatus Act raises at least three constitutional questions: (1) To what extent does the Posse Comitatus Act track constitutional requirements, beyond the power of the President or Congress to adjust or ignore? (2) To what extent do the powers which the Constitution vests in the President limit the power of Congress to enact the Posse Comitatus Act or any other provision restricting the President's discretion to involve the Armed Forces in civilian affairs? (3) What specifically are the military law enforcement activities "expressly authorized in the Constitution" for purposes of the act?

Constitutional Origins

Lord Coke and his colleagues, in crafting the Petition of Right of 1628, found within that chapter of the Magna Carta and subsequent explanatory statutes that are the antecedents of our constitutional due process clauses a prohibition against martial law. In times of peace, this proscription would not abide either the quartering of troops among civilians or any form of martial law, be it imposed by tribunal or more summarily dispatched by soldiers controlling or punishing civilians.

The Declaration of Independence lists the imposition of martial law upon us among those affronts to fundamental liberties that irrevocably ruptured our political ties to Great Britain.

Finally, it is possible to see the protrusions of a larger, submerged constitutional principle which bars the use of the Armed Forces to solve civilian inconveniences in the Second, Third, and Fifth Amendments, with their promises of a civilian militia, freedom from the quartering of troops among us, and the benefits of due process.

This view is not without judicial support. The courts have demonstrated a rather long-standing reluctance to recognize the authority of military tribunals over civilians.[129] And members of the Supreme Court seemed to acknowledge possible components of a larger principle in both *Youngstown Sheet and Tube Co. v. Sawyer*[130] and *Laird v. Tatum.*[131]

But if a larger anti-martial law principle lies beneath constitutional sands, visible only in these amendments and the spirit of the Posse Comitatus Act, it has remained remarkably dormant. Those regions from which it might have been expected to emerge have been characterized most by inactivity. The boundaries of the Third Amendment are virtually uncharted.[132] Until recently, the outreaches of the militia-related Second Amendment appeared only slightly more visible.[133] Even in the inviting context of the Posse Comitatus Act, the courts have generally avoided excursions into areas of its possible constitutional underpinnings.[134]

On the other hand, the Constitution appears to recognize that military force might occasionally be called for in handling domestic affairs. It permits Congress to authorize the use of the militia "to execute the Laws of the Union, suppress Insurrections and repel Invasions."[135] And it guarantees the states protection against invasion or usurpation of their "republican form of government," and, upon the request of the state legislature, against "domestic violence."[136] While states are prohibited from keeping their own standing armies,[137] they retain some control over their militias, subject to any constraints Congress may constitutionally impose, including the authority to call forth those forces to suppress insurrections or quell civil disturbances.[138] The Constitution neither authorized nor proscribes martial law (which is said to exist when civil authority is supplanted by military rule due to war or similar emergency),[139] but it has been proclaimed on rare occasions.[140]

Lesser forms of military involvement in law enforcement have not been commonplace, but have not been particularly rare during the history of the republic.

Without more judicial guidance, it would appear that traditional reservations about military involvement in the execution of civilian law can only clearly be said to rise to the level of constitutional imperative when they take a form that offends some more explicit constitutional prohibition or guarantee such as the right to jury trial, grand jury indictment, or freedom from unreasonable searches and seizures.[141] Consequently, beyond those specific constitutional provisions, Congress's constitutional authority to enact and adjust the provisions of the Posse Comitatus Act is largely a matter of the coordination of congressional and presidential powers.

Presidential vs. Congressional Powers

The case of conflicting congressional and presidential powers is easily stated if not easily resolved. On one hand, the Constitution requires the President to take care to see that the laws are faithfully executed, and designates him as Chief Executive and Commander in Chief of the Armed Forces.[142] In this dual capacity, the presidency is the repository of both extensive responsibilities and broad prerogatives, not the least of which flow from Article IV, Section 4 of the Constitution, which guarantees the states a republican form of government and protection against invasion and domestic violence.[143]

The Supreme Court has made it clear that the President is not dependent upon express constitutional or statutory authorization for the exercise of his powers. Thus, he may meet an emergency by appointing a marshal to protect a threatened Supreme Court Justice, although no statute expressly authorized appointment for such purposes.[144] He must resist invasion by an enemy with force though Congress has yet to declare war.[145] And when an emergency arises threatening the freedom of interstate commerce, transportation of the mails, or some other responsibility entrusted to the federal government, he may call upon "the army of the Nation, and all its militia ... to brush away the obstructions."[146]

Some commentators feel that this implied or incidental constitutional authority to use the Armed Forces not only exists in the absence of congressional direction, but is immune from congressional direction or limitation.[147]

On the other hand, Congress shares constitutional power over the laws and Armed Forces with the President. The Constitution gives Congress the power to make the laws whose faithful execution the President must take care to observe and which carry into execution Congress's own powers and those of the President.[148] It likewise vests Congress with the power to establish, maintain, and regulate the Armed Forces;[149] and with the power to describe the circumstances under which the militia may be called into federal service.[150]

The Supreme Court has shed some light on the coordination of presidential and congressional powers concerning use of the military to enforce civilian law. The Court has pointed out that the President's power under the Guarantee Clause of Article IV, Section 4, which guarantees the states protection against domestic violence, is only provisionally effective until such time as Congress acts.[151] And the President may not always use the

Armed Forces to meet a domestic emergency when Congress has previously resisted an invitation to sanction their employment.[152] Finally, even when Congress has disclaimed any intent to limit the exercise of the President's constitutional powers, the President's inherent and incidental powers will not always trump conflicting, constitutionally grounded claims.[153]

Constitutional Exceptions

The Posse Comitatus Act does not apply "in cases and under circumstances expressly authorized by the Constitution."[154] It has been said that the Constitution contains no provision expressly authorizing the use of the military to execute the law,[155] and that this reference to constitutional exceptions was included as part of a face-saving compromise that consequently should be ignored.[156]

When the phrase was added originally, those who opposed the Posse Comitatus Act believed that the Constitution vested implied and/or inherent powers upon the President to use the Armed Forces to execute the laws; those who urged its passage believed the President possessed no such powers. As initially passed by the House, the bill contained no constitutional exception.[157] The Senate version contained an exception for instances authorized by the Constitution whether expressed or otherwise.[158] The managers of each house described the compromise reached at conference and subsequently enacted as upholding the position of their respective bodies on the issue. While the House manager believed that retention of the word "expressly" was important to prevent the use of the Army wherever implied authority could be inferred,[159] the Senate manager suggested that the term could safely be kept in without affecting the President's ability to act as required by the Constitution.[160]

Early commentaries suggest that the word "expressly" must be ignored, for otherwise in their view the Posse Comitatus Act is a constitutionally impermissible effort to limit the implied or inherent powers of the President.[161] The regulations covering the use of the Armed Forces during civil disturbances do not go quite that far, but they do assert two constitutionally based exceptions—sudden emergencies and protection of federal property.[162]

The question of whether the constitutional exception contained in the Posse Comitatus Act includes instances where the President is acting under implied or inherent constitutional powers or whether it was merely a face-saving device is a question that may turn on whether Congress may constitutionally restrict the President's powers, if any, in the area—a question the courts have yet to answer.

When the Posse Comitatus Act Does Not Apply

In addition to any express constitutional exceptions, the use of the Armed Forces to execute federal law does not violate the Posse Comitatus Act when (1) an act of Congress expressly authorizes use of part of the Army or Air Force as a posse comitatus or otherwise to execute the law; (2) the activity in question does not involve use of part of the Armed Forces covered by the proscription; or (3) the activity in question does not constitute "execution of the law."

Statutory Exceptions

Generally

The Posse Comitatus Act does not apply where Congress has expressly authorized use of the military to execute the law.[163] Congress has done so in three ways: (1) by giving a branch of the Armed Forces civilian law enforcement authority; (2) by establishing general rules for certain types of assistance; and (3) by addressing individual cases and circumstances with more narrowly crafted legislation. Thus it has vested the Coast Guard, a branch of the Armed Forces, with broad law enforcement responsibilities.[164] Second, over time it has enacted a fairly extensive array of particularized statutes, like those authorizing the President to call out the Armed Forces in times of insurrection and domestic violence.[165] Finally, it has passed general legislation permitting the Armed Forces to share information and equipment with civilian law enforcement agencies, subject to restrictions on engaging in direct and active law enforcement.[166]

How explicit must a statutory exception be? If one believes the word "expressly" should be ignored with respect to the constitutionally based exception, consistency might suggest no more is required than that Congress authorize a thing to be done. To those so inclined, the position is further fortified when the statute authorizes executive branch action in circumstances where the President's faithful execution responsibility,[167] coupled with the Administrative Housekeeping Statute,[168] can be called into play. In this rarely espoused view, if an agency has statutory authority to perform a task, the military may be asked to help.

Others maintain that statutes which authorize assistance from federal agencies and departments generally in order to accomplish a particular task qualify as exceptions even if they do not mention the Department of Defense or any part of the military establishment by name.[169] On the one hand, such legislation has ordinarily come into being after the Posse Comitatus Act and thus would ordinarily be thought to amend any conflicting earlier law. On the other hand, the use of military force in civilian affairs is such an extraordinary thing that perhaps it ought not be presumed, but rather found only where Congress has so stated in hoc verba.

The final and more commonly accepted proposition is that the phrase "in cases and under circumstances expressly authorized by ... Act of Congress" demands that the statutory exception specifically refer to some form of military assistance.[170]

The Insurrection Acts

The clearest statutory exceptions to the Posse Comitatus Act are found in the Insurrection Acts, described above, in which Congress has delegated authority to the President to call forth the military during an insurrection or civil disturbance. The modern version has changed little from the original enactments,[171] and is now found in Chapter 15 of Title 10, U.S. Code.[172] The three main authorities differ according to which constitutional provision they are meant to implement, but the provisions have often been used together or without specifying which part of Chapter 15 of Title 10, U.S. Code, provided the authority. In any case where the President considers it necessary to invoke the authority to use the militia or Armed Forces under these provisions, he is required by 10 U.S.C. § 334 to issue a proclamation immediately ordering "insurgents to disperse and retire peaceably to their abodes within a limited time."

The following sections describe the modern authorities and how they have been invoked since the passage of the Posse Comitatus Act, including some instances where a separate authority may have been used for similar purposes.

At the Request of a State

Section 331 of Title 10 authorizes the President to use the military to suppress an insurrection at the request of a state legislature, or its governor, in the event the legislature cannot be convened.[173] It is meant to fulfill the federal government's responsibility to protect states in the event of "domestic violence"[174] (although the term "insurrection" is arguably much narrower than the phrase "domestic violence" in the Constitution). The first request by a governor for troops after enactment of the Posse Comitatus Act appears to have occurred in 1879, when the governor of Nebraska requested a company of troops to help protect a local court where the trial of a prominent outlaw was taking place, which had occasioned concern that the courthouse would be the scene of a rescue attempt by the portion of the band of outlaws still at large. This request was denied, however, as it was framed as a request to use the troops as a posse comitatus, which, according to the Secretary of War, had become unlawful following enactment of the Posse Comitatus Act,[175] although if the situation were to become more dire, the governor could request aid from the President in the form of troops under military command.

Another proclamation was issued under this provision in 1892 due to a miners' strike in Coeur d'Alene, ID.[176] In 1899, President McKinley deployed 500 troops to Coeur D'Alene, ID, at the governor's request, to keep a conflict between union miners and mine owners under control, but did not issue a proclamation required by statute.[177] Although by this time General Hancock's doctrine regarding the relationship between federal and state troops had gained acceptance,[178] state officials directed operations there.[179] When the governor of Colorado requested federal aid to assist state militia to cope with a coal miners' strike, Secretary of War Elihu Root informed the governor that any troops furnished pursuant to the relevant provision of the insurrection statutes would not be at the disposal of the governor, but would remain under the direction of the President.[180]

During the early part of the 20th century, Presidents generally insisted that governors comply with the requirements of the Insurrection Act and the Constitution in formulating requests for the assistance of the Army.[181] After the governor of Nevada requested troops in 1907 to put down violence by a miners' union that was forcibly removing non-union workers from the area, nine companies of infantry were sent there, but told not to act until a proclamation was issued.[182] The mere presence of troops having quieted the unruly element, no proclamation was issued.

President Roosevelt chastised the governor for having requested federal troops without endeavoring to convene the legislature as required under the Constitution and Insurrection Act.[183] In 1914, a miner's strike at Ludlow, CO, led the governor there to request federal troops, which President Wilson granted.[184]

In 1917, after virtually the entire National Guard was called into federal service for the war in Europe,[185] the Secretary of War instituted a "Direct Access Policy" to permit local and state officials to make direct requests for the assistance of federal troops to reduce the burden on states.[186] Between 1919 and 1920, federal troops were employed to assist in putting down labor disputes and other minor disturbances 29 times, all without the issuance of a presidential proclamation.[187] Troops were deployed from the lumber mills of the Northwest to the copper mines in Arizona and New Mexico, and from the coal mines in Appalachia to the oil fields in Texas and Louisiana, justified on the need to keep up production for the war and replace absent state militia.[188] Federal troops also intervened to keep the peace in several cities afflicted by racial quarrels.[189] The policy was revoked in 1921 due to the perception that troops were being misused,[190] and President Harding issued the requisite proclamation in order to send troops to quell a dispute involving West Virginia coal miners.[191] The governor directed state police forces to act under the direction of the U.S. military commander.[192]

At the request of the Commissioners of the District of Columbia, President Hoover used federal troops in 1932 to oust the Bonus Marchers from federal property in Washington, DC, but did not issue a proclamation.[193] President Roosevelt turned down several requests during the 1930s to provide federal troops for strike duty,[194] but directed the Secretary of War in 1941 to seize and operate an aviation plant where a strike threatened wartime fighter plane production.[195] Although the Attorney General likened the situation to an insurrection, the President's order did not make reference to the insurrection statutes,[196] nor was it accompanied by a proclamation to disperse. When faced with losing their deferred status under the draft, the workers promptly returned to the plant and resumed production under military supervision.[197] Other labor disturbances were similarly addressed by having the Army or Navy seize and manage plants or railroads deemed necessary for the war effort, but these occurred under separate authorities.[198]

During the Second World War, racial strife began to contribute once again to civil disturbances,[199] although federal troops were only called in twice. At the request of the Michigan governor, President Roosevelt issued a proclamation and sent federal troops to Detroit[200] to restore order during a race riot there. Troops were also sent to Philadelphia in 1944 to seize and operate the transportation system after white workers went on strike to protest the employment of some black workers as operators.[201] This, however, was done pursuant to a 1916 statute that empowered the President, during time of war, to order the Secretary of War to take over the possession and operation of transportation systems as required for war efforts.[202]

A race riot in Detroit led the Michigan governor to request troops in 1967, which President Johnson provided.[203] Widespread violence in cities across the country following the assassination of Martin Luther King put the military establishment on alert for possible implementation of the government's plan for civil disturbances, Garden Plot.[204] In the end, only the mayor of Washington, DC, and the governors of Illinois and Maryland requested assistance under the insurrection statutes. President Lyndon Johnson issued proclamations in April, 1968 ordering rioters to disperse in Washington, DC,[205] Chicago,[206] and Baltimore.[207] Each proclamation mentioned both the request for assistance and the need to enforce federal law, citing the entire chapter on insurrections in Title 10 among relevant authorities. Regular troops and federalized National Guard were deployed to these cities.[208]

In 1989, reports of widespread looting on the island of St. Croix in the wake of Hurricane Hugo led President George H. W. Bush to issue a proclamation[209] and send troops to the Virgin Islands,[210] as the territorial governor requested federal intervention.[211] The proclamation cited the need to enforce federal law and protect public property, without expressly mentioning the governor's request.[212] Eleven hundred troops (mostly military police) and 80 federal investigators were sent to St. Croix to restore order and investigate reports of looting.[213]

The most recent invocation of 10 U.S.C. § 331 occurred in 1992, when the acquittal of police officers on charges of beating motorist Rodney King sparked rioting in Los Angeles.[214] The California National Guard, already on the scene but unable to control the violence, was federalized, which may have hampered its efforts due to a misunderstanding that the Guard troops under federal control could no longer carry out law enforcement operations due to the Posse Comitatus Act.[215]

To Enforce Federal Law

Section 332 of Title 10 delegates Congress's power under the Constitution to call forth the militia[216] to the President, authorizing him to determine that "unlawful obstructions, combinations, or assemblages, or rebellion against the authority of the United States make it impracticable to enforce the laws of the United States" and to use the Armed Forces as he considers necessary to enforce the law or to suppress the rebellion. Its first application after the enactment of the Posse Comitatus Act involved an appeal by the governor of the Territory of New Mexico in 1878 for federal military assistance in putting an end to the anarchy that characterized the territory due to the operation of bands of robbers who were besieging mail coaches and terrorizing the local populace.[217] After the proclamation to disperse was issued, military forces restored relative order, after which civil authorities reportedly came to depend on U.S. troops for law enforcement to such an extent that they essentially abandoned their own efforts to enforce the law. When the governor complained about the lack of military assistance for arresting lawbreakers, the local commanding general replied that his troops could not be used to make ordinary arrests in situations that did not amount to an insurrection or reach a level of lawlessness that would extend beyond the capacity of the usual civil machinery to handle.[218] This interpretation of the new posse comitatus restriction was adopted by the War Department. The Secretary of War later blamed the Posse Comitatus Act in part for the fact that lawlessness and riots in the territory had reached such a level that military intervention was required.[219]

"Indian outrages" in Arizona led to another proclamation under the Insurrection Act, not at the request of the territorial governor but as a response to news that the governor was proposing to arm citizens to go after Apaches suspected of murder, which would oblige the military to take action to protect the reservation.[220] President Arthur initially requested legislative relief from the Posse Comitatus Act due to his view that its prohibition inhibited an effective military response.[221] Congress declined to repeal the prohibition, however, with the Senate Judiciary Committee pointing out that the Posse Comitatus Act was meant to curb the practice of local marshals and their subordinates employing the Armed Forces to assist them in enforcing the law, but not to prevent the President from himself using any part of the Army under a military chain of command.[222]

Federal troops were called to Chicago in July 1894 to quell riots accompanying the railroad strikes.[223] President Grover Cleveland did not issue a proclamation for rioters to disperse until several days after violence had begun, after learning that troops had been compelled to fire on a mob in the nearby town of Hammond, IL.[224] Another proclamation was issued the next day to remove further obstructions to the mail and execution of U.S. law occasioned by the strike as it spread westward.[225] The governors of the afflicted states did not call for federal assistance; in fact, the governor of Illinois opposed intervention.[226] Rather, the federal marshals and U.S. attorneys notified the Attorney General, who presented the requests to the President. It appears that obtaining civilian deputies to assist marshals against the strikers was made difficult due to the fact that popular sympathies were with the strikers, leading the civilian authorities to prefer shifting the responsibility to the Army.[227] Federal troops were also used to recapture trains stolen by various "industrial armies" of disaffected miners and laborers.[228]

In 1885, resistance in Utah to the "Edmunds law" for the suppression of polygamy caused the governor of that territory to seek federal assistance, which was granted. Animosity toward Chinese railroad laborers and miners led to major disturbances and to calls for federal troops in a number of western states and territories in 1885-1886.[229] Proclamations were issued for the state of Washington,[230] but federal troops sent there met with no resistance.[231] Federal troops were employed in Montana in 1897 to protect a prisoner charged with murder from a potential mob lynching, but this was done on the order of the local commander under "emergency authority," without a presidential proclamation.[232]

A proclamation was issued in 1914 to employ troops to suppress a riot in Arkansas to support the courts and protect government property.[233]

A large task force of regular troops, National Guard, federal marshals, and other police was assembled to protect the Pentagon during the 1967 anti-war demonstration known as the March on the Pentagon.[234] In connection with this effort, the Army authorized a widespread covert intelligence operation to infiltrate protest groups who were planning to march, and radio communications were also monitored.[235] Section 332 was considered in order to provide the legal justification, but rejected because violence was merely projected and a proclamation was thought to be too difficult to frame under such circumstances.[236] In the end, authorities decided to rely on a non-statutory basis regarded as an implicit sovereign right to protect government property, although Section 332 was held in reserve in case the level of violence called for federalizing the National Guard.[237] There were a few clashes between troops and protesters, but the violence did not reach the threshold for invoking Section 332.

The National Guard was called into service during a postal strike in 1970 to "execute the laws of the United States as they relate to the Post Office Department."[238] The cited authority for this action was the Economy Act of 1932, which led to some criticism because that statute does not provide for the use of the Army.[239]

In 1973, the Army became involved in a federal law enforcement operation to quell a civil disturbance on the Pine Ridge Reservation in South Dakota after some 200 members of the American Indian Movement seized and occupied the village of Wounded Knee to demonstrate their grievances. The Attorney General advised President Nixon to send federal troops to the area, presumably under the authority of 10 U.S.C. § 332, but military advisors counseled against the idea.[240] Instead, some 350 federal officers were sent to the scene, including a paramilitary group from the U.S. Marshals Service.[241] Nevertheless, the 82d Airborne Division was tasked to provide a 1,000-man contingency force as well as some observers, and regional National Guard units provided surveillance aircraft and other equipment. The troops from the 82d Airborne were not deployed, but some questioned whether military aid supplied to civilian law enforcement was permissible under the Posse Comitatus Act,[242] leading to litigation and eventually legislation to authorize some types of military support to civil authorities. (See below "Support to Law Enforcement.")

In 1987, President Reagan issued a proclamation to order rioting prisoners in the federal penitentiary in Atlanta, GA, to disperse.[243] He authorized the Secretary of Defense to call up National Guard units or members to suppress the violence, specifying that the law enforcement policies determined by the Attorney General were to be followed.[244] Local authorities were able to negotiate the release of hostages the prisoners had taken and bring an end to the trouble before troops arrived.[245]

Civil Rights Protection

Section 333 of Title 10 permits the President to use the Armed Forces to suppress any "insurrection, domestic violence, unlawful combination, or conspiracy" if law enforcement is hindered within a state, and local law enforcement is unable to protect individuals, or if the unlawful action "obstructs the execution of the laws of the United States or impedes the course of justice under those laws." This section was enacted to implement the Fourteenth Amendment guarantee for equal protection. It does not require the request or even the permission of the governor of the affected state.

The provision lay dormant after the end of Reconstruction until 1957, when President Eisenhower ordered a battle group of the 101st Airborne Division into Little Rock[246] and federalized the entire Arkansas National Guard[247] in order to enforce a court order permitting nine black students to attend a previously white high school. The proclamation to disperse cited both Sections 332 and 333 of Title 10, U.S. Code.[248] By federalizing the Arkansas Guard, the President effectively deprived the governor of forces that had several days previously been used to enforce the governor's view of law and order.[249]

Presidents Kennedy and Johnson followed the Little Rock precedent to deal with resistance to court-ordered desegregation in a number of Southern states. In 1962, after the governor of Mississippi attempted to prevent black student James H. Meredith from registering at the University of Mississippi at Oxford, President Kennedy sought to enforce the court order with federal marshals.[250] When marshals met with resistance from state forces and later a riotous mob, President Kennedy federalized the Mississippi National Guard and ordered active Army troops already gathered in the area to take action.[251] The President's proclamation to disperse named the governor and other state officials as forming the unlawful assemblies obstructing the enforcement of the court order, citing as authority both Sections 332 and 333.[252] President Kennedy followed a similar course of action to confront state resistance to court ordered desegregation in Alabama twice in 1963.[253] President Johnson cited the same authority in 1965 to deploy troops, both regular Army and federalized National Guard, to Alabama to protect civil rights marchers as they made their way from Selma, AL, to Montgomery.[254]

Support to Law Enforcement

In 1981, Congress enacted general law enforcement exceptions[255] to the Posse Comitatus Act prohibitions in order to resolve questions raised by the cases that grew out of the events at Wounded Knee.[256] The take-over and events which occurred during the siege led to four cases[257] involving a series of federal criminal charges including obstructing a law enforcement officer in the lawful performance of his duties during the course of a civil disturbance.[258] Military assistance provided federal authorities at Wounded Knee[259] undermined the prospects of a successful prosecution for obstructing law enforcement officers by casting doubt on whether they were performing their duties lawfully, an element necessary for conviction.

The 1981 legislation contains explicit grants of authority for military assistance to the police— federal, state, and local—particularly in the form of information and equipment, along with restrictions on the use of that authority.[260] These exceptions are found in Chapter

18 of Title 10, U.S. Code, Military Support to Civilian Law Enforcement Agencies (§§ 371-82).

Information: Spies, Advisers, and Undercover Agents

The Wounded Knee cases spawned uncertainty as to the extent to which military authorities might share technical advice, the results of reconnaissance flights, or any other forms of information with civilian law enforcement authorities. Section 371 specifically permits the Armed Forces to share information acquired during military operations and in fact encourages the Armed Forces to plan their activities with an eye to the production of incidental civilian benefits.[261] The section allows the use of military undercover agents and the collection of intelligence concerning civilian activities, however, only where there is a nexus to an underlying military purpose.[262] The committee report suggested that the type of intelligence operations conducted by the Army in preparation for possible civil disturbances in previous decades was not meant to be authorized.[263]

Section 373 permits military personnel to train civilian police on "the operation and maintenance of equipment" and to provide them with "expert advice."[264] The section was originally limited to equipment provided by the Armed Forces,[265] but was expanded in 1988 to include training on any equipment regardless of its origin.[266]

The explanation of what might constitute "expert advice" is limited, but Congress clearly did not use the phrase as a euphemism for active military participation in civilian police activity.[267]

An implementing regulation proposed in 2010 would exclude certain intelligence activities from its purview.[268] Under the proposed regulation, assistance to law enforcement by Defense intelligence and counterintelligence components would be permitted for purposes of investigating or preventing clandestine intelligence activities by foreign powers or international terrorist or narcotics activities.[269] The provision would also permit intelligence elements to cooperate with law enforcement agencies for protecting their own personnel, property, and information, and to provide specialized equipment, technical knowledge, or assistance of expert personnel when lives are endangered.[270]

Equipment and Facilities

Abstractly it might seem that even civilian use—against Americans within the United States—of tanks, missiles, fighter planes, aircraft carriers, and other implements of war offends the Posse Comitatus Act even if use can be accomplished without the direct involvement of military personnel. The arsenal of American military weapons and equipment is "part of the Army and Air Force" even when turned over to civilian authorities before use for civilian purposes. Even if the Posse Comitatus Act were read to apply only to the use of personnel, would the use of military personnel to maintain equipment loaned to civilian authorities violate the act's proscription? The Wounded Knee cases provided conflicting answers.[271]

The 1981 provisions make it clear that the Defense Department may provide civilian police with military equipment[272] and under some circumstances, particularly in drug cases, may also supply military personnel to maintain and, for certain limited purposes (not including searches and seizures),[273] operate such equipment.[274] The provisions also include extraordinary authority to use Navy ships to support Coast Guard drug interdiction on the high seas.[275] In 1996, Congress added authority for military assistance, including the provision of personnel and equipment, for the enforcement of laws prohibiting chemical and biological weapons of mass destruction.[276]

Limitations: Military Preparedness, Reimbursement, and Direct Use

The authority granted in §§ 371-382 is subject to three general caveats. It may not be used to undermine the military capability of the United States.[277] The civilian beneficiaries of military aid must pay for the assistance.[278] And, under § 375, the Secretary of Defense must issue regulations to ensure that the authority under the chapter does not result in use of the Armed Forces to make arrests or conduct searches and seizures solely for the benefit of civilian law enforcement.[279]

For several years, the regulations called for by § 375 appeared in parallel form in the Code of Federal Regulations[280] and in a Defense Department Directive.[281] The heart of the regulations appeared in Subsection 213.10(a)(3):

> Except as otherwise provided in this enclosure, the prohibition on use of military personnel 'as a posse comitatus or otherwise to execute the laws' prohibits the following forms of direct assistance:
>
> (i) Interdiction of a vehicle, vessel, aircraft or other similar activity.
>
> (ii) A search or seizure.
>
> (iii) An arrest, stop and frisk, or similar activity.
>
> (iv) Use of military personnel for surveillance or pursuit of individuals, or as informants, undercover agents, investigators, or interrogators."[282]

Although the provisions have been removed from the C.F.R., the directive remains in effect.[283]

Military Purpose

The Armed Forces, when in performance of their military responsibilities, are beyond the reach of the Posse Comitatus Act and its statutory and regulatory supplements. Analysis of constitutional or statutory exceptions is unnecessary in such cases. The original debates make it clear that the act was designed to prevent use of the Armed Forces to execute *civilian* law. Congress did not intend to limit the authority of the Army to perform its military duties. The legislative history, however, does not resolve the question of whether the act prohibits the Army from performing its military duties in a manner that affords incidental benefits to civilian law enforcement officers.

The courts and commentators believe that it does not.[284] As long as the primary purpose of an activity is to address a military purpose, the activity need not be abandoned simply because it also assists civilian law enforcement efforts. Courts appear to view the location of the activity as particularly indicative of primary purpose; as one court noted, "the power to maintain order, security, and discipline on a military facility is necessary for military operations."[285]

The courts have concluded that, consistent with this legitimate military purpose to maintain order on military installations, military personnel may, without violating the Posse Comitatus Act, turn over to civilian law enforcement authorities armed felons arrested when they flee onto a military base,[286] or drunk drivers arrested on a military base,[287] or firearms stolen from a military installation,[288] as well as any stolen equipment that belongs to a military unit.[289] The courts have likewise found no violation of the act when military personnel arrest civilians on military facilities for crimes committed there,[290] or when military authorities assist a civilian police investigation conducted on a military facility.[291] The military purpose doctrine also permits military law enforcement personnel to investigate the off-base conduct of military personnel,[292] and allows them to assist in investigating the off-base conduct of civilians who are suspected of involvement in a violation of the Uniform Code of Military Justice (UCMJ).[293] The DOD Directive evidences a comparable understanding.[294]

Cases called to apply the military purpose doctrine in cooperative police activities occurring off-base are the most difficult to reconcile. Some seem to require no more than a logical military nexus;[295] others demand a very clear, specific military connection before they will concede the presence of a military purpose;[296] and still others seem to seek a middle ground.[297]

Finally, it is arguable that Congress's authorization for the use of force against those responsible for the September 11 attacks[298] has mooted some of the limitations on the use of the military for law enforcement purposes by recasting them as military operations. Soon after the attacks, the Office of Legal Counsel advised the White House and Defense Department that the Posse Comitatus Act imposed no constraint on the President's use of military forces domestically for anti-terrorism operations against "international or foreign terrorists operating within the United States."[299] This conclusion rested on the determination that the act

> only applies to the domestic use of the Armed Forces for *law enforcement* purposes, rather than for the performance of military functions. The Posse Comitatus Act itself contains an exception that allows the use of the military when constitutionally or statutorily authorized, which has occurred in the present circumstances.[300]

In concluding that the prevention and deterrence of terrorism is "fundamentally military, rather than law enforcement, in character," OLC conceded that distinguishing between military and law enforcement functions when dealing with terrorism is "no easy task." Counter-terrorism operations could therefore "resemble, overlap with, and assist ordinary law enforcement activity."

> Military action might encompass making arrests, seizing documents or other property, searching persons or places or keeping them under surveillance, intercepting electronic or wireless communications, setting up roadblocks, interviewing witnesses, and searching for suspects. Moreover, the information gathered in such efforts could be of considerable use to federal prosecutors if the Government were to prosecute against captured terrorists.[301]

OLC further opined that the President's inherent power to defend the United States supplied a "constitutional exception" to the Posse Comitatus Act,[302] and that statutory exceptions could be found in both the authorization for use of military force[303] and § 333 of the Insurrection Act.[304]

It does not appear, however, that much of this opinion remains the official interpretation of the Justice Department. In 2008, OLC advised that "caution should be exercised before relying in any respect on the Memorandum [regarding the Authority for Use of Military Force to Combat Terrorist Activities Within the United States (Oct. 23, 2001) as a precedent of the Office of Legal Counsel," and that "certain propositions" stated therein "should not be treated as authoritative for any purpose."[305] With respect to the discussion of the Posse Comitatus Act, the superseding memorandum criticized the 2001 memo as "far too general and divorced from specific facts and circumstances to be useful as an authoritative precedent of OLC." Rather than viewing the authorization statute as a statutory exception to the act, the successor memo believed it better to state that the "reasonable and necessary use of military force taken under the authority of the AUMF would be a military action, potentially subject to the established 'military purpose' doctrine, rather than a law enforcement action."[306] Likewise, the revised view of the OLC emphasized that the use of the military to execute the law under the Insurrection Act "would require the presence of an actual obstruction of the execution of federal law or a breakdown in the ability of state authorities to protect federal rights."

The use of the military within the United States for counter-terrorism purposes has been negligible, despite some prodding from Congress to use military forces to apprehend, interrogate, and detain suspected members of Al Qaeda and "associated forces."[307] Consequently, there is more commentary regarding the interplay of the Posse Comitatus Act and what was previously called the "Global War on Terror"[308] than there are judicial decisions to test these theories. One U.S. citizen who was detained by the military without trial after having been designated an "enemy combatant" by the President sought habeas corpus relief, in part on the contention that his confinement by the military violated the Posse Comitatus Act. The reviewing district court judge saw things differently:

> Padilla is not being detained by the military in order to execute a civilian law or for violating a civilian law, not-withstanding that his alleged conduct may in fact violate one or more such laws. He is being detained in order to interrogate him about the unlawful organization with which he is said to be affiliated and with which the military is in active combat, and to prevent him from becoming reaffiliated with that organization.[309]

The decision, however, was reversed on the grounds that the detention violated a more specific statute, but was then vacated by the Supreme Court on procedural grounds. In subsequent proceedings, the petitioner did not rely on the Posse Comitatus Act.[310] It seems safe to say, however, that if the Constitution does not stand in the way of such a measure, the Posse Comitatus Act will not likely impose a greater hurdle.[311]

COVERAGE OF THE POSSE COMITATUS ACT

Willful Use

The act is limited to "willful" misuse of the Army or Air Force.[312] The Senate version of the original act would have limited proscription to "willful and knowing" violations;[313] the House version had no limitation.[314] The compromise that emerged from conference opted to forbid only willful violations, but neither the statements of the managers nor statements elsewhere in the debate explain what the limitation means. In other instances, Congress has used the term "willful" in a number of different contexts and the term has been construed by the courts in a variety of ways, often inconsistent and contradictory.[315] The scattered statements found in the case law under the act are somewhat conflicting and not particularly helpful,[316] although it seems unlikely that a court would convict for anything less than a deliberate disregard of the law's requirements.[317]

Execute the Law

When has the Army or Air Force been used "to execute the laws"? The language of the act by itself seems very sweeping.[318] It is comparable to the instruction of the Constitution that the President "take care that the laws are faithfully executed."[319] Without more, it would seem to prohibit the use of the Army or the Air Force to implement the command or authorization of all state or federal law. It might apply with equal force to delivering the mail or making an arrest.

Existing case law and commentary indicate that "execution of the law" in violation of the Posse Comitatus Act occurs (a) when the Armed Forces perform tasks ordinarily assigned not to them but to an organ of civil government, or (b) when the Armed Forces perform tasks assigned to them solely for purposes of civilian government. (The test that applies in cases where military personnel or units are conducting activities in support of law enforcement authorities is somewhat different, and is covered below.)

While inquiries may surface in other contexts such as the use of the Armed Forces to fight forest fires or to provide assistance in the case of other natural disasters,[320] Posse Comitatus Act questions arise most often when the Armed Forces assist civilian police. This is perhaps not surprising since it is the use that stimulated passage of the act. During the debate, Members complained of various ways in which the Army had been used, essentially as a police force, to break up labor disputes, to collect taxes, to execute search and arrest warrants, and to maintain order at the polls and during state legislative sessions.[321]

At least when suggested that the Armed Forces have been improperly used as a police force, the tests used by most contemporary courts to determine whether military activity in support of civilian authorities violates the Posse Comitatus Act were developed out of disturbances at Wounded Knee on the Pine Ridge Indian Reservation in South Dakota and inquiry:

1. whether civilian law enforcement officials made a "direct active use" of military investigators to "execute the law";
2. whether the use of the military "pervaded the activities" of the civilian officials; or
3. whether the military was used so as to subject "citizens to the exercise of military power which was regulatory, prescriptive, or compulsory in nature."[322]

The vast majority of cases called upon to apply these tests have found that the assistance provided civilian law enforcement did not constitute "execution of the law" in violation of Posse Comitatus Act requirements.[323] Those most likely to fail the tests seem to be those where the activities appear to have a colorable military purpose, but the government fails to make a convincing showing.[324]

The Office of Legal Counsel opined in 1991 that the use of military personnel to conduct aerial infrared monitoring of private property for law enforcement purposes is "aerial reconnaissance" authorized by 10 U.S.C. § 374(b)(2)(B), and is neither inconsistent with 10

U.S.C. § 375 (assistance may not involve military personnel in search, seizure, or arrest) nor prohibited by the Posse Comitatus Act.[325] To reach this conclusion, OLC relied on its interpretation of the legislative history of §§ 371-375 to find that Congress did not mean the term "search" in § 375 to include all conduct that would constitute a search under the Fourth Amendment. Rather, OLC found,

> when Congress used the term "search" in section 375, it intended that the term encompass at most only searches involving physical contact with civilians or their property, and perhaps only searches involving physical contact that are likely to result in a direct confrontation between military personnel and civilians.[326]

The legislative history suggested to OLC that Congress had intended to codify certain court decisions interpreting the Posse Comitatus Act to have as its primary aim the prevention of any "direct confrontation between military personnel and civilians."[327]

Military Coverage

Navy & Marines

The Posse Comitatus Act proscribes use of the Army or the Air Force to execute the law.[328] It says nothing about the Navy, the Marine Corps, the Coast Guard, or the National Guard. The amendment first offered to the Army appropriation bill in 1878 to enact the Posse Comitatus provisions would have prohibited use of "any part of the land or naval forces of the United States" to execute the law.[329] Some commentators believe that sponsors subsequently limited the posse comitatus amendment to the Army appropriation bill in order to avoid challenges on grounds of germaneness.[330] The courts have generally held that the Posse Comitatus Act by itself does not apply to the Navy or the Marine Corps.[331] They maintain, however, that those forces are covered by similarly confining administrative and legislative supplements,[332] the most currently applicable of which appear in the DOD Directive.[333]

Coast Guard

The Posse Comitatus Act likewise says nothing about the Coast Guard. The Coast Guard was formed by merging two civilian agencies, the Revenue Cutter Service and the Lifesaving Service. Although created and used for law enforcement purposes, the cutter service had already been used as part of the military forces of the United States by the time the Posse Comitatus Act was enacted.[334]

The Coast Guard is now a branch of the Armed Forces, located within the Department of Homeland Security,[335] but relocated within the Navy in time of war or upon the order of the President.[336] The act does not apply to the Coast Guard while it remains part of the Department of Homeland Security.[337] While part of the Navy, it is subject to the orders of the Secretary of the Navy,[338] and consequently to any generally applicable directives or instructions issued under the Department of Defense or the Navy.

As a practical matter, however, the Coast Guard is statutorily authorized to perform law enforcement functions.[339] Even while part of the Navy its law enforcement activities would come within the statutory exception to the posse comitatus restrictions, and the restrictions applicable to components of the Department of Defense would apply only to activities beyond those authorized.[340]

National Guard

The act is silent as to what constitutes "part" of the Army or Air Force for purposes of proscription. There is little commentary or case law to resolve questions concerning the coverage of the National Guard, the Civil Air Patrol, civilian employees of the Armed Forces, or regular members of the Armed Forces while off duty.

Strictly speaking, the Posse Comitatus Act predates the National Guard only in name, for the Guard "is the modern Militia reserved to the States by Art. I, § 8, cls.15, 16, of the Constitution," which has become "an organized force, capable of being assimilated with ease into the regular military establishment of the United States."[341] There seems every reason to consider the National Guard part of the Army or Air Force, for purposes of the Posse Comitatus Act, when in federal service.[342] When not in federal service, historical reflection might suggest that it is likewise covered. Recall that it was the state militia, called to the aid of the marshal enforcing the Fugitive Slave Act, which triggered Attorney General Cushing's famous opinion.[343] And that the Posse Comitatus Act's reference to "posse comitatus or otherwise" is a "they-are-covered-no-matter-what-you-call-them" response to the assertion derived from Cushing's opinion that troops could be used to execute the law as long as they were acting as citizens and not soldiers.

On the other hand, the National Guard is a creature of both state and federal law, a condition which as the militia it has enjoyed since the days of the Articles of Confederation.[344] And the courts have said that members of the National Guard when not in federal service are not covered by the Posse Comitatus Act.[345] Similarly, the DOD Directive is only applicable to members of the National Guard when they are in federal service.[346]

Off Duty Military, Acting as Citizens & Civilian Employees

The historical perspective fares little better on the question of whether the Posse Comitatus Act extends to soldiers who assist civilian law enforcement officials in a manner which any other citizen would be permitted to provide assistance, particularly if they do so while off duty.

Congress passed the act in response to cases where members of the military had been used based on their civic obligations to respond to the call as the posse comitatus. The debate in the Senate, however, suggests that the act was not intended to strip members of the military of all civilian rights and obligations.[347]

The Senate debate may have influenced some reviewing courts, particularly in earlier decisions interpreting the Posse Comitatus Act, which held that a soldier who does no more than any other citizen might do to assist civilian law enforcement has not been used in violation of the Posse Comitatus Act.[348] The more recent decisions under similar facts, with the endorsement of the commentators,[349] have focused on the nature of the assistance provided and whether the assistance is incidental to action taken primarily for a military purpose.[350]

Some have questioned whether civilian employees of the Armed Forces should come within the proscription of the act,[351] but most, frequently without comment, seem to consider them "part" of the Armed Forces for purposes of the Posse Comitatus Act.[352] The current Defense Department Directive expressly includes civilian employees "under the direct command and control of a military officer" within its Posse Comitatus Act policy restrictions,[353] while the Office of Legal Counsel considers that civilian employees are not "part of" the Armed Forces and may be assigned to duties with law enforcement organizations without violating the Posse Comitatus Act.[354] The Office of Legal Counsel has also opined that military members who operate under civilian command and control are not "part of" the Armed Forces, at least so long as they are not still subject to the military chain of command.[355]

Geographical Application

It seems unlikely that the Posse Comitatus Act, by itself, applies beyond the confines of the United States, its territories, and possessions.[356] As a general rule, acts of Congress are presumed to apply only within the United States, its territories, and possessions unless Congress has provided otherwise or unless the purpose of Congress in enacting the legislation evidences an intent that the legislation enjoy extraterritorial application.[357]

The Posse Comitatus Act contains no expression of extraterritorial application. Congress enacted it in response to problems occurring within the United States and its territories, problems associated with the American political process and military usurpation of civilian law enforcement responsibilities over Americans. It seems unlikely that its extraterritorial application was either anticipated or intended.

The first court to consider the question agreed, but it arose in occupied territory overseas in which an American military government had temporarily displaced civil authorities.[358] For some time subsequent decisions either declined to resolve the issue or ignored it.[359]

Congress does appear to have intended the authority and restrictions contained in 10 U.S.C. §§ 371-382 to apply both in the United States and beyond its borders. Certainly, the provisions directing the placement of members of the Coast Guard on Navy ships for drug interdiction purposes[360] evidence an understanding that the Posse Comitatus Act's statutory shadow, the restrictions on arrests and similar direct law enforcement activities under 10 U.S.C. § 375, applies at least on the high seas.[361] In fact, in some instances it initially contemplated that various provisions would only apply overseas.[362]

The regulations implementing 10 U.S.C. § 375 address only assistance to law enforcement officials of the several states, the United States, or its territories or possessions,[363] without any explicit declaration that the ban applies only within this country.[364] In the case of assistance provided overseas to foreign law enforcement officials, the so-called Mansfield Amendment[365] creates something of an overseas version of the Posse Comitatus Act, at least for drug enforcement purposes.[366]

Consequences of Violation

Prosecution

The Posse Comitatus Act is a criminal statute under which there has never been an officially reported prosecution,[367] although it appears there were two prosecutions shortly after the act was passed.[368] While some courts have concluded that it does not provide a private right of action on behalf of anyone who claims to have suffered some injury due to its violation,[369] it has been invoked with varying degrees of success to challenge the jurisdiction of the courts; as a defense in criminal prosecutions for other offenses; as a ground for the suppression of evidence; as the grounds for, or a defense against, civil liability; and as an impediment to proposed actions by the Armed Forces.

Exclusion of Evidence

Allegations that the Posse Comitatus Act has been violated are made most often by defendants seeking to exclude related testimony or physical evidence. The case law begins with *United States v. Walden*,[370] where the U.S. Court of Appeals for the Fourth Circuit found that the Treasury Department's use of three Marines as undercover agents in an investigation of firearms offenses violated Navy regulations that made the act applicable to use of the Marines, but declined to order the exclusion of evidence obtained by the Marines.

The court found no "conscious, deliberate or willful intent on the part of the Marines or the Treasury Department's Special Investigator to violate" the regulation or the act.[371] It also noted that the regulation contained no enforcement mechanism and the Posse Comitatus Act provided only for criminal prosecution, and that case before lacked the elements which had led to the adoption of the Fourth Amendment exclusionary rule. Finally, the court felt the use of the Marines had been aberrational; that subsequent similar transgressions were unlikely; and that the regulation would be amended to provide an enforcement component. But the court warned, "should there be evidence of widespread or repeated violations in any future case, or ineffectiveness of enforcement by the military, we will consider ourselves free to consider whether adoption of an exclusionary rule is required as a future deterrent."[372]

Later defendants have focused upon the *Walden* court's warning; later courts have emphasized the refusal to adopt an exclusionary rule. Most cases note the absence of an exclusionary rule either to avoid deciding whether the Posse Comitatus Act was violated or to conclude that no relief is available irrespective of any violation.[373] Three states' cases have required the suppression of evidence resulting from the use of military undercover agents to target civilian drug dealing without establishing any connection to activities on a military installation or sales to military personnel other than the undercover agents.[374] Where the defendant is a member of the armed services and military investigators take part in an investigation, it has been held that an attorney's failure to make an effort to exclude evidence on the basis of an alleged Posse Comitatus Act violation does not give rise to a claim for ineffective assistance of counsel.[375]

Jurisdiction & Criminal Defenses

The first criminal defendants to seek refuge in the Posse Comitatus Act claimed unsuccessfully that use of the military to transport them back to the United States for trial violated the act and vitiated the jurisdiction of American courts to try them. Ordinarily, criminal trials are not barred simply because the defendant was unlawfully seized and carried into the jurisdiction of the trial court.[376] There are indications that the same rule applies when the defendant challenges the court's jurisdiction on the grounds of Posse Comitatus Act violations. In the early posse comitatus cases, the defendants' arguments were further undermined by the fact that the countries from which they were returned, Germany and Japan, were under American military rule at the time.[377]

In later cases, some of which began beyond the territorial confines of the United States, although none in occupied territory, the courts noted that dismissal would not be an appropriate remedy for a posse comitatus violation.[378]

Defendants have found the act more helpful in prosecutions where the government must establish the lawfulness of its conduct as one of the elements of the offense charged, a rare feature of criminal prohibitions.[379] Thus, several defendants at Wounded Knee were able to persuade the court that evidence of possible Posse Comitatus Act violations precluded their convictions for obstructing law enforcement officials "lawfully engaged" in the performance of their duties.[380]

Civil Liability

Some time ago, the Eighth Circuit found that a violation of the act might constitute an unreasonable search and seizure for purposes of the Fourth Amendment, thereby giving rise to a *Bivens* cause of action against offending federal officers or employees.[381] A Posse Comitatus Act violation, however, also provides the government with a defense to a claim under the Federal Tort Claims Act (FTCA) since the government is not liable under the FTCA for injuries inflicted by federal officers or employees acting outside the scope of their authority.[382] It appears that plaintiffs asserting violations against state or local law enforcement officers also face an uphill battle.[383] On balance, the Posse Comitatus Act is only rarely placed in issue in civil cases.

COMPLIANCE

The most significant impact of the Posse Comitatus Act is attributable to compliance by the Armed Forces. As administrative adoption of the act for the Navy and Marines demonstrates, the military has a long-standing practice of avoiding involvement in civilian affairs which it believes are contrary to the act.[384]

End Notes

[1] For a review of the changed role of the military, see William C. Banks, *The Normalization of Homeland Security after September 11: The Role of the Military in Counterterrorism Preparedness and Response*, 64 LA. L. REV. 745 (2004).

[2] P.L. 107-56, 115 Stat. 272 (2001).

[3] *Id.* § 104 (amending 18 U.S.C. § 2332e).

[4] Homeland Security Act of 2002, P.L. 107-296, § 886, 116 Stat. 2248 (2002)(codified at 6 U.S.C. § 466).

[5] *See* Lisa Grow Sun, *Disaster Mythology and the Law*, 96 CORNELL L. REV. 1131 (2011); William C. Banks, *Providing "Supplemental Security"—The Insurrection Act and the Military Role in Responding to Domestic Crises*, 3 J. NAT'L SECURITY L. & POL'Y 39 (2009)(both articles recounting history behind the short-lived amendment to the Insurrection Act enacted in response to Hurricane Katrina).

[6] Magna Carta, ch. 39 (1225)[ch.29 in the Charter of King John (1215)], *reprinted in* WILLIAM F. SWINDLER, MAGNA CARTA: LEGEND AND LEGACY 315-16 (1965)("No freeman shall be taken, or imprisoned, or be disseised *of any freehold, or liberties, or free customs*, or outlawed, or banished, or in any *other* way destroyed, nor will we go or send against him, except by the lawful judgment of his peers or by the law of the land")(language added to ch.29 of the Charter of King John in the reissuance by King Henry III appears in italics). Although the Magna Carta in the modified version of King Henry III remains in effect, the language quoted above is generally cited as "chapter 29." *See, e.g.*, FAITH THOMPSON, MAGNA CARTA: ITS ROLE IN THE MAKING OF THE ENGLISH CONSTITUTION 1300-1629, at 68 (1948); SIR MATTHEW HALE, THE HISTORY OF THE COMMON LAW OF ENGLAND 49 (1716 ed.); 1 SIR EDWARD COKE, THE SECOND PART OF THE INSTITUTES OF THE LAWS OF ENGLAND 45 (1797 ed.); I SIR WILLIAM BLACKSTONE, COMMENTARIES ON THE LAWS OF ENGLAND 400 (1765 ed.).

[7] 25 Ed. III. Stat. 5, ch. 4 (1352), *reprinted in* 1 STATUTES OF THE REALM, 1231-1377 321 (1993):

> Whereas it is contained in the Great Charter of the Franchises of England, that none shall be imprisoned nor put out of his Freehold, nor of his Franchises nor free Custom, unless it be by the Law of the Land; It is accorded assented, and established, That from henceforth none shall be taken by Petition or Suggestion made to our Lord the King, or to his Council, unless it be by Indictment or Presentment of good and lawful People of the same neighbourhood where such Deeds be done, in due Manner, or by Process made by Writ original at the Common Law; nor that none be out of his Franchises, nor of his freeholds, unless he be duly brought into answer, and forejudged of the same by the Course of the Law; and if any thing be done against the same, it shall be redressed and holden for none.

[8] 28 Ed. III. chs. 1, 3 (1354), *reprinted in* 1 STATUTES OF THE REALM, 1231-1377 at 345 (1993)("the Great Charter ... [shall] be kept and maintained in all Points.... No Man of what[ever] Estate or Condition that he be, shall be put out of land or Tenement, nor taken, nor imprisoned, nor disinherited, nor put to Death, without being brought in Answer by due Process of the Law").

[9] *See* THOMPSON, *supra* footnote 6, at 347-50; David E. Engdahl, *Soldiers, Riots, and Revolution: The Law and History of Military Troops in Civil Disorders*, 57IOWA L. REV.1 (1971). Coke's Institutes make the same point; proceedings under martial law are not proceedings under the "law of the land" (*lex terrae*). *See* I COKE, *supra* footnote 6, at 50 ("And so if two English men doe goe into a foreine kingdome, and fight there, and the one murder the other, *lex terrae* extendeth not hereunto, but this offense shall be heard, and determined before the constable, and marshall [i.e. at martial law], and such proceedings shall be there, by attaching of the body, and otherwise, as the law, and custom of that court have been allowed by the lawes of the realme, [13 H.IV. ch.5 (1412)]").

[10] For a more expansive examination, see Engdahl, *supra* footnote 9.

[11] Restating the relevant guarantees of the Magna Carta and subsequent statutes, Parliament declared:

> [N]everthess of late time divers commissions under your Majesty's great seal have issued forth, by which certain persons have been assigned and appointed commissioners with power and authority to proceed within the land, according to the justice of martial law, against such soldiers or mariners, or other dissolute persons joining with them, as should commit any murder, robbery, felony, mutiny, or other outrage or misdemeanour whatsoever, and by such summary course and order as is agreeable to martial law, and as is used in armies in time of war, to proceed to the trial and condemnation of such offenders, and them to cause to be executed and put to death according to the law martial.... They do therefore humbly pray your most excellent Majesty ... that your Majesty would be pleased to remove the said soldiers and mariners, and that your people may not be so burdened in time to come; and that the aforesaid commissions, for proceeding by martial law, may be revoked and annulled; and that hereafter no commissions of like nature may issue forth to any person or persons whatsoever to be executed as aforesaid, lest by colour of them any of your Majesty's subjects be destroyed or put to death contrary to the laws and franchise of the land.

Petition of Right, 3 Car. I, c.1, §§ 3, 4, 7, 10, *reprinted in* WILLIAM STUBBS, SELECT CHARTERS AND OTHER ILLUSTRATIONS OF ENGLISH CONSTITUTIONAL HISTORY FROM THE EARLIEST TIMES TO THE REIGN OF EDWARD THE FIRST 515-17 (8th ed. 1895); and 5 STATUTES OF THE REALM 23, 24 (1993).

The Petition of Right was understood to have established, with respect to martial law,

> *First*, That in truth and reality it is not a law, but something indulged rather than allowed as a law; the necessity of government, order and discipline in an army, is that only which can give those laws a countenance. *Secondly*, This indulged law was only to extend to members of the army, or to those of the opposite army, and never was so much indulged as intended to be (executed or) exercised upon others; for others were not listed under the army, had no colour of reason to be bound by military constitutions, applicable only to the army; whereof they were not parts, but they were to be ordered and governed according to the laws to which they were subject, though it were a time of war. *Thirdly*, That the exercise of martial law, whereby any person should lose his life or member, or liberty, may not be permitted in time of peace, when the King's courts are open for all persons to receive justice, according to the laws of the land.

HALE, *supra* footnote 6, at 39-40.

According to Blackstone,

the necessity of order and discipline in an army is the only thing which can give ... countenance [to martial law]; and therefore it ought not to be permitted in time of peace, when the king's courts are open for all persons to receive justice according to the laws of the land.... And it is laid down, that if a lieutenant, or other, that hath commission of martial authority, doth in time of peace hang or otherwise execute any one by colour of martial law, this is murder; for it is against the magna carta. And the petition of right enacts, that no soldier shall be quartered on the subject without his own consent; and that no commission shall issue to proceed within this land according to martial law. And whereas, after the restoration, king Charles the second kept up about five thousand regular troops, by his own authority, for guards and garrisons; which king James the second by degrees increased to no less than thirty thousand, all paid from his own civil list; it was made one of the articles of the bill of rights, that the raising or keeping of a standing army within the kingdom in time of peace, unless it be with the consent of the parliament, is against the law.

I BLACKSTONE, *supra* footnote 6, at 400.

[12] HILLER B. ZOBEL, THE BOSTON MASSACRE 135 (1987) ("The soldiers, one ought always to remember, went into Boston not as an occupying army but rather as a force of uniformed peace-keepers, or policemen. Their role as even the radicals conceived it was to assist the executive and if necessary the courts to maintain order.").

[13] *See* Engdahl, *supra* footnote 9, at 24-25:

The last die was cast when two regiments of troops were quartered in Boston at the end of the decade. Boston was a hotbed of colonial discontent. The assemblage of military troops for control of possible disorders aggravated the discontent, not only because it affronted the English tradition against domestic use of military troops, but also because it was without warrant in the charter of Massachusetts Bay. The unwelcome troops were frequently taunted and vilified, and the ultimate and inevitable outrage soon occurred. A crowd of angry Bostonians ... blocked the path of a detachment of soldiers marching to their post. The soldiers made ready to force their passage, but were ordered back to the main guard.... The crowd approached the main guard with angry and opprobrious taunts. A sentinel struck one particularly bothersome boy with the butt of his musket, and quickly a crowd converged on that spot throwing snowballs and rocks at the sentinel along with verbal threats on his life. The sentinel loaded his musket and waved it at the mob, a squad of soldiers were sent to his aid. The soldiers, soon joined by a colonel, loaded their muskets as the crowd hooted and jeered and berated them and dared them to shoot. They kept the crowd back a time with bayonets, but then suddenly fired. It was never made clear – it never is – whether they had fired on their officer's order, or upon their own compulsion. In any event, five Americans lay dead and several others seriously wounded.... Members of a distrusted standing army, whose quartering was in violation of the Petition of Right, and whose preparation to militarily suppress possible civil disorder was inconsistent with the oldest of England's own traditions, had slain English civilians in a time of peace.

[14] This last charge presumably refers to the results of the murder trials of the officer and soldiers involved in the Boston Massacre. Two of the soldiers were convicted of manslaughter, branded on the hand and released; the officer and the other soldiers were acquitted. *See* ZOBEL, *supra* footnote 12, at 241-94.

[15] *See, e.g.*, ARTS. OF CONF. VI, VII, & IX.

No vessels of war shall be kept up in time of peace by any State, except such number only, as shall be deemed necessary by the United States in Congress assembled, for the defence of such State, or its trade; nor shall any body of forces be kept up by any State, in time of peace, except such number only, as in the judgment of the United States, in Congress assembled, shall be deemed requisite to garrison the forts necessary for the defence of such State; but every State shall always keep a well regulated and disciplined militia, sufficiently armed and accoutered, and shall provide and constantly have ready for public use, in public stores, a due number of field pieces and tents, and a proper quantity of arms, ammunition and camp equipage.... When land-forces are raised by any State for the common defence, all officers of or under the rank of colonel, shall be appointed by the Legislature of each State respectively by whom such forces shall be raised, or in such manner as such State shall direct, and all vacancies shall be filled up by the State which first made the appointment.... The United States in Congress assembled shall never ... appoint a commander in chief of the army or navy, unless nine States assent to the same....

[16] U.S. CONST. art. II, § 2; art. I, § 8, cls. 12, 13, 14. The Constitution treats the militia similarly. The President is the Commander in Chief of the militia while it is in federal service, and Congress is empowered to approve its organization, arms and discipline, U.S. CONST. art. II, § 2; art. I, § 8, cl.16.

[17] U.S. CONST. amend. III.

[18] U.S. CONST. amend. II.

[19] U.S. CONST. art. I, § 8, cl.15. Congress is further empowered to organize, arm, and discipline the militia, and to govern any part of militia in federal service, but the power to appoint officers and train the militias remains with the states. *Id.* cl. 16.

[20] *See* Jay S. Bybee, *Insuring Domestic Tranquility:* Lopez, *Federalization of Crime, and the Forgotten Role of the Domestic Violence Clause*, 66 GEO.WASH. L. REV. 1, 40 (1997).

[21] The Latin phrase literally means attendants with the capacity to act from the words *comes* and *posse* meaning companions or attendants (*comes*) and to be able or capable (*posse*). Among the Romans comitatus referred to one who accompanied the proconsul to his province. Later, comes (sometimes referred to as comites or counts) meant the king's companions or his most trusted attendants and comitatus came to refer to the districts or counties entrusted to their care. BOUVIER'S LAW DICTIONARY AND CONCISE ENCYCLOPEDIA 529, 2635 (1914).

[22] At common law, the sheriff of every county was obligated "to defend his county against any of the king's enemies when they come into the land; and for this purpose, as well as for keeping the peace and pursuing felons, he may command all the people of his county to attend him; which is call the posse comitatus, or power of the county; which summons every person above fifteen years old, and under the degree of a peer, is bound to attend upon warning, under pain of fine and imprisonment." 1 BLACKSTONE, *supra* footnote 6, at 332.

[23] For example, to counter the infamous Burr conspiracy in 1806, President Jefferson issued a proclamation "enjoin[ing] and requir[ing] all officers, civil and military, of the United States, or of any of the states or territories, and especially all governors and other executive authorities, all judges, justices and other officers of the peace, all military officers of the Army or Navy of the United States, or officers of the militia, to be vigilant, each within his respective department and according to his functions, in searching out and bringing to condign punishment all persons engaged in[a military expedition against Spanish territory], in seizing and detaining ... all vessels, arms military stores ... and in general in preventing the carrying on such expedition or enterprise by all lawful means within their power...." FREDERICK T. WILSON, FEDERAL AID IN DOMESTIC DISTURBANCES, 1903-22, at 38, S. DOC.NO. 67-263 (1922) (hereinafter "S. DOC.NO 67-263").

[24] Eighteenth and nineteenth century instances are collected, along with related proclamations and other documentation, in FREDERICK T. WILSON, FEDERAL AID IN DOMESTIC DISTURBANCES: 1787-1903, S. DOC.NO 57-209 (1903); updated to include early 20th century incidents in U.S. ARMY JUDGE ADVOCATE GENERAL, FEDERAL AID IN DOMESTIC DISTURBANCES, 1903-22, S. DOC. NO. 67-263 (1922); *see also* BENNET MILTON RICH, PRESIDENTS AND CIVIL DISORDER (1941); CLAYTON D. LAURIE AND RONALD H. COLE, THE ROLE OF FEDERAL MILITARY FORCES IN DOMESTIC DISORDERS: 1877-1945 (1997); PAUL SCHEIPS, THE ROLE OF FEDERAL MILITARY FORCES IN DOMESTIC DISORDERS, 1945-1992 (2005).

[25] 1 Stat. 96 (1789); 1 Stat. 121 (1790).

[26] Calling Forth Act of 1792, ch. 28, 1 Stat. 264 (repealed 1795); the Militia Act of 1795, ch. 36, 1 Stat. 424 (repealed in part 1861 and current version at 10 U.S.C. §§ 331-335). The constitutional and statutory authority to use military force in case of insurrection seems to have been in direct response to a perceived weakness in government under the Articles of Confederation. In 1787, a group of farmers in western Massachusetts, led by a Revolutionary War veteran named Daniel Shays and feeling oppressed by tax and creditor protection policies within the Commonwealth, had harassed the state courts and constabulary, and had attempted to storm the federal arsenal at Springfield before being repulsed by the militia. Some saw the insurrection as evidence of the need for a stronger central government and implicitly, confirmation that domestic tranquility might be more readily ensured if backed by centralized military capability. *See* SAMUEL ELIOTT MORISON, ET AL., I THE GROWTH OF THE AMERICAN REPUBLIC 242 (7th ed. 1980)("Nevertheless, Shays's Rebellion had a great influence on public opinion.... When Massachusetts appealed to the Confederation for help, [the Continental] Congress was unable to do a thing. That was the final argument to sway many Americans in favor of a stronger federal government"); CHRISTOPHER COLLIER & JAMES LINCOLN COLLIER, DECISION IN PHILADELPHIA: THE CONSTITUTIONAL CONVENTION OF 1787, at 13 (1986)("To men like Madison and Washington, Shays's Rebellion was an imperative. It hung like a shadow over the old Congress, and gave both impetus and urgency to the Constitutional Convention. It was the final, irrefutable piece of evidence that something had gone badly wrong. For some time these men had known that the deficiencies of the American government must be remedied. Shays's Rebellion made it clear to them that it must be done now."); CATHERINE DRINKER BOWEN, MIRACLE AT PHILADELPHIA: THE STORY OF THE CONSTITUTIONAL CONVENTION MAY TO SEPTEMBER 1787, at 10 (1966) ("Shays's Rebellion had been in the public mind when Congress, after debating the Annapolis report, had voted in favor of a convention in Philadelphia.").

[27] Calling Forth Act of 1792, ch. 28, § 1, 1 Stat. 264 (repealed 1795 and current version now at 10 U.S.C. § 331). It is unclear why Congress limited the ability of states to request assistance to circumstances of insurrection rather than "domestic violence" as permitted in Article IV, § 4 of the Constitution. Perhaps "domestic violence" was interpreted to be restricted to violence of a sufficient magnitude to constitute an insurrection, or the word "insurrection" was meant to convey armed violence that did not amount to a rebellion or revolution seeking to overthrow the government in part or all of a state. *See* RICH, *supra* footnote 24, at 21 n. 1 (citing definition of insurrection as including resistance to government authority smaller in scope and purpose than those described by the terms "rebellion" and "revolution").The guarantee of a "republican form of government" would seem to require federal intervention in the event of a rebellion against a state government even without its request.

[28] *Id.* § 2 (repealed 1795 and current version now at 10 U.S.C. § 332).

[29] *Id.* § 3 (repealed 1795 and current version now at 10 U.S.C. § 334).

[30] *See* Presidential Proclamations of Aug. 7, 1794 and Sept. 25, 1794, 1 JAMES D. RICHARDSON, A COMPILATION OF THE MESSAGES AND PAPERS OF THE PRESIDENTS 158-62 (1896); THOMAS P. SLAUGHTER, THE WHISKEY REBELLION: FRONTIER EPILOGUE TO THE AMERICAN REVOLUTION (1986); STEVEN R. BOYD, THE WHISKEY REBELLION: PAST AND PRESENT PERSPECTIVES (1985).

[31] The Militia Act of 1795, ch. 36, 1 Stat. 424 (repealed in part 1861).

[32] *See* Engdahl, *supra* footnote 9, at 49-50 (noting that prior to the Civil War, military troops were more commonly employed to assist civil officers in the enforcement of civilian laws rather than as soldiers privileged to use force).

[33] The Insurrection Act of 1807, ch. 39, 2 Stat. 443 provided that:

> in all cases of insurrection, or obstruction to the laws, either of the United States, or of any individual state or territory, where it is lawful for the President of the United States to call forth the militia for the purpose of suppressing such insurrection, or of causing the laws to be duly executed, it shall be lawful for him to employ, for the same purposes, such part of the land or naval force of the United States, as shall be judged necessary, having first observed all the pre-requisites of the law in that respect.

[34] *See* RICH, *supra* footnote 24, at 25-26 (noting lack of resistance to armed troops, whose presence terrorized local inhabitants, partly due to the inability of the commanding general to maintain strict discipline among his troops).

[35] Proclamation of March 12, 1799, *reprinted in* S. DOC. 67-263, *supra* footnote 23, at 35.

[36] Proclamation of May 21, 1800, *reprinted in* S. DOC. 67-263, *supra* footnote 23, at 36.

[37] *See* RICH, *supra* footnote 24, at 21 (attributing need for increased revenue to pending war with France).

[38] 2 Stat. 451.

[39] S. DOC. NO. 67-263, *supra* footnote 23, at 40-44. The federal marshal was to attempt to enforce the law with the use of the posse comitatus, and if that failed, the Secretary of War was to request the governor to issue a proclamation furnished by the President and then call on the state militia. *Id.* at 41. The President's proclamation to disperse drew ire from the local population, which drew up their own memorial protesting the characterization of the situation as an "insurrection and rebellion." RICH, *supra* footnote 24, at 32. Militia troops sent in by the governor proved unwilling to enforce the laws against their neighbors, and after a skirmish between militia troops and a group of smugglers, President Jefferson sent in troops from the regular Army. When similar opposition to the embargo arose in New York, the President did not issue a proclamation, attempting instead to persuade the governor to take action, but promising to reimburse the state for its assistance in enforcing federal law. *Id.* at 33.

[40] 2 Stat. 506, 510 (1809) (also known as the "Force Bill") (repealed).

[41] *See* ROBERT W. COAKLEY, THE ROLE OF FEDERAL MILITARY FORCES IN DOMESTIC DISORDERS, 1789-1878, at 89 (1989). Congress replaced the Embargo Act with a new measure to interdict trade with Great Britain and France, 2 Stat. 528, which authorized military force to compel ships from those countries to depart U.S. ports but did not permit the use of federal or state military forces to prevent any illicit trade.

[42] *See* RICH, *supra* footnote 24, at 38-39.

[43] *Id.*; ANDREW JACKSON, COPIES OF THE PROCLAMATION AND PROCEEDINGS IN RELATION TO SOUTH CAROLINA, S. DOC. NO. 22-30, at 38 (1833).

[44] 4 Stat. 632 (authorizing the President "to employ such part of the land or naval forces, or militia of the United States, as may be deemed necessary").

[45] *See generally* CHARLES FENWICK, THE NEUTRALITY LAWS OF THE UNITED STATES 15-18 (1913) (describing political situation accompanying President Washington's neutrality proclamation and early neutrality statutes).

[46] Act of June 5, 1794, 1 Stat. 381, renewed, 1 Stat. 497 (March 2, 1797) and 2 Stat. 54 (April 24, 1800), repealed 3Stat. 447, 450 (1818).

[47] *Id.* §7, 1 Stat. 384.

[48] *See* COAKLEY, *supra* footnote 41, at 25-28 (describing government circular to governors requesting militia support to suppress neutrality violations).

[49] *See supra* footnote 23; Thomas Jefferson, Message to Congress on the Burr Conspiracy, January 22, 1807, *available online at* The American Presidency Project, http://www. presidency.ucsb.edu/ws/?pid=65721 ("Orders were dispatched to every interesting point on the Ohio and Mississippi from Pittsburg to New Orleans for the employment of such force either of the regulars or of the militia and of such proceedings also of the civil authorities as might enable them to seize on all the boats and stores provided for the enterprise, to arrest the persons concerned, and to suppress effectually the further progress of the enterprise."); Thomas Jefferson, Sixth Annual Message, December 2, 1806, *available online at* The American Presidency Project, http://www.presidency.ucsb.edu/ws/?pid=29448 (suggesting additional statutory authority for prevention of such expedition might be in order). The President's desire to employ federal troops along with state militia led him to use the neutrality law rather than the insurrection act, although President believed the conspiracy amounted to an insurrection aimed at separating western territories from the United States. *See* COAKLEY, *supra* footnote 41, at 83. The Insurrection Act was thereafter amended to permit the use of regular troops as well as militia. *Id.*, *see supra* footnote 33.

[50] FENWICK, *supra* footnote 45, at 32-33 (describing Francesco de Miranda's efforts to organize expeditions).

[51] S. DOC. NO.67-263, *supra* footnote 23, at 39.

[52] S. DOC. NO. 67-263, *supra* footnote 23, at 49-50.

[53] Neutrality Act of April 20, 1818, § 8, 3 Stat. 447, 449. Prior to enactment of the 1818 statute, the general practice entailed a presidential appeal to state governors for aid in arresting violators. *See* VII JOHN BASSET MOORE, DIGEST OF INTERNATIONAL LAW §1321 (1906). After enactment of the 1818 Act, the President called on district attorneys and U.S. marshals or on states' attorneys-general to assist in enforcement, *see id.*, sometimes with the aid of military forces.

[54] S. DOC. NO. 67-263, *supra* footnote 23, at 51-53.

[55] V JAMES D. RICHARDSON, A COMPILATION OF THE MESSAGES AND PAPERS OF THE PRESIDENTS 7-8 (1897).

[56] The first of the so-called filibuster expeditions led by Narciso Lopez was disbanded without force by the Navy and civil authorities in 1849. *See* Louis N. Feipel, *The Navy and Filibustering in the Fifties*, 44 U.S. NAVAL INST. PROC.767 (1918). A second expedition in 1851 evaded U.S. naval forces only to have two of its vessels captured by Spanish men-of-war, but the captured filibusterers were eventually released back to American forces after some diplomatic exchange. *Id.* at 1016, 1026. A third expedition managed to land in Cuba in 1851 but was not met with local enthusiasm according to plan and was defeated, ending in the trial and execution of the main instigators. *Id.* at 1027-29.

[57] Proclamation of Oct. 12, 1870, 16 Stat. 1136; FENWICK, *supra* footnote 45, at 52 (stating object of proclamation).

[58] *See* COAKLEY, *supra* footnote 41, at 105.

[59] *Id.* at 105-06.

[60] RICH, *supra* footnote 24, at 53.

[61] *Id.*

[62] *Id.* at 74-75. Pennsylvania militia sent to suppress a riot in Pittsburgh instead inflamed the situation and were forced to withdraw, leaving the city in anarchy.

[63] The insurrection involved striking railroad workers, who seized control of the railroad in Martinsburg, WV. *See* RICH, *supra* footnote 24, at 73. The President sent federal troops, instructing their commanders not to act until his proclamation to disperse had been published. *See* S. DOC. NO. 67-263, *supra* footnote 23, at 163; 20 Stat. 803-04 (proclamation).

[64] A confrontation between militia and strike sympathizers in Baltimore, which resulted in 10 deaths, was the impetus for sending in troops. *See* RICH, *supra* footnote 24, at 74; 20 Stat. 804 (proclamation).

[65] The Illinois governor requested assistance in the proper form, and President Hayes promptly promised to supply it, but apparently not wanting to issue a proclamation, gave orders that troops were to be used to protect government property and enforce the orders of federal courts. *See* RICH, *supra* footnote 24, at 80.

[66] S. DOC. NO. 67-273, *supra* footnote 23, at 171-72.

[67] *See* RICH, *supra* footnote 24, at 80-81. The disturbance in California resulted from resentment against Chinese immigrants.

[68] *See id.* at 78 (listing the President's criteria for a formal request, which consisted of a certification that (1) disorder existed; (2) state authorities were incapable of preserving the peace; (3) the legislature was not in session; (4) the legislature could not be convened in time to meet the emergency; and (5) the appeal to the President was to protect the state against domestic violence).

[69] *See* S. DOC. NO. 67-263, *supra* footnote 23, at 170 (reporting that General Hancock determined that such assistance was not authorized, the governor not having requested it, unless troops were formally summoned by the sheriff as a posse comitatus).

[70] *See* RICH, *supra* footnote 24, at 82-83.

[71] *See* JERRY M. COOPER, THE ARMY AND CIVIL DISORDER 62-64 (1980).

[72] S. DOC. NO. 67-273, *supra* footnote 23, at 171-72. Although no proclamation under the Insurrection Act was issued, President Hayes ordered that officers in charge were to command insurgents to disperse prior to taking any action. *Id.*

[73] *See* RICH, *supra* footnote 24, at 78.

[74] Telegram from Major-General Hancock to Adjutant-General of the Army, July 24, 1877, *reprinted in* S. DOC. NO. 67-263, *supra* footnote 23, at 275.

[75] Telegram from Major-General Hancock to Secretary of War George W. McCrary, July 24, 1877, *reprinted in* S. DOC. NO. 67-263, *supra* footnote 23, at 275, 276.

[76] *See* RICH, *supra* footnote 24, at 76-77.

[77] *See, e.g.,* War Department Document No. 882, Office of the Adjutant General, Military Protection The Use of Organized Bodies in the Protection and Defense of Property During Riots, Strikes, and Civil Disturbances 63 (1919) (stating that "federal troops can not take orders from civil authorities" and that "a degree of martial law actually exists whenever Federal troops go on duty" for the purpose of riot duty, even where martial law has not been declared); *see also A Comprehensive Study of the Use of Military Troops in Civil Disorders with Proposals for Legislative Reform*, 43 U. COLO. L. REV. 399, 410 (1972) (arguing that the use of military during the Civil War led to erosion of notion that military troops used to execute laws were ordinarily subordinate to civil authority). This phenomenon may have been more pronounced at the state level. *See* Henry Winthrop Ballantine, *Unconstitutional Claims of Military Authority*, 5 J. AM. INST. CRIM. L. &

CRIMINOLOGY 718 (1915) (reporting instances of military intervention in labor disputes, mostly by state militias).

78 S. DOC. NO. 67-263, *supra* footnote 23, at 74-77.

79 *Id.* at 72-76, 247.

80 *Id.* at 78.

81 *Id.* at 78 (citing H.R. EX. DOC. NO. 25, 32d Cong., 2d sess.).

82 *Id.* (federal forces were originally to act as posse comitatus to aid newly appointed civilian government).

83 *Id.* at 79.

84 Proclamation of April 6, 1858, 11 Stat. 796.

85 S. DOC. NO. 67-263, *supra* footnote 23, at 45-46, related documents at 223-25.

86 11 Stat. 791 (1856).

87 S. DOC. NO. 67-263, *supra* footnote 23, at 69-71.

88 *Id.* at 71.

89 *See* Engdahl, *supra* footnote 9, at 53.

90 *See id.*

91 *Id.* at 53-54. The Supreme Court declared such use of the military in loyal states to be unconstitutional. *Ex parte* Milligan, 71 U.S. (4 Wall.) 2 (1866).

92 Act of July 29, 1861, 12 Stat. 281. *See* Engdahl, *supra* footnote 9, at 55-56 (describing changes).

93 *See* Gary Felicetti and John Luce, *The Posse Comitatus Act: Setting the Record Straight on 124 Years of Mischief and Misunderstanding Before Any More Damage Is Done*, 175 MIL. L. REV. 86, 100-09 (2003) (describing "counter-reconstruction" efforts and widespread racial terrorism); S. DOC. NO. 67-263, *supra* footnote 23, chapters V – VIII (describing employment of military during Reconstruction period and post-Reconstruction political disturbances during the years between 1866 and 1876).

94 *See* COAKLEY, *supra* footnote 41, at 341.

95 P.L. 42-22, 17 Stat. 13 (1871) (current version codified at 10 U.S.C. § 333).

96 17 Stat. 949. A previous proclamation under the existing authority to assist states South Carolina in putting down domestic violence on application of the governor did not bring about the desired result, 16 Stat. 1138 (March 24, 1871).

97 17 Stat. 950.

98 17 Stat. 951.

99 S. DOC. NO. 67-263, *supra* footnote 23, at 103.

100 *See, e.g.*, 1 Stat. 87 (1789)("a marshal shall be appointed in and for each district ... whose duty it shall be ... to execute throughout the district, all lawful precepts directed to him, and issued under the authority of the United States, and he shall have the power to command all necessary assistance in the execution of his duty...."); Calling Forth Act, § 9, 1 Stat. 265 (1792)("the marshals of the several districts and their deputies shall have the same powers in executing the laws of the United States, as sheriffs and their deputies in the several states have by law, in executing the laws of their respective states").

101 *See* WILLIAM WINTHROP, MILITARY LAW AND PRECEDENTS 866 (1920).

102 Act of Feb. 12, 1793, Respecting fugitives from justice, and persons escaping from the service of their masters, 1 Stat. 302, as amended by 9 Stat. 462 (1850).

103 Laws permitting the President to use military forces to execute particular laws were apparently understood to place the forces so employed under the direction of civil authorities. *See, e.g.*, Neutrality Act of April 30, 1818, § 8-9, 3 Stat.447, 449 (authorizing President or his designee to employ militia or land or naval forces to detain certain vessels, prevent military expeditions, and compel departure of foreign ships). In 1849, President Taylor used this authority to call upon "every officer in the military, civil or military, to use all efforts in his power to arrest for trial and punishment every such offenders of [neutrality laws, with respect to an expedition to invade Cuba]," V JAMES D. RICHARDSON, A COMPILATION OF THE MESSAGES AND PAPERS OF THE PRESIDENTS 7-8 (1907).

104 9 Stat. at 463.

105 S. DOC. NO. 67-263, *supra* footnote 23, at 62; 9 Stat. 1006 (President Millard Fillmore's proclamation urging all officers, civil and military, to assist in enforcement of the Fugitive Slave Act in 1851).

106 *Id.*

107 *See* COAKLEY, *supra* footnote 41, at 130 (citing VI JAMES D. RICHARDSON, A COMPILATION OF THE MESSAGES AND PAPERS OF THE PRESIDENTS 2637-46 (1897)). He further suggested that the requirement to issue a proclamation in connection with calling forth the militia should be dispensed with in cases where such a proclamation might defeat the purpose of the law to be executed by alerting persons whose arrest was sought.

108 *Id.*

109 *Id.*; S. REP.NO. 31-320 (1851). The Committee suggested that statutory authority to call forth the military or the regular military forces to enforce due execution of the laws would be rarely used, only after civil power (with the aid of military units as a posse comitatus) were to prove inadequate. *Id.* at 1.

110 S. DOC. NO. 67-263, *supra* footnote 23, at 64.

[111] *Id.* at 63-65 (recounting the "Anthony Burns" riots and a similar incident that occurred in Racine, Wisconsin in 1854).

[112] *See* COAKLEY, *supra* footnote 41, at 133-137 (reporting that Cushing's opinion was drafted in the midst of widespread resistance in Boston to the rendition of Anthony Burns, which became the occasion for the largest military posse comitatus ever assembled, albeit not under the effective direction of the marshal).

[113] 6 Op. Att'y Gen. 466, 473 (1854). Cushing's citation to Lord Mansfield is apparently a reference to the remarks of the English Chief Justice during debate in the House of Lords concerning the validity of use troops to quell rioters in London:

> Lord Mansfield ... went on: '....[I]t appears most clearly to me, that every man may legally interfere to suppress a riot, much more to prevent acts of felony, treason, and rebellion, in his private capacity, but he is bound to do it as an act of duty; and if called upon by a magistrate, is punishable in case of refusal.... A private man, if he sees a person committing an unlawful act, ... may apprehend the offender, and ... may use force to compel him, not to submit to him, but to the law. What a private man may do, a magistrate or peace officer may clearly undertake; and according to the necessity of the case ... , any number of men assembled or called together for the purpose are justified to perform. This doctrine I take to be clear and indisputable, with all the possible consequences which can flow from it, and to be the true foundation for calling in of the military power to assist in quelling the late riots.
>
> The persons who assisted in the suppression of those riots and tumults, in contemplation of law, are to be considered as mere private individuals, acting according to law, and upon any abuse of the legal power with which they are invested, are amendable to the laws of their country.
>
> ... On the whole, my lords, while I ... sincerely lament the cause which rendered it indispensably necessary to call out the military to assist in the suppression of the late disturbances, I am clearly of the opinion, that no steps have been taken which were not strictly legal, as well as fully justifiable in point of policy.... The military have been called in, ... not as soldiers, but as citizens: no matter whether their coats be red or brown, they have been called in aid of the laws, not to subvert them, or overturn the constitution, but to preserve both."

XXI HANSARD, THE PARLIAMENTARY HISTORY OF ENGLAND FROM THE EARLIEST PERIOD TO THE YEAR 1803, at 690-98 (June 19, 1780). Cushing seemed to turn Lord Mansfield's point on its head when he wrote that, "the fact that they are organized as military bodies, under the immediate command of their own officers, does not in any wise affect their legal character." English law prohibited martial law, the use of military force domestically, in peacetime England. Lord Mansfield justified an apparent breach of the martial law proscription by asserting that the soldiers had acted as individuals called, commanded, and governed exclusively by the dictates of law applicable to civilians. Civilians are not organized as military units and are not subject to the command of military officers. Lord Mansfield's justification could only hold as long as the soldiers were not organized as military bodies and were not acting under the command of their officers. The fact that they were organized as military bodies, under the immediate command of their own officers, was the critical determinant of their legal character.

[114] President Pierce told Congress:

> The Constitution requiring [the Executive] to take care that the laws of the United States be faithfully executed, if they be opposed in the Territory of Kansas he may, and should, place at the disposal of the marshal any public force of the United States which happens to be within the jurisdiction, to be used as a portion of the posse comitatus; and if that do not suffice to maintain order, then he may call forth the militia of one or more States for that object, or employ for the same object any part of the land or naval force of the United States. So, also, if the obstruction be to the laws of the Territory, and it be duly presented to him as a case of insurrection, he may employ for its suppression the militia of any State or the land or naval force of the United States.

V JAMES D. RICHARDSON, A COMPILATION OF THE MESSAGES AND PAPERS OF THE PRESIDENTS 358 (1897); *see also* EDWARD CORWIN, THE PRESIDENT: OFFICE AND POWERS, 1787-1984, 155 (5th ed. 1984) (calling Cushing's opinion an ingenious means of virtually eliminating the proclamation requirement under the Insurrection Act by enabling marshals to summon both state militia and U.S. regular forces within their precincts to assist in enforcing the law, noting President Pierce's use of new doctrine to declare it his duty to place U.S. forces in Kansas at the disposal of marshal).

[115] By the proposed legislation, would Congress would have given itself final authority to select which of the contending governments to recognize:

> But Congress hereby disapproving the code of alleged laws officially communicated to them by the President, and which are represented to have been enacted by a body claiming to be the Territorial Legislature of Kansas; and also disapproving of the manner in which said alleged laws have been enforced by the authorities of said Territory, expressly declare that, until those alleged laws shall have been affirmed by the Senate and House of Representatives as having been enacted by a legal Legislature, chosen in conformity with the organic law, by the people of Kansas, no part of the military force of the United States shall be employed in aid of their enforcement, nor shall any citizen of Kansas be required,

under those provisions to act as a part of the posse comitatus of any officer acting as a marshal or sheriff in said Territory.
CONG. GLOBE 34th Cong., 1st & 2d Sess. 1813 (1856).

[116] Members of the two political parties understandably disagreed as to whether the presence of federal troops in the South tainted or insured the integrity of the political process; compare, "[O]ur Army, degraded from its high position of the defenders of the country from foreign and domestic foes, has been used as a police; has taken possession of polls and controlled elections; has been sent with fixed bayonets into the halls of State Legislatures in time of peace and under the pretense of threatened outbreak; has been placed under the control of subordinate State officials, and, under the instructions of the Attorney General, has been notified to obey the orders of deputy United States marshals, 'general and special,' appointed in swarms to do dirty work in a presidential campaign," 5 CONG. REC. 2117 (remarks of Rep. Banning), with, "Nor do I think, sir, that the use of troops in the States recently in rebellion was uncalled for or inconsistent with the spirit of republican liberty. If they were recalled before every man, white and black, was safe – safe and truly free, with all his civil rights in their fullest extent – they were recalled too soon." 7 CONG. REC. 3616 (remarks of Rep. Philips).

[117] Section 5 of H.R. 4691, as passed by the House, provided, "That no part of the money appropriated by this act, nor any money heretofore appropriated, shall be applied to the pay, subsistence, or transportation of troops used, employed, or to be used or employed, in support of the claim[s of various individuals and bodies purporting to comprise the valid government of Louisiana]; nor in the aid of the execution of any process in the hands of the United States marshal in said State issued in aid of and for the support of any such claims. Nor shall the Army, or any portion of it, be used in support of the claims, or pretended claim or claims, of any State government, or officer thereof, in any State, until the same shall have been duly recognized by Congress. Any person offending against any of the provisions of this act shall be guilty of a misdemeanor, and, upon conviction thereof, shall be imprisoned at hard labor for not less than five years or more than ten years." 5 CONG. REC. 2119 (1877).

[118] *See* Presidential Proclamation of May 5, 1877, 20 Stat. 803 (1877), calling Congress into session.

[119] The bill contained no posse comitatus provisions because the President had withdrawn federal troops from Louisiana and South Carolina and because of concern over disturbances on the Mexican border and over Indian uprisings. 6 CONG. REC. 287 (remarks of Rep. Atkins) (1877).

[120] "From and after the passage of this act it shall not be lawful to employ any part of the Army of the United States as a *posse comitatus* or otherwise under the pretext or for the purpose of executing the laws, except in such cases and under such circumstances as such employment of said forces may be expressly authorized by act of Congress; and no money appropriated by this act shall be used to pay any of the expenses incurred in the employment of any troops in violation of this section; and any person violating the provisions of the this section shall be deemed guilty of a misdemeanor, and on conviction thereof shall be punished by a fine not exceeding $10,000 or imprisonment not exceeding two years, or both such fine and imprisonment." 7 CONG.REC. 3845 (1878).

[121] The "pretext" language was stricken because it was thought to be "in the nature of a reflection upon the past administration of the Government." 7 CONG. REC. 4648 (remarks of Sen. Sargent). Instances of express Constitutional authority were added to the statutory exception, although then as now the precise effect of this change was a matter of dispute; the penalty was applicable only to willful violations, although a Senate requirement that the penalty be restricted to willful and knowing violations was not accepted. *Id.*

[122] *See* WINTHROP, *supra* footnote 101, at 867.

[123] *See id.*

[124] *See* Engdahl, *supra* footnote 9, at 62-64 ("By the end of the [19th] century it had become thoroughly established in the common understanding that wherever and whenever military troops were employed, it was equivalent to war.").

[125] *Cf* Felicetti & Luce, *supra* footnote 93, at 91(arguing that "courts analyzing the Act [have written] about the law as if it was the only law or principle that limited the use of the armed forces in a law enforcement role. Some, therefore, have claimed to discern a broader policy or 'spirit' behind the Act that is not supported by the historical record or the statute's text. While these wider policies are sound, they are embodied in federalism, the law concerning federal arrest authority, election law, and especially fiscal law. The ... Posse Comitatus Act ... doesn't have to do all the work, a view that even the Act's original proponents appeared to recognize. Trying to force-fit all these other principles into the surviving part of the Act has only created a need to 'discover' a number of implied exceptions and has sowed a great deal of confusion.").

[126] *See* Rutherford B. Hayes, Second Annual Message to Congress, 8 CONG. REC. 5 (1878) (noting recommendation of the Secretary of War that the provision be repealed or amended); 1 Annual Report of the Secretary of War for 1878, at VI-VII (advising repeal of posse comitatus provision or expansion of exceptions to permit employment of the Army to counter lawlessness in Arizona territory); *see also* Chester A. Arthur, First Annual Message to Congress, 13 CONG. REC. 28 (1881) (advising an exception permitting the military to assist the civil Territorial authorities in enforcing the laws of the United States); Chester A. Arthur, Special Message, 13 CONG. REC. 3355 (1882) (same). Congress declined to exempt the territories at that time, apparently due to the belief that sufficient authority existed in insurrection statutes to permit military intervention to execute federal

law, albeit under presidential authority rather than that of the federal marshal. *See* 13 CONG. REC. 3457-58 (1882) (statement by Senator Edmunds, reporting conclusion of the Senate Judiciary Committee). In 1900, however, Congress enacted an exemption for the District of Alaska, Act of June 6, 1900, 31 Stat. 330.

[127] For some time the act was contained in Title 10 of the United States Code and Alaska, while the Alaskan territory was exempted, 10 U.S.C. § 15 (1940 ed.). When Title 10 was recodified and the section transferred to Title 18, the Air Force, previously covered while it was part of the Army, was expressly added to the act, 70A Stat. 626 (1956).

Over the years, Congress has adjusted the impact of the Posse Comitatus Act by enlarging the number of statutes which expressly authorize the use of the Army or Air Force to execute the law. These are sometimes referred to as "amendments" to the Posse Comitatus Act. Since they do not change language of the act itself, it seems to be more accurate to characterize them as expansions of authority under the statutory exception to the Posse Comitatus Act rather than as amendments or changes in the act itself.

[128] "The Secretary of Defense shall prescribe such regulations as may be necessary to ensure that any activity (including the provision of any equipment or facility or the assignment or detail of any personnel) under this chapter [10 U.S.C. §§ 371-382] does not include or permit direct participation by a member of the Army, Navy, Air Force, or Marine Corps in a search, seizure, arrest, or other similar activity unless participation in such activity by such member is otherwise authorized by law." 10 U.S.C. § 375.

Soon after the enactment of Section 375, the Secretary of Defense promulgated such regulations which, subject to designated exceptions, prohibited: "(i) Interdiction of a vehicle, vessel, aircraft or other similar activity. (ii) A search or seizure, (iii) An arrest, stop and frisk, or similar activity. (iv) Use of military personnel for surveillance or pursuit of individuals, or as informants, undercover agents, investigators, or interrogators." 32 C.F.R. 213(10)(a)(3), 47 Fed. Reg. 14899, 14902 (April 7, 1982). Some years later the regulations were removed, 53 Fed. Reg. 23776 (April 28, 1993) and replaced with a new regulation combining various authorities related to domestic operations, 32 C.F.R. Part 185, 58 Fed. Reg. 52667 (Oct. 12, 1993), which in turn refers to relevant DOD Directives setting forth regulations in greater detail. Proposed 32 C.F.R. Part 182 (a)(iii) would add "(4) Evidence collection, security functions, and crowd and traffic control" to the above list of exceptions. 75 Fed. Reg. 81,547 (December 28, 2010).

[129] *Ex parte* Milligan, 71 U.S. (4 Wall.) 3, 123-25 (1866); Toth v. Quarles, 350 U.S. 11 (1955); Reid v. Covert, 354 U.S. 1 (1957); Kinsella v. Singleton, 361 U.S. 234 (1960); Grisham v. Hagan, 361 U.S. 278 (1960); McElroy v. Guagliardo, 361 U.S. 281 (1960); O'Callahan v. Parker, 395 U.S. 258 (1969); *but see* Solorio v. United States, 483 U.S. 435 (1987) (holding that the jurisdiction of military tribunals depends upon whether the accused was a member of the Armed Forces at the time of alleged misconduct and, contrary to *O'Callahan*, not whether the crime was "service connected").

[130] 343 U.S. 579 (1952).

> Article II, Section 2 make the Chief Executive the Commander in Chief of the Army and Navy. But our history and tradition rebel at the thought that the grant of military power carries with it authority over civilian affairs.

343 U.S. at 632 (Douglas, J., concurring).

> Time out of mind, and even now in many parts of the world, a military commander can seize private housing to shelter his troops. Not so, however, in the United States, for the Third Amendment says, 'No Soldier shall, in time of peace be quartered in any house, without the consent of the Owner, nor in time of war, but in a manner to be prescribed by law.' Thus, even in war time, his seizure of needed military housing must be authorized by Congress. It also was expressly left to Congress to 'provide for calling forth the Militia to execute the laws of the Union, suppress Insurrections and repel Invasions...." Such a limitation on the command power, written at a time when the militia rather than a standing army was contemplated as the military weapon of the Republic, underscores the Constitution's policy that Congress, not the Executive, should control utilization of the war power as an instrument of domestic policy. Congress, fulfilling that function, has authorized the President to use the army to enforce certain civil rights. On the other hand, Congress has forbidden him to use the army for the purpose executing general laws except when *expressly* authorized by the Constitution or Act of Congress.

343 U.S. at 644-45 (Jackson, J., concurring)(emphasis in the original).

In *Youngstown*, the Court held that, when Congress had specifically refused to grant such authority by statute, the President's constitutional and statutory powers as President and Commander in Chief were not sufficient to support an executive order authorizing the Secretary of Commerce use the resources of the federal government, including its Armed Forces, to seize and operate the country's steel mills which were then threatened by a nation-wide strike.

[131] 408 U.S. 1 (1972).

> The concerns of the Executive and Legislative Branches in response to disclosure of the Army surveillance activities – and indeed the claims alleged in the complaint – reflect a traditional and strong resistance of Americans to any military intrusion into civilian affairs. That tradition has deep roots in our history and found early expression, for example, in the Third Amendment's explicit prohibition against quartering soldiers in private homes without consent and in the constitutional provisions for civilian

control of the military. Those prohibitions are not directly presented by this case, but their philosophical underpinnings explain our traditional insistence on limitations on military operations in peacetime.

Id. at 15-6.

In *Laird v. Tatum*, the Court refused to order the military to stop collecting information about civilians unless the civilians could show how they had been hurt by what the military was doing. (More precisely the Court held that, in the absence of any showing of specific harm or the realistic threat of specific harm, a claim, that the data gathering activities of the military services had been conducted so as to chill the First Amendment rights of the targets of those intelligence collection efforts, was nonjusticiable).

[132] *See* Tom W. Bell, *The Third Amendment, Forgotten But Not Gone*, 2 WM & MARY BILL RTS. J. 117 (1993); William S. Fields and David T. Hardy, *The Third Amendment and the Issue of the Maintenance of Standing Armies: A Legal History*, 35 AM. J. LEGAL HIST. 393 (1991); William Sutton Fields, *The Third Amendment: Constitutional Protection From the Involuntary Quartering of Soldiers*, 124 MIL. L. REV. 195 (1989). In one of the few reported Third Amendment cases, striking state correctional officers brought a civil rights action against state authorities who had used the officers' prison facility resident quarters to house replacement national guard troops. The district court dismissed, Engblom v. Carey, 522 F. Supp. 57, 70 (S.D.N.Y. 1981), the appellate court reversed on the ground that it could not hold as a matter of law that the officers had no Third Amendment possessory interest in the resident quarters, 677 F.2d 957, 964 (2d Cir. 1982). On remand the district court dismissed based on the qualified immunity of the defendant state officials in light of the uncertainty of the right with respect to Third Amendment questions, 572 F. Supp. 44, 49 (S.D.N.Y.), *aff'd*, 724 F.2d 28 (2d Cir. 1983). The implications of the case prior to remand are discussed in *The Third Amendment's Protection Against Unwanted Military Intrusions*, 49 BROOK. L. REV. 857 (1983).

[133] The Second Amendment might be seen as evidence of the founders' preference for the Minute Men over Hessian mercenaries as a means of common defense. Story, speaking of the Second Amendment, noted the distaste in the early Republic not simply for a standing army's involvement in domestic affairs but for existence of a standing army at all:

The militia is the natural defence of a free country against sudden foreign invasions, domestic insurrections, and domestic usurpations of power by rulers. It is against sound policy for a free people to keep up large military establishments and standing armies in time of peace, both from the enormous expenses, with which they are attended, and the facile means, which they afford to ambitious and unprincipled rulers, to subvert the government, or trample upon the rights of the people. The right o f the citizens to keep and bear arms has justly been considered, as the palladium of the Liberties of a republic; since it offers a strong moral check against the usurpation and arbitrary power of rulers; and will generally, even if these are successful the first instance, enable the people to resist and triumph over them.

III JOSEPH STORY, COMMENTARIES ON THE CONSTITUTION OF THE UNITED STATES § 1890 (1833). At one time, scholars disagreed over whether the Second Amendment's predominant theme is the right to bear arms or this perceived need for a well regulated militia. *See* William Van Alstyne, *The Second Amendment and the Personal Right to Bear Arms*, 43 DUKE L. J. 1236 (1994); Andrew D. Herz, *Gun Crazy: Constitutional False Consciousness and Dereliction of Dialogic Responsibility*, 75 B.U. L. REV. 57 (1995). The Supreme Court seems to have resolved the matter in favor of the former. District of Columbia v. Heller, 554 U.S. 570 (2008).

[134] *See, e.g.*, United States v. Walden, 490 F.2d 372, 376 (4th Cir. 1974)("we do not find it necessary to interpret relatively unexplored sections of the Constitution in order to determine whether there might be constitutional objection to the use of the military to enforce civilian laws").

[135] U.S. CONST. art I, § 8, cl. 15.

[136] U.S. CONST. art IV, § 4.

[137] U.S. CONST. art. I, § 10, cl.3.

[138] *See* Luther v. Borden, 48 U.S. (7 How.) 1, 45 (1849) ("[U]nquestionably a State may use its military power to put down an armed insurrection too strong to be controlled by the civil authority.").

[139] *See, e.g.*, George B. DAVIS, A TREATISE OF THE MILITARY LAW OF THE UNITED STATES 300 (3d ed. 1913)(describing "martial law" as a term applied to the "temporary government, by military authority, of a place or district in which, by reason of the existence civil disorder, or a state of war and the pendency of military operations, the civil government is, for the time being, unable to exercise its functions.")

[140] *See* Jason Collins Weida, Note, *A Republic of Emergencies: Martial Law in American Jurisprudence*, 36 CONN. L. REV. 1397 (2004); Kirk L. Davies, *The Imposition of Martial Law in the United States*, 49 A.F. L. REV. 67, 111 (2000); George M. Dennison, *Martial Law: The Development of a Theory of Emergency Powers, 1776-1861*, 18 AM. J. LEGAL HIST. 52, 56-58 (1974). Until recently, federal regulation provided for martial law in certain circumstances. *See* former 32 C.F.R. Part 501 (2007). According to former 32 C.F.R. § 501.4:

When Federal Armed Forces are committed in the event of civil disturbances, their proper role is to support, not supplant, civil authority. Martial law depends for its justification upon public necessity. Necessity gives rise to its creation; necessity justifies its exercise; and necessity limits its duration. The extent of the military force used and the actual measures taken, consequently, will depend upon the actual threat to order and public safety which exists at the time.

The regulation went on to say that declarations of martial law are ordinarily made by the President, but that the decision could be made "by the local commander on the spot, if the circumstances demand immediate action, and time and available communications facilities do not permit obtaining prior approval from higher authority." *Id.* The regulation was withdrawn in 2008. 73 Fed. Reg. 23,350 (Apr. 30, 2008) (noting that the responsibility to prepare for civil disturbances has been transferred to Office of the Assistant Secretary of Defense for Homeland Defense). Until 1993, 32 C.F.R. Part 185, Defense Support of Civil Defense, contained a provision authorizing senior military to impose martial law where the President had not done so in the event of a complete breakdown of civil governance. The regulation further stated that military resources could not be employed for law enforcement purposes unless martial law had been proclaimed or a serious breakdown of law and order impelled civil authorities to request military assistance to prevent loss of life or wanton destruction of property. 32 C.F.R. § 185.4 (1993).

141 *See* James P. O'Shaughnessy, Note, *The Posse Comitatus Act: Reconstruction Politics Reconsidered*, 13 AM. CRIM. L. REV. 703, 712-13 (1976).

142 U.S. CONST. art. II, § 1 ("[t]he executive Power shall be vested in a President of the United States of America"), §2 ("[t]he President shall be Commander in Chief of the Army and Navy of the United States, and of the Militia of the several States, when called into actual Service of the United States"), §3 ("[The President] shall take Care that the Laws be faithfully executed").

143 "The United States shall guarantee to every State in this Union, a Republican Form of Government, and shall protect each of them against Invasion; and on Application of the Legislature, or of the Executive (when the Legislature cannot be convened) against domestic Violence." U.S. CONST. art. IV, § 4.

144 *In re* Neagle, 135 U.S. 1, 62-4 (1890).

145 The Prize Cases, 67 U.S.(2 Black) 635, 668 (1863).

146 *In re* Debs, 158 U.S. 364, 381 (1895).

147 *See, e.g.*, Walter A. Lorence, *The Constitutionality of the Posse Comitatus Act*, 8 U. KAN. CITY L. REV. 164, 185-91 (1940); H.W.C. Furman, *Restrictions Upon Use of the Army Imposed by the Posse Comitatus Act*, 7 MIL. L. REV. 85, 91-2 (1960); CORWIN, *supra* footnote 114, at 152-61.

148 U.S. CONST. art. I, § 8, cl.18.

149 U.S. CONST. art. I, § 8, cls.12, 13, & 14

150 U.S. CONST. art. I, § 8, cls.15 & 16.

151 *See* Texas v. White, 74 U.S. (7 Wall.) 700 (1869).

152 *See* Youngstown Sheet & Tube Co. v. Sawyer, 343 U.S. 579 (1952). In *Youngstown*, President Truman attempted to invoke his powers as Commander in Chief and Chief Executive to seize and operate most of the Nation's steel mills during the Korean conflict when it appeared they might be shut down by a labor dispute. Congress had earlier specifically refused to grant the President such power legislatively.

153 *See* United States v. United States District Court, 407 U.S. 297 (1972). Congress had established a warrant procedure to be used by law enforcement officials to permit wiretapping in criminal cases. In doing so, it expressly disclaimed any intent to "limit the constitutional power of the President to take such measures as he deems necessary to protect the Nation against actual or potential attack or other hostile acts of a foreign power, to obtain foreign intelligence information deemed essential to the security of the United States, or to protect national security information against foreign intelligence activities [or] to take such measures as he deems necessary to protect the United States against the overthrow of the Government by force or other unlawful means, or against any clear and present danger to the structure or existence of the Government," 18 U.S.C. § 2511(3)(1970 ed.). Even in the absence of congressionally asserted counter authority, a unanimous Court declined to accept the argument that President's inherent and incidental constitutional powers permitted a failure to comply with the Fourth Amendment's warrant requirements when gathering intelligence concerning purely domestic threats to national security.

154 18 U.S.C. § 1385.

155 H.R. REP. NO. 97-71, at 6 n.3, *reprinted in* 1981 U.S.C.C.A.N. at 1789 n.3 ("The statute permits Constitutional exceptions. However, there are none"); G. NORMAN LIEBER, THE USE OF THE ARMY IN AID OF THE CIVIL POWER 17 (1898); John P. Coffey, Note, *The Navy's Role in Interdicting Narcotics Traffic: War on Drugs or Ambush of the Constitution?*, 75 GEO. L.J. 1947, 1951 (1987); John D. Gates, Note, *Don't Call Out the Marines: An Assessment of the Posse Comitatus Act*, 13 TEX. TECH. L. REV. 1467, 1486 (1982); O'Shaughnessy, *supra footnote 141*, at 712.

The Constitution does empower Congress "to provide for calling forth the Militia to execute the laws of the Union, suppress insurrections and repel invasions," U.S. CONST. art. I, § 8, cl. 15; but since this express grant of authority can only be activated by an act of Congress, it adds nothing to the "act of Congress" exception also included within the Posse Comitatus Act.

156 The act also provides that the Army and Air Force can be used on the basis of an *express constitutional* authorization. This language reflects a compromise reached in the debate over the act. It is a meaningless proviso since the Constitution does not expressly authorize such a use of troops.

In any event, if the Constitution provided the President with authority over a purely executive function, Congress could not disable the President from acting on the basis of it, whether the authorization was express or implied. But since the Constitution provides Congress with the power to control military intervention in domestic affairs, the President's actions can be limited to the express terms of a statutory authorization. *Honored in the Breech: Presidential Authority to Execute the Laws with Military Force*, 83 YALE L. J. 130, 143-44 (1973). *See also* O'Shaugnhessy, *supra* footnote141, at 712-13.

[157] 7 CONG. REC. 3877 (1878). As introduced, the measure provided:

From and after the passage of this act it shall not be lawful to employ any part of the army of the United Sates as a *posse comitatus* or otherwise under the pretext or for the purpose of executing the laws, *except in such cases and under such circumstances as such employment of said force may be expressly authorized by act of Congress*; and no money appropriated by this act shall be used to pay any of the expenses incurred in the employment of any troops in violation of this section; and any person violating the provisions of this section shall be deemed guilty of a misdemeanor, and on conviction thereof shall be punished by a fine of not exceeding $10,000 or imprisoned not exceeding two years, or by both such fine and imprisonment. (Emphasis added).

[158] 7 CONG. REC. 4303-304 (1878). The Senate version would have provided:

From and after the passage of this act it shall not be lawful to employ any part of the army of the United Sates as a *posse comitatus* or otherwise for the purpose of executing the laws, *except in such cases and under such circumstances as such employment of said force may be authorized by the Constitution or by act of Congress*; and no money appropriated by this act shall be used to pay any of the expenses incurred in the employment of any troops in violation of this section. (Emphasis added).

[159] As the House manager viewed the matter:

But these [compromises on other differences in the Army appropriation bill] are all minor points and insignificant questions compared with the great principle which was incorporated by the House in the bill in reference to the use of the Army in time of peace. The Senate had already conceded what they called and what we might accept as principle; but they had stricken out the penalty and had stricken out the word 'expressly,' so that the Army might be used in all cases where implied authority might be inferred. The House committee planted themselves firmly upon the doctrine that rather than yield this fundamental principle, for which for three years this House had struggled, they would all the bill to fail—notwithstanding the reforms which we had secured; regarding these reforms as of but little consequence alongside the great principle in all its length and breadth, including the penalty which the Senate had stricken out. We bring you back, therefore, a report with the alteration of a single word, which the lawyers assure me is proper to be made, restoring to this bill the principle for which we have contended so long, and which is so vital to secure the rights and liberties of the people.

7 CONG. REC. 4686 (1878)(remarks of Rep. Hewitt).

[160] The manager in the Senate described the compromise as follows:

With reference to the provisions of the bill inserted by the House prohibiting the use of the Army, ... Senators will remember that it was amended in the senate so as to strike out ['pretext' and 'expressly,' and the penalty, and amended] so as to read 'by the Constitution or by act of congress.'... We found considerable difficulty in agreeing upon this section, but the modification which the Senate had made in it made it possible to come to an understanding.... As it now stands, the House yielded that the words 'under the pretext of' should go out, which we contended were in the autre of a reflection upon the past administration of the government, and we could not consent that anything in the nature of a reflection, and which was entirely useless for any practical purpose, should remain in the bill....

With reference to the word 'expressly.' we restored it and allowed it to go in, so that now the employment of such force must be expressly authorized by the Constitution or by act of Congress, they assenting that the words 'the Constitution or by' before the words 'act of Congress' might remain in, so that if the power arises under either the Constitution or the laws it may be exercised and the Executive would not be embarrassed by the prohibition of Congress so to act where the Constitution requires him to act; and the embarrassments would not have the effect of restraining the action of an upright and energetic Executive, but still might raise a question which he would desire to avoid if possible....

7 CONG. REC. 4648 (1878) (remarks of Sen. Sargent).

[161] *See* LIEBER, *supra* footnote 155, at 14-15.

The debate [on the Posse Comitatus section] was an interesting one, but too long to follow in detail. An attempt was made to strike out the word "expressly," but that failed. But, manifestly, the clause, as enacted, recognizes the Constitution as a direct source of authority for the employment of the Army. This is a very important consideration in the construction of the legislation. And another matter of great importance is also to be observed with reference to it. The enactment prescribes that it shall be unlawful to employ any part of the Army as a *posse comitatus*, or otherwise, for the purpose of executing the laws, except when it is *expressly* authorized by the Constitution or by act of Congress. Now, it is evident that the word 'expressly' can not be construed as placing a restriction on any constitutional power. If authority so to use the Army is included in a constitutional power, although it be not expressly named, it can not, of course, be taken away by legislation.

Lorence, *supra* footnote 147, at 185-86.

But it is evident that the word *expressly* in the Posse Comitatus Act cannot be construed as placing a restriction on the constitutional Power of the President, because even though not expressly named, such constitutional power cannot be taken away by legislation.... Thus, the Posse Comitatus Act appears to be a rather singular statute to pass, saying that the Army of the United States shall not be used for the purpose of executing the laws, in view of the fact that the Constitution expressly makes the President the Commander-in-Chief of the Army and Navy, and expressly makes it his duty to take care that the laws are faithfully executed.

[162] According to 32 C.F.R. 215.4(b),(c)(1),

(b) Aside from the constitutional limitations of the power of the Federal Government at the local level, there are additional legal limits upon the use of military forces within the United States. The most important of these from a civil disturbance standpoint is the Posse Comitatus Act (18 U.S.C. § 1385), which prohibits the use of any part of the Army or the Air Force to execute or enforce the laws, except as authorized by the Constitution or Act of Congress.

(c) The Constitution and Acts of Congress establish six exceptions generally applicable within the entire territory of the United States, to which the Posse Comitatus Act prohibition does not apply.

(1) The constitutional exceptions are two in number and are based upon the inherent legal right of the U.S. Government – a sovereign national entity under the Federal Constitution – to insure the preservation of public order and the carrying out of governmental operations within its territorial limits, by force if necessary.

(i) The emergency authority. Authori[z]es prompt and vigorous Federal action, including use of military force to prevent loss of life or wanton destruction of property and to restore governmental functioning and public order when sudden and unexpected civil disturbances, disasters, or calamities seriously endanger life and property and disrupt normal governmental functions to such an extent that duly constituted local authorities are unable to control the situation.

(ii) Protection of Federal property and functions. Authorizes Federal action, including the use of military forces, to protect Federal property and Federal governmental functions when the need for protection exists and duly constituted local authorities are unable or decline to provide adequate protection."

For a discussion of instances when the emergency, "immediate response authority" has been used, see Jim Winthrop, *The Oklahoma City Bombing: Immediate Response Authority and Other Military Assistance to Civil Authority (MAC)*, ARMY LAW., July 1997, at 3.

[163] "Whoever, *except in cases and under circumstances expressly authorized by* the Constitution or *Act of Congress*, willfully uses any part of the Army or the Air Force as a posse comitatus or otherwise to execute the laws shall be fined under this title or imprisoned not more than two years, or both." 18 U.S.C. § 1385 (emphasis added).

[164] 14 U.S.C. § 2 provides:

The Coast Guard shall enforce or assist in the enforcement of all applicable Federal laws on, under, and over the high seas and waters subject to the jurisdiction of the United states; shall engage in maritime air surveillance or interdiction to enforce or assist in the enforcement of the laws of the United States; shall administer laws and promulgate and enforce regulations for the promotion of safety of life and property on and under the high seas and waters subject to the jurisdiction of the United States covering all matters not specifically delegated by law to some other executive department; shall develop, establish, maintain and operate with due regard to the requirements of national defense, aids to maritime navigation, icebreaking facilities, and rescue facilities for the promotion of safety on, under, and over the high seas and waters subject to the jurisdiction of the United States; shall, pursuant to international agreements, develop, establish, maintain, and operate icebreaking facilities on, under, and over the waters other than the high seas and waters subject to the jurisdiction of the Untied States; shall engage in oceanographic research on the high seas and in waters subject to the jurisdiction of the United Stats; and shall maintain a state of readiness to function as a specialized service in the Navy in time of war, including the fulfillment of Maritime Defense Zone command responsibilities.

Coast Guard personnel are also considered customs officers for purpose of customs law enforcement, 19 U.S.C. § 1401(i)("When used in this subtitle [relating to administrative provisions concerning customs duties] or in part I of subtitle II of this chapter [relating to the miscellaneous provisions of the Tariff Act of 1930] ... (i) The terms 'officer of the customs' and 'customs officer' mean ... any commissioned, warrant, or petty officer of the Coast Guard ... "); 19 U.S.C. § 1709(b) (Coast Guard officers are customs officials for purposes of the Anti-Smuggling Act). The Coast Guard has explicit law enforcement powers under 14 U.S.C. § 89 ("The Coast Guard may make inquiries, examinations, inspections, searches, seizures, and arrests upon the high seas and waters over which the United States has jurisdiction, for the prevention, detection, and suppression of violations of laws of the United States."); 14 U.S.C. § 91 (empowering Secretary of the respective department in which the Coast Guard is operating to provide for safety and security of U.S. naval vessels). *See generally* Greg Shelton, Note, *The United States Coast Guard's Law Enforcement Authority Under 14 U.S.C. § 89: Smugglers' Blues or Boaters' Nightmare?*, 34 WM. & MARY L. REV. 933 (1993); Christopher A. Abel, Note, *Not Fit for Sea Duty: The Posse Comitatus Act, the United States Navy, and Federal Law Enforcement at Sea*, 31 WM. & MARY L. REV. 445 (1990).

[165] Statutory exceptions to the Posse Comitatus Act include:

5 U.S.C. App. (Inspector General Act of 1978) § 8(g) (Department of Defense Inspector General is not limited by the Posse Comitatus Act (18 U.S.C. § 1385) in carrying out audits and investigations under the act);

10 U.S.C. §§ 331-335 (President may use the militia and Armed Forces to suppress insurrection and enforce federal authority in the face of rebellion or other forms of domestic violence); *10 U.S.C. § 12406* (President may call National Guard units or members into federal service to repel an invasion, suppress a rebellion, or execute federal laws when he is unable to execute them using the regular forces);

16 U.S.C. § 23 (Secretary of the Army may detail troops to protect Yellowstone National Park upon the request of the Secretary of the Interior);

16 U.S.C. § 78 (Secretary of the Army may detail troops to protect Sequoia and Yosemite National Parks upon the request of the Secretary of the Interior);

16 U.S.C. § 593 (President may use the land and naval forces of the United States to prevent destruction of federal timber in Florida);

16 U.S.C. § 1861(a) (Secretary of Homeland Security (or the Secretary of the Navy in time of war) may enter into agreements for the use of personnel and resources of other federal or state agencies—including those of the Department of Defense—for the enforcement of the Magnuson Fishery Conservation and Management Act);

18 U.S.C. §§ 112, 1116 (Attorney General may request the assistance of federal or state agencies—including the Army, Navy and Air Force—to protect foreign dignitaries from assault, manslaughter and murder);

18 U.S.C. § 351 (FBI may request the assistance of any federal or state agency—including the Army, Navy and Air Force—in its investigations of the assassination, kidnapping or assault of a Member of Congress);

18 U.S.C. § 1751 (FBI may request the assistance of any federal or state agency—including the Army, Navy and Air Force—in its investigations of the assassination, kidnapping or assault of the President);

18 U.S.C. § 3056 note (Director of the Secret Service may request assistance from the Department of Defense and other federal agencies to protect the President);

22 U.S.C. § 408 (President may use the land and naval forces of the United States to enforce Title IV of the Espionage Act of 1917 (arms embargoes) (22 U.S.C. §§ 401-408));

22 U.S.C. § 461 (President may use the land and naval forces and militia of the United States to enforce parts of the Neutrality Act, 22 U.S.C. §§ 461-465 and 18 U.S.C. §§ 958-962);

22 U.S.C. § 462 (President may use the land and naval forces and militia of the United States to detain or compel departure of foreign ships under the provisions of the Neutrality Act);

25 U.S.C. § 180 (President may use military force to remove trespassers from Indian treaty lands);

42 U.S.C. § 97 ("officers of the United States shall faithfully aid in the execution of [state] quarantines and health laws, according to their respective powers and within their respective precincts, and as they shall be directed, from time to time, by the Secretary of Health and Human Services");

42 U.S.C. § 1989 (magistrates issuing arrest warrants for civil rights violations may authorize those serving the warrants to call for assistance from bystanders, the posse comitatus, or the land or naval forces or militia of the United States);

42 U.S.C. 5170b (Governor of state in which a major disaster has occurred may request the President to direct the Secretary of Defense to permit the use of DOD personnel for emergency work necessary for the preservation of life and property, but DOD does not consider this provision to authorize law enforcement measures);

43 U.S.C. § 1065 (President may use military force to remove unlawful enclosures from the public lands);

48 U.S.C. § 1418 (President may use the land and naval forces of the United States to protect the rights of owners in guano islands);

48 U.S.C. § 1422 (Governor of Guam may request assistance of senior military or naval commander of the Armed Forces of the United States in cases of disaster, invasion, insurrection, rebellion or imminent danger thereof, or lawless violence);

48 U.S.C. § 1591 (Governor of the Virgin Islands may request assistance of senior military or naval commander of the Armed Forces of the United States in the Virgin Islands or Puerto Rico in cases of disaster, invasion, insurrection, rebellion or imminent danger thereof, or of lawless violence);

49 U.S.C. § 324 (Secretary of Transportation may provide for participation of military personnel in carrying out duties);

50 U.S.C. § 220 (President may use the Army, Navy or militia to prevent the unlawful removal of vessels or cargoes from customs areas during times of insurrection).

[166] Military assistance available to civilian law enforcement entitles includes the following provisions: *10 U.S.C. § 371* (Secretary of Defense may provide federal, state, or local civilian law enforcement officials with information collected during military training operations or training);

10 U.S.C. § 372 (Secretary of Defense may make equipment and facilities available to federal, state, and local law enforcement operations);

10 U.S.C. § 373 (Secretary of Defense may train federal, state, and local law enforcement officials to operate and maintain equipment);

10 U.S.C. § 374 (Secretary of Defense may provide personnel to maintain and operate equipment and facilities in support of certain federal, state and local law enforcement operations;)
10 U.S.C. § 374 note (§1004 of the National Defense Authorization Act for 1991, as amended) (during fiscal years 1991 through 2011, the Secretary of Defense was authorized to provide counter-drug activity assistance upon request of federal or state law enforcement agencies);
10 U.S.C. § 382 (the Secretary of Defense may provide assistance to the Department of Justice in emergency situations involving chemical or biological weapons of mass destruction);
10 U.S.C. § 382 note (§1023 of the National Defense Authorization Act for Fiscal Year 2000) (during fiscal years 2000 through 2004, the Secretary of Defense was authorized to provide assistance to federal and state law enforcement agencies to respond to terrorism or threats of terrorism);
18 U.S.C. § 831 (Attorney General may request assistance from the Secretary of Defense for enforcement of the proscriptions against criminal transactions in nuclear materials if an emergency is deemed to exist); 18 U.S.C. §§ 175a, 229E, and 2332e cross reference to the Attorney General's authority under 10 U.S.C. § 382 to request assistance from the Secretary in an emergency involving biological weapons, chemical weapons, and weapons of mass destruction respectively.
42 U.S.C. § 98 (Secretary of the Navy at the request of the Public Health Service may make vessels or hulks available to quarantine authority at various U.S. ports).

[167] U.S. CONST. art. II, § 3, cl.3 ("[T]he President] shall take care that the laws be faithfully executed.").

[168] 5 U.S.C. § 301 ("The head of an Executive department or military department may prescribe regulations for the government of his department, the conduct of its employees, the distribution and performance of its business, and the custody, use, and preservation of its records, papers, and property....").

[169] *E.g.*, 21 U.S.C. § 873(b)("[w]hen requested by the Attorney General, it shall be the duty of any agency or instrumentality of the Federal Government to furnish assistance, including technical advice, to him for carrying out his functions under this subchapter; except that no such agency or instrumentality shall be required to furnish the name of, or other identifying information about, a patient or research subject whose identity it has undertaken to keep confidential").

[170] The Department of Defense Directive, for example, lists only the military-aid-specific statutes in its inventory of statutory exceptions, DOD Dir. No. 5525.5 (Encl.4) A.2.e.

[171] The 109th Congress changed the name of the U.S. code chapter from "Insurrection Act" to "Enforcement of the Laws to Restore Public Order" and amended § 333 to expand the circumstances in which it might be invoked, John Warner National Defense Authorization Act for Fiscal Year 2007, P.L. 109-364 § 1076, 120 Stat. 2083, 2404, (October 17, 2006)). The revised § 333 explicitly covered instances of "domestic violence" where public order is disrupted due to a "natural disaster, epidemic, or other serious public health emergency, terrorist attack or incident, or other condition." It authorized the President to employ federal troops to "restore public order and enforce the laws of the United States," without a request from the governor or legislature of the state involved, in the event he were to determine that local authorities were unable to maintain public order, where, as before, either the enjoyment of equal protection of the laws were impeded or the execution of federal law and related judicial process were obstructed. The President's recourse to "any other means" was eliminated, and the relevant state was to be deemed to have denied constitutional equal protection any time the authority was exercised outside of the newly described disaster scenario. The 110th Congress repealed these changes in the Defense Authorization Act for Fiscal Year 2008, P.L. 110-181 § 1068, 122 Stat. 3, 325 (January 28, 2008), returning the language of § 333 to its previous state.

[172] The relevant DOD regulation is DOD Dir. No. 3025.12, "Employment of Military Resources in the Event of Civil Disturbances," February 4, 1994.

[173] 10 U.S.C. § 331 provides:

> Whenever there is an insurrections in any State against its government, the President may, upon the request of its legislature or of its governor if the legislature cannot be convened, call into Federal service such of the militia of the other States, in the number requested by that State, and use such of the armed forces, as he considers necessary to suppress the insurrection.

[174] U.S. CONST. art. IV, § 4. See *supra* footnote 143 for text.

[175] *See* S. DOC NO. 67-263, *supra* footnote 23, at 181.

[176] *Id.* at 192 (noting that troops were used to assist civil officers in making arrests and guarding prisoners); 27 Stat. 1030. It appears that federal troops were essentially employed as posse comitatus to assist state officials in breaking the miner's union rather than restoring order. *See* COOPER, *supra* footnote 71, at 168.

[177] Felicetti & Luce, *supra* footnote 93, at 124. A proclamation was apparently prepared but withheld unless circumstances required its issue, which were deemed not to have occurred. *See* S. DOC NO. 67-263, *supra* footnote 23, at 215. Troops were nevertheless used to pursue the perpetrators of violence, who had fled the area, in aid of state deputies. Felicetti & Luce, *supra* footnote 93, at 124-25. A congressional investigation of the legality of the Army's actions split along party lines, with the Republican majority holding that no proclamation was necessary under the insurrection laws unless the President declared martial law. *Id.* at 125; *Coeur D'Alene Labor Troubles*, H.R. REP.NO. 56-1999 (1900).

[178] *See supra* footnote 75; RICH, *supra* footnote 24, at 191.

[179] *See* RICH, *supra* footnote 24, at 191 (attributing this state of affairs to the President's "lack of careful supervision").

[180] *Report on Labor Disturbances in the State of Colorado from 1880 to 1904, Inclusive, With Correspondence Relating Thereto*, S. DOC.NO. 58-122, at 10-11.

[181] *See, e.g.*, *id.* at 10-14 (correspondence between War Department and Colorado governor questioning existence of actual insurrection that could not be overcome using forces available to state).

[182] *See* S. DOC NO. 67-263, *supra* footnote 23, at 310.

[183] *Id.* at 311.

[184] 38 Stat. 1994 (1914). Federal intervention was requested after the Colorado National Guard had engaged the miners in a pitched battle during which a number of persons were killed. *See* S. DOC NO. 67-263, *supra* footnote 23, at 312. President Wilson requested the governor to withdraw state forces once federal troops arrived, explaining that his request was compelled by the "manifest disadvantage of having two military forces under separate sources of control."

[185] 40 Stat. 1681 (1917).

[186] Felicetti & Luce, *supra* footnote 93, at 126 (commenting that the policy amounted to a reestablishment of the Cushing Doctrine for nearly four and a half years, without evoking any congressional opposition); LAURIE AND COLE, *supra* footnote 24, at 229-30 (reporting that insurrection statutes and the Posse Comitatus Act were negated, and that soldiers were authorized to make arrests); CORWIN, *supra* footnote 114, at 157-58 (calling policy a deliberate and sustained neglect of the formalities required by Article IV and the Insurrection Acts).

[187] *See* S. DOC NO. 67-263, *supra* footnote 23, at 317 (stating that in no case was it deemed necessary to issue a proclamation under Section 5300 of the Revised Statues, the predecessor to 10 U.S.C. § 334).

[188] *See* LAURIE AND COLE, *supra* footnote 24, at 312.

[189] RICH, *supra* footnote 24, at 152. In Washington, D.C., rioting was apparently sparked by the use of soldiers, sailors, and marines to conduct a manhunt for a black man suspected of having attacked a white woman. *Id.* at 153. The Secretary of War ordered that troops should be used to assist civilian police, and military intelligence assets were deployed in an effort to learn about planned attacks. *Id.* Riots also occurred in Gary, Indiana, and Omaha, Nebraska. *Id.* at 155-57.

[190] *See* LAURIE AND COLE, *supra* footnote 24, at 252.

[191] 42 Stat. 2247 (1921). President Harding at first declined a number of requests from the governor, finding military intervention unwarranted; however, after state constabulary forces exchanged fire with a group of miners, the Army sent in several detachments of troops, who were able to restore order without resorting to force. RICH, *supra* footnote 24, at 158-67.

[192] *See* RICH, *supra* footnote 24, at 91.

[193] *Id.* at 170-71. The "Bonus Army" consisted of needy veterans from all parts of the country who descended on Washington, D.C., to demand immediate payment of the soldiers' bonus Congress had promised. *Id.*

[194] *Id.* at 177. A 1941 request from the governor of Wisconsin for federal intervention in another strike went unanswered because it did not explicitly ask for troops. *See id.* at 192.

[195] Exec. Order No. 8773, 6. Fed. Reg. 2777 (June 9, 1941). President Roosevelt asserted that he was acting under the Constitution and laws of the United States, but did not mention any specific statutes. Congress later enacted the War Labor Disputes Act of 1943, P.L. 78-89, 57 Stat. 163, which provided authority for government seizure and operation of facilities deemed necessary for the war effort, §3, 57 Stat. at 164. That authority expired under its own terms on the termination of hostilities, 57 Stat. 165. The Supreme Court later held that the omission of seizure authority from subsequent labor relations and defense production statutes precluded the President's resort to seizure of production facilities under a claim of inherent executive power. Youngstown Sheet & Tube Co. v. Sawyer, 343 U.S. 579 (1952).

[196] *See* RICH, *supra* footnote 24, at 183-84.

[197] *Id.* at 185-86. War department seizures of manufacturing plants where war materials were under production continued during the war, which effectively precluded the need to send troops in the event of a strike. *See* SCHEIPS, *supra* footnote 24, at 3. There were twelve such cases between September 1945 to January 1953, *id.* at 4.

[198] *See* SCHEIPS, *supra* footnote 24, at 17 (describing the practice as a "legal remedy" that did not involve sending in troops); LAURIE AND COLE, *supra* footnote 24, ch. 17.

[199] *See* SCHEIPS, *supra* footnote 24, at 17 (asserting that demands for equality on the part of black Americans and the resulting backlash on the part of white Americans led to a series of racial conflicts that sometimes became violent).

[200] Proclamation No. 2588, 8 Fed. Reg. 8733 (June 25, 1943).

[201] *See* Allan M. Winkler, *The Philadelphia Transit Strike of 1944*, 59 J. AM. HIST. 73 (1972).

[202] Exec. Ord. No. 9459, 3 C.F.R. 320 (1943-1948) (citing the Act of August 29, 1916, 39 Stat. 645, among other authorities). That authority still exists and is codified at 10 U.S.C. § 2644.

[203] Proclamation 3795, 32 Fed. Reg. 10905 (July 24, 1967) (citing governor's request as well as a need to execute federal law); Exec. Ord. No. 11364, 32 FR 10907 (July 24, 1967); *see also* SCHEIPS, *supra* footnote 24, at 190-91.

[204] *See* SCHEIPS, *supra* footnote 24, at 271-72. "Garden Plot" was the nickname for the Army's successive civil disturbance plans beginning in 1968 through 2001. The 1968 version contained an Intelligence Annex which provided guidance for commands to gather intelligence with respect to local "dissident elements" who might conspire to instigate a riot. *See id.* at 228. Army surveillance and intelligence operations targeting civil rights leaders and antiwar activists under the guise of planning for possible civil disturbances was a subject of scrutiny of the Church Committee. *See Improper Surveillance of Private Citizens by the Military*, *in* Supplementary Detailed Staff Reports on Intelligence Activities and the Rights of Americans, Book III, of the Final Report of the Senate Select Committee to Study Governmental Operations with Respect to Intelligence Activities, SEN.REP.NO. 94-755 (1976) (hereinafter "Church Committee Report"]. The Senate Subcommittee on Constitutional Rights rejected the contention that the authority to conduct such political surveillance flowed from the Insurrection Act. *Id.* at 794.

[205] Proclamation No. 3840, 33 Fed. Reg. 5495 (April 5, 1968).

[206] Proclamation No. 3841, 33 Fed. Reg. 5497 (April 7, 1968).

[207] Proclamation No. 3842, 33 Fed. Reg. 5499 (April 7, 1968).

[208] *See* SCHEIPS, *supra* footnote 24, at 338 (reporting that 23,008 regular Army troops and 15,586 Guardsmen participated in the federal response).

[209] Proclamation No. 6023, 54 Fed. Reg. 39,151 (Sep. 20, 1989).

[210] Exec. Order No. 12690, 54 Fed. Reg. 39153 (Sep. 20, 1989).

[211] *See* SCHEIPS, *supra* footnote 24, at 441.

[212] The President may have issued the order for troops prior to any request from the territorial governor. *See* Dennis Hevesi, *Bush Dispatches Troops to Island in Storm's Wake*, N.Y. TIMES, Sept. 21, 1989 (reporting that Governor Alexander Farrelly had told reporters he had not asked for federal troops).

[213] *See* Jeffrey Schmalz, *3 Weeks After Storm, St. Croix Still Needs Troops*, N.Y. TIMES, Oct. 9, 1989.

[214] Proclamation No. 6427, 57 Fed. Reg. 19,359 (May 1, 1992) (citing California governor's notification and request related to rioting in Los Angeles, and also determining that the "domestic violence and disorder are also obstructing the execution of the laws of the United States"); Exec. Order No. 12804, 57 Fed. Reg. 19361 (May 1, 1992).

[215] *See* SCHEIPS, *supra* footnote 24, at 447 (citing the findings of the Webster Commission, an advisory board set up to investigate the police and military handling of the riots).

[216] U.S. CONST. art. I, § 8, cl. 14.

[217] *See* S. DOC NO. 67-263, *supra* footnote 23, at 178-180. Because New Mexico was a territory and not yet a state, the provisions of § 331 were not applied, but President Rutherford B. Hayes asserted military force was necessary to overcome resistance to U.S. laws. Proclamation of October 7, 1878, 20 Stat. 806, 807.

[218] *See* S. DOC NO. 67-263, *supra* footnote 23, at 179.

[219] Annual Report of the Secretary of War, 1878 ("In those new regions the Army is the power chiefly relied upon by the law-abiding people for protection and chiefly feared by the lawless classes. Numerous instances might be cited, but the recent occurrences in Lincoln County, N. Mex., constitute a striking example. The inability of the officer in command of the troops at that vicinity to aid the officers of the law in making arrests was one of the principal causes which led to the most disgraceful scenes of riot and murder, amounting, in fact, to anarchy.").

[220] *See* S. DOC NO. 67-263, *supra* footnote 23, at 182; 22 Stat. 1035 (proclamation).

[221] Felicetti & Luce, *supra* footnote 93, at 119-20; *see supra* footnote 126.

[222] Felicetti & Luce, *supra* footnote 93, 120 (citing 13 CONG. REC. 3458 (1882) (remarks of Sen. Edmunds on behalf of the Judiciary Committee)). The Senate also disagreed with the Administration's interpretation that the authority to use the Army to execute federal law did not include local territorial laws, making the suggested addition of territories to the authority to provide assistance to states when requested moot. *See supra* footnote 126.

[223] S. DOC NO. 67-263, *supra* footnote 23, at 195-96; 12 Stat. 1249 (1894).

[224] S. DOC NO. 67-263, *supra* footnote 23, at 197.

[225] 28 Stat. 1250 (proclaiming unlawful obstructions in North Dakota, Montana, Idaho, Washington, Wyoming, Colorado, California, and the territories of Utah and New Mexico).

[226] *See* LIEBER, *supra* footnote 155, at 43-44 & appendix C.

[227] *See* COOPER, *supra* footnote 71, at 103 (noting that correspondence between Attorney General and federal judges and marshals suggested that using the Army would save the Justice Department substantial funds).

[228] *See id.* at 106-14.

[229] *See* S. DOC NO. 67-263, *supra* footnote 23, at 189-90.

[230] 24 Stat. 1027-28.

[231] *See* S. DOC NO. 67-263, *supra* footnote 23, at 190.

[232] *See* LIEBER, *supra* footnote 155, at 46 & n. 1 (describing incident and Army regulation authorizing commanders to intervene in sudden emergencies where there was no time to await instructions from headquarters). This emergency authority was also used in Denver in 1894 after the governor of Colorado appealed directly to the local commander. *See* S. DOC NO. 67-263, *supra* footnote 23, at 193. General McCook, Commander of the Department of the Colorado, sent troops into Denver and advised the governor to withdraw state militia, which the governor declined to do. Federal troops were told their mission was to protect federal property only and not assist the National Guard's efforts to retake the city hall until the governor asked for and received assistance under the insurrection statute. *Id.* at 193-94.

[233] 38 Stat. 2035 (1914).

[234] *See* SCHEIPS, *supra* footnote 24, at 237-53.

[235] *See* Church Committee Report, *supra* footnote 204, at 796. The intelligence operation targeted groups in Washington, D.C., as well as groups who were planning to travel there to participate, and began weeks before the demonstration was scheduled to occur. *See id.*; SCHEIPS, *supra* footnote 24, at 247-48.

[236] *See* SCHEIPS, *supra* footnote 24, at 239.

[237] *See id.* at 239-41. It was apparently felt that the operation would comply with the Posse Comitatus Act so long as troops remained under military command and subject to presidential direction, and were not placed under the direction of civilian officials. *See id.* at 240.

[238] Proclamation 3972, Declaring a National Emergency, 35 Fed. Reg. 5001 (March 24, 1970).

[239] *See* SCHEIPS, *supra* footnote 24, at 433. It was envisioned that the troops might be required to restore order if the strike were to turn violent, but since no violence occurred, the military contribution consisted of helping to sort and move mail.

[240] *See* SCHEIPS, *supra* footnote 24, at 436-37.

[241] *Id.* at 434-35.

[242] *Id.* at 436.

[243] Proclamation No. 5748, 52 Fed. Reg. 46730 (Dec. 9, 1987).

[244] Exec. Ord. No. 12,616, 52 Fed. Reg. 46,729 (Nov. 24, 1987).

[245] *See* SCHEIPS, *supra* footnote 24, at 441.

[246] *See* SCHEIPS, *supra* footnote 24, at 40.

[247] Exec. Ord. No. 10,730, 22 Fed. Reg. 7628 (Sept. 24, 1957).

[248] Proclamation No. 3204, 22 Fed. Reg. 7628 (Sept. 24, 1957).

[249] Robert W. Coakley, *Federal Use of Militia and the National Guard in Civil Disturbances*, in BAYONETS IN THE STREETS, 17, 30 (Robin Higham, ed. 1989). The governor had ordered the National Guard to enforce segregation by preventing students from entering any high school that had previously been used exclusively for students of another race, in defiance of a federal court order. *See* SCHEIPS, *supra* footnote 24, at 34.

[250] *See* SCHEIPS, *supra* footnote 24, at 86-87.

[251] *Id.* at 87-93; Exec. Ord. No. 11053, 27 Fed. Reg. 9693 (Oct. 2, 1962).

[252] Proclamation No. 3497, 27 Fed. Reg. 9681 (Oct. 2, 1962).

[253] Proclamation 3542, 28 Fed. Reg. 5705 (June 12, 1963); Exec. Order No. 11,111, 28 Fed. Reg. 5709 (June 12, 1963); Proclamation 3554, 28 Fed. Reg. 9861 (Sept. 11, 1963); Exec. Order 11,118, 28 Fed. Reg. 9863 (Sept. 11, 1963).

[254] Proclamation No. 3645, 30 Fed. Reg. 3739 (Mar. 20, 1965); Exec. Ord. No. 11,207, 30 Fed. Reg. 3743. The governor was enjoined by court order from interfering with the march, and he refused to call out the Alabama National Guard to protect the marchers on the grounds that he did not want the state to foot the bill. *See* SCHEIPS, *supra* footnote 24, at 162-63.

[255] P.L. 97-86, Title IX, 95 Stat. 1115 (1981), *codified as amended at* 10 U.S.C. §§ 371-82.

[256] H.R. REP. NO. 97-71, pt.2, 5-6, *reprinted in* 1981 U.S.C.C.A.N. 1785, 1788 ("Although the military activities challenged in each case were identical, the courts in *Banks* and *Jaramillo* found those activities to be in violation of the [Posse Comitatus] Act, while the lower court in *Red Feather* found those activities to be permissible").

[257] United States v. Jaramillo, 380 F. Supp. 1375 (D. Neb. 1974), *app. dism'd*, 510 F.2d 808 (8th Cir. 1975); United States v. Banks, 383 F. Supp. 368 (D.S.D. 1974); United States v. Red Feather, 392 F. Supp. 916 (D.S.D. 1975); United States v. McArthur, 419 F. Supp. 186 (D.N.D.), *aff'd sub nom.* United States v. Casper, 541 F.2d 1275 (8th Cir. 1976).

[258] 18 U.S.C. § 231(a)(3)(1970 ed.) provided:

> Whoever commits or attempts to commit any act to obstruct, impede, or interfere with any fireman or law enforcement officer lawfully engaged in the lawful performance of his official duties incident to and during the commission of a civil disorder which in any way or degree obstructs, delays, or adversely affects commerce or the movement of any article or commodity in commerce or the conduct or performance of any federally protected function – shall be fined not more than $10,000 or imprisoned not more than five years, or both.

[259] One court described the military assistance as follows:

The evidence of military involvement contained in the transcripts [of the Wounded Knee trial cases], in essence, falls into the following categories: use by federal civil law enforcement officers of material and equipment furnished by the United States Army and the South Dakota National Guard; the presence of United States Army personnel who were ordered to Wounded Knee to observe and report to the President through the Department of Defense the necessity of calling in federal troops; the drafting by military personnel of contingency plans to be used by the United States Army in the event that federal military intervention was ordered by the President; aerial photographic reconnaissance service provided by the United States Air Force and the Nebraska National Guard; the advice, urging and counsel given by the United States Army personnel to Department of Justice personnel on the subjects of negotiations, logistics and rules of engagement; and the maintenance of military vehicles performed by members of the Nebraska National Guard.

McArthur, 419 F. Supp. at 193 n.3.

[260] 10 U.S.C. §§ 371-382.

[261] 10 U.S.C. § 371 provides:

(a) The Secretary of Defense may in accordance with other applicable law, provide to Federal, State or local civilian law enforcement officials any information collected during the normal course of military training or operations that may be relevant to a violation of any Federal or State law within the jurisdiction of such officials.

(b) The needs of civilian law enforcement officials for information shall, to the maximum extent practicable, be taken into account in the planning and execution of military training or operations.

(c) The Secretary of Defense shall ensure, to the extent consistent with national security, that intelligence information held by the Department of Defense and relevant to drug interdiction or other civilian law enforcement matters is provided promptly to appropriate civilian law enforcement officials.

According to its legislative history:

The phrase 'in accordance with other applicable law' as used in section 371 is meant to continue the application of the Privacy Act to this type of intelligence sharing.... [Congress did] not intend the military to engage in the routine collection of intelligence information about United States residents ... [and] nothing in this section [was] intended to modify in any way existing law with respect to the military's authority (or lack thereof) to collect and disseminate intelligence information about American citizens and residents here and abroad. *See e.g.*, Exec. Order No. 12,036.

H.R. REP. NO. 97-71 pt.2, 8, *reprinted in* 1981 U.S.C.C.A.N. 1785, 1790-91.

[262] The House of Representatives Armed Services Committee, in reporting the Defense Authorization Act of 1982, H.R. 3519, 97th Cong. with the amendment providing for military cooperation with civilian law enforcement officials:

adopted the view of the Department of Justice that the weight of authority on the Posse Comitatus Act 'prohibits the use of military personnel as informants, undercover agents, or non-custodial interrogators in a civilian criminal investigation that does not involve potential military defendants or is not intended to lead to any official action by the armed forces.' ... [W]hen military personnel become aware of violations of civilian laws as an incidental result of other military operations, such information may be voluntarily disclosed.

Examples of this type of information sharing include situations such as investigations of military and non-military coconspirators and the observation by military personnel of illegal conduct during a routine military mission or training operation.

The Committee anticipates, however, that an increased sensitivity to the needs of civilian law enforcement officials, particularly in drug enforcement, will permit more compatible mission planning and execution. For example, the scheduling of routine training missions can easily accommodate the need for improved intelligence information concerning drug trafficking in the Caribbean. The committee does not intend the military to engage in the routine collection of intelligence information about United States residents. Thus, the legislation creates no risk that the military will return to the abuses exposed in previous Congressional hearings. *See* Hearings on *Federal Data Banks, Computers and the Bill of Rights* before the Committee on Constitutional Rights, Committee on the Judiciary, United States Senate, 92d Cong., 1st sess.

H.R. REP.NO. 97-71, 8 & n.1.

[263] In connection with the hearings noted by the Armed Services Committee in recommending the language, a staff report noted that:

the U.S. Army had for several years maintained a close and pervasive watch over most civilian protest activity throughout the United States. At its height during the late 1960's, the monitoring drew upon the part-time services of at least 1,500 plainclothes agents of the Army Intelligence Command, and an unspecified number of agents from the Continental Army Command. Their reports, which described the nonviolent political activities of thousands of individuals and organizations unaffiliated with the armed forces were amassed in scores of data centers.... The picture is that of a runaway intelligence bureaucracy unwatched by its civilian superiors, eagerly grasping for information about political dissenters of all kinds and totally oblivious to the impact its spying could have on the constitutional liberties it had sworn to defend.

Military Surveillance of Civilian Politics: A Report of the Subcommittee on Constitutional Rights of the Senate Committee on the Judiciary, 93d Cong., 1st Sess. 10 (1973)(Comm. Print). For a more contemporary examination of the issues associated with military surveillance of off-base political protests, see Paul M. Peterson, *Civilian Demonstrations Near the Military Installation: Restraints on Military Surveillance and Other Activities*, 140 MIL.L. REV. 113 (Spring, 1993). For a review of the history of the domestic use of military personnel to collect intelligence, see Stephen Dycus, *The Role of Military Intelligence in Homeland Security*, 64 LA. L. REV. 779 (2004).

[264] 10 U.S.C. § 373 provides:

The Secretary of Defense may, in accordance with other applicable law, make Department of Defense personnel available – (1) to train Federal, State, and local civilian law enforcement officials in the operation and maintenance of equipment, including equipment made available under section 372 of this title; and (2) to provide such law enforcement officials with expert advice relevant to the purposes of this chapter.

[265] "Nothing in this section contemplates the creation of large scale or elaborate training programs.... [This section would not authorize the routine use of a Green Beret training course for urban SWAT teams.] ... Rather this section anticipates the continuing need for the military to train civilians in the operation and maintenance of the equipment lent under proposed section 372," H.R. REP. NO. 97-71, at 10, *reprinted in* 1981 U.S.C.C.A.N. 1785, 1792-793 (footnote 2 of the report in brackets).

[266] "Paragraph (1) clarifies current law to provide that the Secretary of Defense, in accordance with applicable law, may make Department of Defense personnel available to train Federal, State, and local civilian law enforcement officials in the operation of maintenance of equipment, including equipment made available under section 372," H.R. REP.NO. 100-989, 451, *reprinted in* 1988 U.S.C.C.A.N. 2503, 2579. According to DOD regulations,

[t]he Military Departments and Defense Agencies may provide training to Federal, State, and local civilian law enforcement officials, Such assistance may including training in the operation and maintenance of equipment made available under section E3.1. of enclosure 3. This does not permit large scale or elaborate training, and does not permit regular or direct involvement of military personnel in activities that are fundamentally civilian law enforcement operations, except as other wise authorized in this enclosure."

Training of Federal, State, and local civilian law enforcement officials shall be provided under the following guidance:

[1] This assistance shall be limited to situations when the use of non-DoD personnel would be unfeasible or impractical form a cost or time perspective and would not otherwise compromise national security or military preparedness concerns.

[2] Such assistance may not involve DoD personnel in a direct role in a law enforcement operation, except as otherwise authorized by law.

[3] Except as otherwise authorized by law, the performance of such assistance by DoD personnel shall be at a location where there is not a reasonable likelihood of a law enforcement confrontation.

DOD Dir. No. 5525.5 (Encl.4) E.4.

[267] "Neither does the authority to provide expert advice create a loophole to allow regular or direct involvement of military personnel in what are fundamentally civilian law enforcement operations," H.R. REP. NO. 97-71, at 10, *reprinted in* 1981 U.S.C.C.A.N. 1785, 1792. "Paragraph (2) restates current law permitting advice. Such training and expert advice may extend to instruction in the operation of equipment, scientific analysis, translations, and assistance in strategic planning, but may not extend to direct, active involvement in specific law enforcement operations," H.R. REP. NO. 100-989, 451, reprinted in 1988 U.S.C.C.A.N. 2503, 2579. *See also* DOD Dir. No. 5525.5 (Encl.4) E4.1.5.,"Military Departments and Defense Agencies may provide expert advice to Federal, State, or local law enforcement in accordance with 10 U.S.C. §§ 371-378 (reference (d)). This does not permit regular or direct involvement of military personnel in activities that are fundamentally civilian law enforcement operations, except as otherwise authorized in this enclosure."

[268] 75 Fed. Reg. 81547, proposed 32 CFR Part 182.2(d)(4)(excepting Defense intelligence and counterintelligence activities when providing assistance in accordance with paragraph 2.6. of Executive Order 12333).

[269] E.O 12333 para. 2.6 provides:

Elements of the Intelligence Community are authorized to:

(a) Cooperate with appropriate law enforcement agencies for the purpose of protecting the employees, information, property, and facilities of any element of the Intelligence Community;

(b) Unless otherwise precluded by law or this Order, participate in law enforcement activities to investigate or prevent clandestine intelligence activities by foreign powers, or international terrorist or narcotics activities;

(c) Provide specialized equipment, technical knowledge, or assistance of expert personnel for use by any department or agency, or when lives are endangered, to support local law enforcement agencies.

Provision of assistance by expert personnel shall be approved in each case by the general counsel of the providing element or department; and

(d) Render any other assistance and cooperation to law enforcement or other civil authorities not precluded by applicable law.

Executive Order 12333, United States Intelligence Activities (As amended by Executive Orders 13284 (2003), 13355 (2004) and 13470 (2008)).

270 *Id.*

271 Compare *Jaramillo*, 380 F. Supp. at 1379 ("It is the use of military personnel, not materiel, which is proscribed by [the Posse Comitatus Act].") and *Red Feather*, 392 F. Supp. at 923 (loans of military equipment and materiel not proscribed) *with Banks*, 383 F. Supp. at 386 (rejecting Government's argument that loan of equipment was authorized by the Economy Act); and *McArthur*, 419 F. Supp. at 194 (finding not only that the "government policy of loaning equipment between branches of the government" was permissible, but that it "extends to the loaning of expert advisors").

272 10 U.S.C. § 372 provides:

The Secretary of Defense may, in accordance with other applicable law, make available any equipment (including associated supplies or spare parts), base facility, or research facility of the Department of Defense to any Federal, State, or local civilian law enforcement official for law enforcement purposes.

See also 10 U.S.C. § 380 (mandating annual briefing of state law enforcement personnel to familiarize them with the types of assistance and equipment available from the Department of Defense and means for obtaining same).

273 10 U.S.C. § 374(b)(2) (listing permitted functions, *see infra*); 10 U.S.C. § 375 (listing limitations); 10 U.S.C. § 382(d)(2)(a). *See* United States v. Johnson, 410 F.3d 137 (4th Cir. 2005) (use of Armed Forces Institute of Pathology resources to conduct blood tests for civilian law enforcement authorities permitted so long as military personnel do not operate laboratory equipment to conduct the testing on blood extracted from a civilian suspect).

274 10 U.S.C. § 374 authorizes the Secretary of Defense to make military personnel available to federal, state, and local civilian law enforcement officials to maintain military equipment; to make personnel available to federal law enforcement agencies for the purposes of:

- Detection, monitoring, and communication of the movement of air and sea traffic or surface traffic outside the geographic boundary of the United States and within the United States not to exceed 25 miles of the boundary if the initial detection occurred outside the boundary.
- Aerial reconnaissance.
- Interception of vessels or aircraft detected outside the land area of the United States to direct such vessels and aircraft to go to a location designated by appropriate civilian officials.
- Operation of equipment to facilitate communications in connection with authorized law enforcement programs
- The transportation of civilian law enforcement personnel and the operation of a base of operations for them, subject to high-level approval.

Other support may be made available only if it "does not involve direct participation by such personnel in a civilian law enforcement operation unless such direct participation is otherwise authorized by law."

10 U.S.C. § 381 mandates the Secretary of Defense to establish procedures for procuring equipment for state and local agencies for counter-drug, homeland security, and emergency response activities, to be paid for by the receiving government.

275 10 U.S.C. § 379.

276 10 U.S.C. § 382 provides that the Secretary of Defense, upon the request of the Attorney General, may provide assistance in support of law enforcement activities during an emergency situation involving a biological or chemical weapon of mass destruction, if such assistance is absolutely necessary and will not adversely affect the military preparedness of the United State, and the Department of Defense is reimbursed. Assistance authorized includes the operation of equipment to monitor, contain, disable, or dispose of the weapon involved or elements of the weapon. Regulations required to implement the provision are not to authorize arrest or direct participation in conducting a search for or seizure of evidence or the collection of intelligence for law enforcement purposes.

277 10 U.S.C. § 376 provides that no assistance to civilian law enforcement official can be provided that will adversely affect the military preparedness of the United States.

278 10 U.S.C. § 377 requires reimbursement under the Economy Act, 31 U.S.C. § 1531, unless waived by the Secretary of Defense, which is permissible if the assistance is provided in the normal course of military training or operations or if it provides benefits similar to what the participating personnel would obtain from operations or training.

279 10 U.S.C. § 375 provides:

The Secretary of Defense shall prescribe such regulations as may be necessary to ensure that any activity (including the provision of any equipment or facility or the assignment or detail of any personnel) under this chapter does not include or permit direct participation by a member of the Army, Navy, Air Force, or

Marine Corps in a search, seizure, arrest, or other similar activity unless participation in such activity by such member is otherwise authorized by law.

[280] 47 Fed. Reg. 14,899 (April 7, 1982), *codified at* 32 C.F.R. pt.213, *removed by* 58 Fed. Reg. 25,776 (April 28, 1993).

[281] Department of Defense Directive No. 5525.5 (January 15, 1986), as amended December 12, 1989 (hereinafter DOD Dir. No. 5525.5). Prior to enactment of 10 U.S.C. §§ 371 *et seq.*, the Navy had operated under a Navy Department Instruction of similar import, SECNAVINST 5400.12 (January 17, 1969), *see* United States v. Walden, 490 F.2d 372, 373-74 (4th Cir. 1974).

[282] 32 C.F.R. §213.10(a)(3)(July 1, 1992).

[283] The provision in DOD Dir. No. 5525.5 (Encl.4) notes the following forms of direct assistance are prohibited: a. Interdiction of a vehicle, vessel, aircraft, or other similar activity. b. A search or seizure. c. An arrest, apprehension, stop and frisk, or similar activity. d. Use of military personnel for surveillance or pursuit of individuals, or as undercover agents, informants, investigators, or interrogators. DOD Dir. No. 5525.5 (Encl.4) para. E.1.4.3. Proposed 32 C.F.R. Part 182.6 (a)(iii) would add "(4) Evidence collection, security functions, and crowd and traffic control" to the above list of exceptions. 75 Fed. Reg. 81547-01 (2010).

[284] Logic might suggest that the military purpose doctrine is simply the largest of the statutory exceptions, that is, that the doctrine merely encompasses the military authority vested in the Armed Forces under the Code of Military Justice and the other statutes which grant them military authority. Neither the commentators nor the courts have ordinarily clearly limited their analyses in such terms, *see, e.g.,* Clarence I. Meeks, *Illegal Law Enforcement: Aiding Civil Authorities in Violation of the Posse Comitatus Act*, 70 MIL.L.REV. 83, 124-26 (1975); Paul Jackson Rice, *New Laws and Insights Encircle the Posse Comitatus Act*, 104 MIL.L.REV. 109, 128-35 (1984); Hayes v. Hawes, 921 F.2d 100,103 (7th Cir. 1990); Taylor v. State, 640 So.2d 1127, 1136 (Fla. App. 1994); State v. Pattioay, 896 P.2d 911, 915-18 (Haw. 1995).

[285] Eggleston v. Dept. of Revenue, 895 P.2d 1169, 1170 (Colo. App. 1995)(*citing* Cafeteria & Restaurant Workers Union Local v. McElroy, 367 U.S. 886 (1961)).

[286] Harker v. State, 663 P.2d 932, 936 (Alaska 1983).

[287] Brune v. Administrative Director of Courts, 110 Hawai'i 172, 130 P.3d 1037 (Haw. 2006); Eggleston v. Dept. of Revenue, 895 P.2d 1169, 1170 (Colo. App. 1995)(military police also administered breath test and provided local law enforcement officers with the results); McNeil v. State, 787 P.2d 1036, 1037 (Alaska App. 1990); Anchorage v. King,754 P.2d 283, 286 (Alaska App. 1988).

[288] United States v. Griley, 814 F.2d 967, 976 (4th Cir. 1987).

[289] United States v. Chon, 210 F.3d 990, 994 (9th Cir. 2000).

[290] United States v. Banks, 539 F.2d 14, 16 (9th Cir. 1976); United States v. Santana, 175 F. Supp. 2d 153 (D.P.R. 2001).

[291] United States v. Allen, 53 M.J. 402 (C.A.A.F. 2000)(Air Force investigators assisted local law enforcement to investigate military member's use of government computer for pornography); People v. Caviano, 560 N.Y.S.2d 932, 936-37 (N.Y. 1990)(Navy personnel made a sailor available for questioning at naval station facilities; the interrogation was conducted by civilian police who subsequently arrested the sailor for an out of state robbery); United States v. Hartley, 678 F.2d 961, 978 (11th Cir. 1982)(military inspectors who discovered evidence of fraudulent conduct by defense contractors "aided the civilian employee in charge of the investigation only to the extent of activities normally performed in the ordinary course of their [military] duties"); State v. Trueblood, 265 S.E.2d 662, 664 (N.C.App. 1980)(military search (with consent) of on-base quarters in connection with a civilian investigation of off-base drug dealing by military personnel); State v. Nelson, 298 N.C. 573, 260 S.E.2d 629 (1979)(military inventory of personal effects of AWOL soldier were conducted primarily for a military purpose pursuant to a regulation designed to safeguard private property and protect service against claims); Commonwealth v. Shadron, 471 Pa. 461, 465, 370 A.2d 697, 699 (1977)(military police acting within the scope their authority did not violate the Posse Comitatus Act by making a soldier available, at the Air Force base where he was stationed, to civilian investigators for interrogation by the civilian officers and by permitted the civilians to search the defendant's possessions with his consent).

[292] Davidson v. State, 249 S.W.3d 709 (Tex. App. Austin 2008)(Air Force involvement in off-base investigation of the murder of a service member not prohibited, even though civilian wife was eventually implicated in the crime); United States v. Griley, 814 F.2d 967, 976 (4th Cir. 1987)(off-base military investigation of concerning property stolen on-base by military personnel); Applewhite v. United States, 995 F.2d 997, 1001 (10th Cir. 1993)(military police off-base drug sting targeting military personnel); State v. Hayes, 102 N.C. App. 777, 779-81, 404 S.E.2d 12, 13-15 (1991)(off-base purchase of drugs by a military undercover agent from an AWOL soldier); State v. Poe, 755 S.W.2d 41, 44-45 (Tenn. 1988)(military investigation of the off-base murder of a soldier by other soldiers).

[293] United States v. Hitchcock, 286 F.3d 1064, 1070 (9th Cir. 2002)("Military participation in Hitchcock's investigation for the purpose of determining the extent to which his LSD was being used and distributed on the military base was justified [as serving a valid military purpose].").

[294] DOD Dir. No. 5525.5 (Encl. 4) E4.1.2 provides:

Permissible direct assistance. The following activities are not restricted by reference (v) [the Posse Comitatus Act, 18 U.S.C. 1385].
E4.1.2.1. Actions that are taken for the primary purpose of furthering a military or foreign affairs function of the United States, regardless of incidental benefits to civilian authorities. This provisions must be used with caution, and does not include actions taken for the primary purpose of aiding civilian law enforcement officials or otherwise serving as a subterfuge to avoid the restrictions of reference (v). Actions under this provision may include the following, depending on the nature of the DoD interest and the authority governing the specific action in question:
E4.1.2.1.1. Investigations and other actions related to enforcement of the Uniform Code of Military Justice (UCMJ)(reference (d)).
E4.1.2.1.2. Investigations and other actions that are likely to result in administrative proceedings by the Department of Defense, regardless of whether there is a related civil or criminal proceeding. See DoD Directive 5525.7 (reference (w)) with respect to matters in which the Departments of Defense and Justice both have an interest.
E4.1.2.1.3. Investigations and other actions related to the commander's inherent authority to maintain law and order on a military installation or facility.
E4.1.2.1.4. Protection of classified military information or equipment.
E4.1.2.1.5. Protection of DoD personnel, DoD equipment, and official guests of the Department of Defense.
E4.1.2.1.6. Such other actions that are undertaken primarily for a military or foreign affairs purpose.
32 C.F.R. §213.10(2)(i)(July 1, 1992) was identical except for styles used to designate subsections, paragraphs and subparagraphs, and that the C.F.R. contained no cross reference citations except to the Code of Military Justice. Proposed 32 C.F.R. § 182.6 contains in substance the same list of permissible types of direct assistance, except that the last catch-all activity for military or foreign affairs is moved to the introductory paragraph describing the "Military Purpose Doctrine." 75 Fed. Reg. 81550 (2010).

[295] State v. Sanders, 303 N.C. 608, 613, 281 S.E.2d 7, 10 (1981)("military policeman Lambert's duty [during joint patrol with civilian police off-base] was not to execute civilian law but to assist the police department in returning apprehended military personnel to Fort Bragg"); State v. Short, 113 Wash.2d 35, 38-40, 775 P.2d 458, 459-60 (1989)(where civilian Naval Investigative Services (NIS) agent participated in a joint drug operation with local law enforcement agencies by working undercover at a local restaurant frequented by military personnel, the agent did not arrest the defendant, and "any personnel, equipment, and information provided to local law enforcement did not constitute direct participation," no improper military involvement in the investigation was found); People v. Wells, 175 Cal.App.3d 876 (1985)(where, in order to minimize the flow of drugs into Camp Pendleton, the N.I.S. initiated a joint investigation with the local police, in which military policemen made undercover solicitations for drugs but any detention or arrest of a suspect was conducted by a civilian police officer, the court found no "subjugation of citizens to the exercise of military power of a regulatory, prescriptive or compulsory nature" that would implicate statutory restrictions).

[296] In *United States v. Walden*, for example, where a Treasury agent was found to have used Marines as undercover agents to secure evidence against civilian firearms offenders, the court found a breach of the posse comitatus requirements without even acknowledging the government's military purpose argument. 490 F.2d 372 (4th Cir. 1974). *See* Meeks, *supra* footnote 284, at 115 ("the Government argued [in *Walden*] that the Act had not been violated because the investigation was 'related directly to the maintenance of order and security' on the base and that such undercover assistance to civilian authorities does not constitute 'execution of the law'"); Rice, *supra* footnote 284, at 129 ("[i]f the court considered the government's argument that the activities of the Marines were related to the maintenance, order and security of the base, it had rejected it. However, the sale of the weapons occurred immediately off the base in the town of Quantico. If the base authorities were aware of this fact and that the illegally sold weapons were being purchased by Marines and being brought on the base, then what may they do to insure order and discipline? Clearly, they can notify local authorities. But would the purchase in question by an undercover Marine be for the primary purpose of furthering a military function? Order, discipline, and security of a base is a military function"). Other courts have expressly rejected assertions that military purpose justifies law enforcement against civilians unless a verifiable nexus exists. *See* People v. Tyler, 854 P.2d 1366, 1369 (Colo. App. 1993)("before the military may directly participate in an undercover investigation of these civilians and their off-base activities, the state carries the burden of demonstrating that there exists a nexus between drug sales off base by civilians to military personnel and the military base at which the purchasers are stationed"), *rev'd on other grounds* 874 P.2d 1037 (Colo. App. 1994); State v. Pattioay, 78 Haw. 455, 464-65, 896 P.2d 911, 920-21 (1995)("[w]here the target of a military investigation is a civilian and there is no verified connection to military personnel, the PCA prohibits military participation in activities designed to execute civilian laws.... In fact, the apparent justification for the military involvement in the instant case was to facilitate the enforcement of civilian laws.... Hence, the prosecution has the duty to present evidence to show that, when a military investigation was undertaken, the targeted drug transactions involved military personnel or were connected to sales conducted on a military installation.... That the military has a valid interest in ferreting out those who supply drugs to military personnel, does not

automatically qualify its aid to civilian drug law enforcement as having the 'primary purpose of furthering a military ... function'")(internal citations omitted).

[297] United States v. Hitchcock, 286 F.3d 1064, 1070 (9th Cir. 2002)(where it was undisputed that the defendant had sold LSD to a Marine, who distributed the substance to other soldiers, the court stated that "the proposition that the sale of LSD to persons who might use the drug on a military base or sell it to others on the base implicates the maintenance of law and order on a military installation is unassailable"); Moon v. State, 785 P.2d 45, 48 (Alaska App. 1990)("[I]t seems to us that the army had a valid military purpose in preventing illicit drug transactions involving active duty personnel even if the transaction took place off base. The investigation was not begun until the military was satisfied that drug dealers at the Palace Hotel had targeted military personnel as a market. It was also reasonable to infer that a substantial quantity of illicit drugs was finding its way onto the base"); State v. Maxwell, 174 W.Va. 632, 635, 328 S.E.2d 507, 509 (W.Va. 1985)("The fact that the Navy's internal investigation happened to uncover wrongs by civilians does not bring the case within the scope of 18 U.S.C. § 1385 or render the Navy agents incompetent as witnesses."); State v. Presgraves, 174 W.Va. 683, 328 S.E.2d 699 (W.Va. 1985)(same); Hayes v. Hawes, 921 F.2d 100, 103-104 (7th Cir. 1990)(no violation where Navy undercover agent, who had "received information" that a sailor had purchased drugs at an off-base arcade, joined local police with several other military agents for surveillance of the arcade, made a drug buy in cooperation with local police who made the arrest and conducted the search of civilian).

[298] P.L. 107-40, 115 Stat. 224 (2001).

[299] Office of Legal Counsel, Authority For Use Of Military Force To Combat Terrorist Activities Within The United States, October 23, 2001, *available at* 2001 WL 36190674 (O.L.C.).

[300] *Id.* (emphasis in the original).

[301] *Id.* at *15.

[302] *Id.* at * 18 ("In light of [the opinion's earlier] review of the President's inherent powers, it should be clear that the PCA's constitutional exception has been triggered.").

[303] *Id.* ("This authorization does not distinguish between deployment of the military either at home or abroad, nor does it make any distinction between use of the Armed Force for law enforcement or for military purposes.").

[304] *Id.* at *19 ("We think it plain that the President could find that the present circumstances justify the invocation of § 333. Here, an unlawful terrorist group has hijacked civilian airliners and used them to kill thousands of civilians by crashing them into the World Trade Center and the Pentagon. These terrorists have engaged in 'domestic violence' within the states of New York and Virginia and have violated numerous federal laws.").

[305] Office of Legal Counsel, October 23, 2001 OLC Opinion Addressing the Domestic Use of Military Force to Combat Terrorist Activities, October 6, 2008, *available at* 2008 WL 6060107 (O.L.C.).

[306] *Id.* at *2.

[307] Congressional encouragement for a broader military role in domestic counterterrorism is most visible in the provisions of the National Defense Authorization Act for FY2012 (P.L. 112-81) and the surrounding legislative debates. For an overview of those provisions and related issues, see CRS Report R42143, *The National Defense Authorization Act for FY2012: Detainee Matters*, by Jennifer K. Elsea and Michael John Garcia.

[308] *See, e.g.*, Gregory E. Maggs *Assessing the Legality of Counterterrorism Measures Without Characterizing Them as Law Enforcement or Military Action*, 80 TEMP. L. REV. 661 (2007); Christopher J. Schmidt and David A. Klinger, *Altering the Posse Comitatus Act: Letting the Military Address Terrorist Attacks on U.S. Soil*, 39 CREIGHTON L. REV. 667 (2006); William C. Banks, *The Normalization of Homeland Security After September 11: The Role of the Military in Counterterrorism Preparedness and Response*, 64 LA. L. REV. 735 (2004); Tom A. Gizzo, Esq. and Tama S. Monoson, *A Call to Arms: The Posse Comitatus Act and the Use of the Military in the Struggle Against International Terrorism*, 15 PACE INT'L L.REV. 149 (2003); Nathan Canestaro, *Homeland Defense: Another Nail in the Coffin for Posse Comitatus*, 12 WASH.U.J.L. & POL'Y 99 (2003); Ronald J. Sievert, *War on Terrorism or Global Law Enforcement Operation?*, 78 NOTRE DAME L. REV. 307 (2003).

[309] *See* Padilla *ex rel.* Newman v. Bush, 233 F. Supp. 2d 564, 588 n.9 (S.D.N.Y. 2002, *rev'd sub nom.* Padilla v. Rumsfeld, 352 F.3d 695 (2d Cir. 2003), *rev'd*, 542 U.S. 426 (2004).

[310] Padilla v. Hanft, 389 F. Supp. 2d 678 (D.S.C. 2005), *rev'd*, 423 F.3d 386 (4th Cir.), *cert. denied*, 547 U.S. 1062(2006). The case was ultimately made moot by the government's transfer of the petitioner into civil custody to stand trial.

[311] For more background and analysis of the constitutionality of military detention of terrorism suspects in the United States, see CRS Report R42337, *Detention of U.S. Persons as Enemy Belligerents*, by Jennifer K. Elsea.

[312] Whoever, except in cases and under circumstances expressly authorized by the Constitution or Act of Congress, *willfully* uses any part of the Army or the Air Force as a posse comitatus or otherwise to execute the laws shall be fined under this title or imprisoned not more than two years, or both. 18 U.S.C. § 1385 (emphasis added).

[313] 7 CONG. REC. 4302 (1878).

[314] 7 CONG. REC. 4181 (1878).

[315] The Senate Judiciary Committee noted that:

The courts have defined a 'willful' act as an act done voluntarily as distinguished from accidentally, an act done with specific intent to violate the law, an act done with bad purpose, an act done without justifiable excuse, an act done stubbornly, an act done without grounds for believing it is lawful, and an act done with careless disregard whether or not one has the right so to act.

S. REP. NO. 97-307, at 63-64 (1981). Supreme Court cases seem to caution against a broad interpretation of the term "willful" or any of the other state-of-mind elements in federal criminal statute, Bryan v. United States, 524 U.S. 184, 191-92 (1998)("The word willfully is sometimes said to be a word of many meanings whose construction is often dependent on the context in which it appears.... As a general matter, when used in the criminal context, a willful act is one undertaken with a bad purpose. In other words, in order to establish a willful violation of a statute, the Government must prove that the defendant acted with knowledge that his conduct was unlawful")(*citing* Ratzlaf v. United States, 510 U.S. 135, 137 (1994)).

[316] United States v. Bacon, 851 F.2d 1312, 1313 (11th Cir. 1988)("even if the participation by military personnel [as undercover solicitors of drugs from civilians] in this drug investigation is to be considered a violation of the Posse Comitatus Act, it was not a willful violation of the spirit of the Act"); United States v. Walden, 490 F.2d 372, 376 (4th Cir. 1974)("there is totally lacking any evidence that there was a conscious, deliberate or willful intent on the part of the Marines or the ... Special Investigator to violate the Instruction or the spirit of the Posse Comitatus Act. From all that appears, the Special Investigator acted innocently albeit ill-advisedly"); State v. Danko, 219 Kan. 490, 548 P.2d 819, 822 (1976)("the statute is limited to deliberate use of armed force for the primary purpose of executing civilian laws")(quoting Furman, *supra* footnote 147, at 128; Kim v. State, 817 P.2d 467, 469 n.2 (Alaska, 1991)(Rabinowitz, J. dissenting)("A will to violate the Act is not required, but only the wilful use of military personnel").

[317] *See, e.g,* Riley v. Newton, 94 F.3d 632, 636 (11th Cir. 1996). The court found that officers faced with civil suit for alleged violation of posse comitatus restrictions were entitled to qualified immunity because

The law of this circuit has not been developed to make it obvious to law enforcement officers what constitutes "wilful use" of the Army "to execute the laws." Specifically, our case law does not make obvious what activities constitute "executing the law" for purposes of the Act; it does not delineate at what point or under what circumstances a joint investigation with military personnel would violate the Posse Comitatus Act. And even more importantly here, our case law does not give any guidance as to what constitutes "wilful use" in the event that the military person's actions would clearly constitute "executing the law."

In any event, it is not generally the person accused of posse comitatus violations who is facing prosecution. *See infra* "Consequences of Violation." Thus, even in cases where it seems obvious that military personnel were "willfully" used to "execute the law," courts have found no need to engage in lengthy analysis. *See* United States v. Wooten, 377 F.3d 1134, 1139-40 (10th Cir. 2004):

There appears to be no dispute in this case that the United States Attorney for the Western District of Oklahoma 'willfully use[d]' ... an active duty member of the Army and Staff Judge Advocate, to assist in 'execut[ing] the laws' of the United States. In particular, [an Army captain] was appointed as an SAUSA and, in that role, participated in the investigation, grand jury proceedings, and trial of this case. The question is whether [the captain's] appointment and participation fall within the scope of the PCA's express exception.... The Court declines to answer this question, in part because it concludes that it does not have to do so in order to resolve this appeal.... Assuming [a violation of the] PCA, the question then becomes to what relief, if any, [the defendant] would be entitled. The answer is "none."

[318] "Whoever, except in cases and under circumstances expressly authorized by the Constitution or Act of Congress, willfully *uses any part of the Army or the Air Force as a posse comitatus or otherwise to execute the laws* shall be fined under this title or imprisoned not more than two years, or both." 18 U.S.C. § 1385 (emphasis added).

[319] U.S. CONST. art. II, § 3.

[320] *See, e.g.*, John J. Copelan and Steven A. Lamb, *Disaster Law and Hurricane Andrew: Government Lawyers Leading the Way to Recovery*, 27 URB. LAW. 1 (1995); Francis A. Delzompo, *Warriors on the Fire Line: The Deployment of Service Members to Fight Fire in the United States*, ARMY LAW., April 1995, at 51; Federal Disaster Assistance: Report of the Senate Task Force on Funding Disaster Relief, S. DOC.NO. 104-4 (1995).

Congress has established provisions that at first glance might appear to be a blanket statutory exception to the prohibition of military assistance to civil authorities. For example, P.L. 102-484,§ 1081(b)(1), Oct. 23, 1992, 106 Stat. 2515, required the Secretary of Defense to establish a program to be known as the 'Civil-Military Cooperative Action Program' in order to use the "skills, capabilities, and resources of the armed forces to assist civilian efforts to meet the domestic needs of the United States," 10 U.S.C. § 410(a))(repealed by P.L. 104-106, Div. A, Title V, § 571(a)(1), Feb. 10, 1996, 110 Stat. 353). Closer examination reveals, however, that legislation sought to encourage activity that would not previously have violated the Posse Comitatus Act or its supplementary statutory and regulatory provisions:

The programs shall have the following objectives: (1) To enhance individual and unit training and morale in the armed forces through meaningful community involvement of the armed forces. (2) To encourage cooperation between civilian and military sectors of society in addressing domestic needs. (3) To advance equal opportunity. (4) To enrich the civilian economy of the United States through education, training, and transfer of technological advances. (5) To improve the environment and economic and social conditions. (6) To provide opportunities for disadvantaged citizens of the United States.... Nothing in this section shall be construed as authorizing – (1) the use of the armed forces for civilian law enforcement purposes; or (2) the use of Department of Defense personnel or resources for any program, project, or activity that is prohibited by law.

Former 10 U.S.C. § 410(b),(e); S. REP.NO. 102-352, 278-82 (1992); H.R. REP.NO. 102-966, 762, reprinted in 1992 U.S.C.C.A.N. 1769, 1853. The provision that replaced it, 10 U.S.C. § 2012, likewise provides that "[n]othing in this section shall be construed as authorizing—(1) the use of the armed forces for civilian law enforcement purposes or for response to natural or manmade disasters; or (2) the use of Department of Defense personnel or resources for any program, project, or activity that is prohibited by law," subsection i. *See* W. Kent Davis, *Innovative Readiness Training under 10 U.S.C. § 2012: Understanding The Congressional Model for Civil-military Projects*, ARMY LAW., July 2001, at 21.

[321] 5 CONG. REC. 2113 (1877); 6 CONG. REC. 294-307, 322; 7 CONG. REC. 3538, 3581-582, 3850, 4245 (1878).

[322] Taylor v. State, 640 So.2d 1127, 1136 (Fla. App. 1994); *see also* United States v. Kahn, 35 F.3d 426, 431 (9th Cir. 1994); United States v. Yunis, 924 F.2d 1086, 1094 (D.C. Cir. 1991); Hayes v. Hawes, 921 F.2d 100, 104 (7th Cir. 1990); United States v. Gerena, 649 F. Supp. 1179, 1182 (D. Conn. 1986); United States v. Hartley, 678 F.2d 961, 978 n.24 (8th Cir. 1982); United States v. Jaramillo, 380 F. Supp. 1375, 1379-380 (D. Neb. 1974), *appeal dismissed*, 510 F.2d 808 (8th Cir. 1975)(whether the use of military personnel affected or materially contributed to the activities of civilian law enforcement officials); United States v. Banks, 383 F. Supp. 368, 375 (D.S.D. 1974)(whether there was active participation of military personnel in civilian law enforcement activities); United States v. Red Feather, 392 F. Supp. 916, 921 (D.S.D. 1975)(whether there was direct active use of military personnel by civilian law enforcement officers); United States v. McArthur, 419 F. Supp. 186, 194-95 (D.N.D. 1976), *aff'd sub nom.* United States v. Casper, 541 F.2d 1275, 1278 (8th Cir. 1976)(whether "Army or Air Force personnel [were] used by the civilian law enforcement officers in such manner that the military personnel subjected the citizens to the exercise of military power which was regulatory, prescriptive, or compulsory in nature, either presently or prospectively").

[323] United States v. Yunis, 924 F.2d 1086, 1094 (D.C. Cir. 1991)(Navy transportation of prisoner in the custody the FBI); Hall v. State, 557 N.E.2d 3, 4-5 (Ind. App. 1990)(Air Force personnel acting as undercover agents to assist local police in drug investigations involving a controlled buy of cocaine did not "display the unauthorized exercise of military power that is 'regulatory, prescriptive, or compulsory in nature'")(citing United States v. McArthur, 419 F. Supp. 186 (D.N.D. 1975), *aff'd*, 541 F.2d 1275 (8th Cir. 1976); United States v. Bacon, 851 F.2d 1312, 1313-14 (11th Cir. 1988)(concluding there was no 'military permeation of civilian law enforcement where "an active-duty army investigator assumed an undercover role in working jointly with the ... Sheriff's Department to ferret out a source of some of the cocaine being supplied to [the area for] both civilians and army personnel.... Army funds were used for some of the undercover drug 'buys.' ... All drugs and other evidence gathered by Army Investigator Perkins were turned over to the state and local investigators for evidence in the prosecution of [the] drug distributor.....' "). Courts do not seem to have accepted the proposition that military undercover participation without a primary military purpose is a per se violation of the Posse Comitatus Act or at least of DOD Dir. No. 5525.5 (Encl.4) A.3. ("except as otherwise provided in this enclosure, [e.g., when done primarily for a military purpose], the prohibition on the use of military personnel 'as a posse comitatus or otherwise to execute the laws prohibits ... d. Use of military personnel for surveillance... or as undercover agents...." United States v. Hartley, 796 F.2d 112, 115 (5th Cir. 1986)(Air Force assistance to a customs agent tracking an aircraft suspected of smuggling marijuana into the United States); United States v. Gerena, 649 F. Supp. 1179, 1182 (D. Conn. 1986)(military transport of prisoner in the custody of the Marshals Service); People v. Bautista, 115 Cal. App.4th 229 (2004) (military drug detection dog alert that led to police search of airport locker was not direct participation); Airway Heights v. Dilley, 45 Wash. App. 87, 92, 724 P.2d 407, 410 (1986)(use of Air Force technician and equipment to administer breathalyzer test).

[324] *E.g., accord,* Taylor v. State, 645 P.2d 522, 525 (Okla. Crim. App. 1982). *See also*, United States v. Walden, 490 F.2d 372 (4th Cir. 1974); Taylor v. State, 640 So.2d 1127, 1136 (Fla. App. 1994)("Cases addressing [restrictions on military assistance to law enforcement under 18 U.S.C. § 1385 and 10 U.S.C. § 375] have ruled that where military involvement is limited and there is an independent military purpose, 'the coordination of military police efforts with those of civilian law enforcement officials does not violate either [section 1385 or section 375].' Hayes v. Hawes, 921 F.2d 100, 103 (7th Cir. 1990) (finding that Naval Investigative Service (NIS) agents' activities impermissibly "permeated the initial stages of the homicide investigation" where agents obtained authorization to arrest a sailor suspected of homicide on pretextual grounds for unauthorized absence, traveled to Virginia to interview appellant's family members and kept them under surveillance, questioned him about the homicides and took oral and written statements from him, seized his clothing and other personal effects, and then transported appellant to Jacksonville, where they returned him over to the civilian authorities).

[325] Military Use of Infrared Radars Technology to Assist Civilian Law Enforcement Agencies, 15 U.S. Op. Off. Legal Counsel 36 (1991). DOD presented the question to the Justice Department after receiving several requests for assistance from DEA to deploy Forward Looking Infrared Radar (FLIR) to identify illicit narcotics production.

[326] *Id.* at 39-40. OLC found noteworthy that the original version of 10 U.S.C. § 375 prohibited military personnel from participating in "an interdiction of a vessel or aircraft, *a search and seizure*, arrest, or other similar activity." *Id.* at 41 (citing P.L. 97-86, tit. IX, § 905(a)(1), 95 Stat. 1099, 1116 (1981)(emphasis added)). OLC reasoned that:

The coupling of "search" and "seizure" through use of the conjunctive "and," and the reference to the two as a single event (i.e., "a search and seizure"), strongly suggests that Congress was referring to searches of persons or objects that had been seized and thus were in the custody of law enforcement officers. Searches of seized persons or objects almost always involve physical contact.

Id. While OLC thought the later amendment of the statute, which deleted the "and" between "search" and "seizure," was meant to clarify that it prohibited even searches that did not result in a seizure, the OLC's conclusion that the kind of searches to be prohibited encompassed only those involving physical contact remained unaffected.

[327] *Id.* at 42-46 (citing H.R. Rep. No. 71, 97th Cong., 1st Sess., pt. 2 (1981) and S. Rep. No. 58, 97th Cong., 1st Sess. (1981) to conclude that Congress intended to codify the distinction articulated in United States v. Red Feather, 392 F. Supp. 916 (D.S.D. 1975) between "indirect passive" assistance and "direct active" involvement in law enforcement activity).

[328] Whoever, except in cases and under circumstances expressly authorized by the Constitution or Act of Congress, willfully uses *any part of the Army or the Air Force* as a posse comitatus or otherwise to execute the laws shall be fined under this title or imprisoned not more than two years, or both. 18 U.S.C. § 1385 (emphasis added).

[329] *See* 7 CONG. REC. 3586 (1878).

[330] *See* Coffey, *supra* footnote 155, at 1955 (1987); Meeks, *supra* footnote 284, at 101. Under long standing rules of the House, an amendment that deals with a subject different from those contained in the bill which it seeks to amend is nongermane and subject to challenge. If the sponsors adjusted their amendment solely for reasons of germaneness, one would expect to find a comparable amendment in the Navy appropriation bill before the Congress at the same time. No such amendment was offered to the Navy bill, 46 Stat. 48 (1878).

[331] United States v. Mendoza-Cecelia, 963 F.2d 1467, 1477 (11th Cir. 1992); United States v. Yunis, 924 F.2d 1086, 1093 (D.C. Cir. 1991); State v. Short, 113 Wash.2d 35, 38, 775 P.2d 458, 459 (1989); United States v. Ahumedo-Avendano, 872 F.2d 367, 372 n.6 (11th Cir. 1989); Schowengerdt v. General Dynamics Corp., 823 F.2d 1328, 1339-340 (9th Cir. 1987); United States v. Roberts, 779 F.2d 565, 567 (9th Cir. 1986); United States v. Walden, 490 F.2d 372, 374 (4th Cir. 1974).

[332] United States v. Kahn, 35 F.3d 426, 431 (9th Cir. 1994)("[t]hus the Posse Comitatus Act applies to the Navy through section 375 [of title 10 of the United States Code] and 32 C.F.R. §213.10"); Taylor v. State, 640 So.2d 1127, 1136 (Fla.App. 1994)("[m]ilitary participation in civilian law enforcement activities is restricted by the federal Posse Comitatus Act, 18 U.S.C. § 1385, and by 10 U.S.C. § 375"); United States v. Yunis, 924 F.2d 1086, 1094 (D.C. Cir. 1991)) ("[r]egulations issued under 10 U.S.C. § 375 require Navy compliance with the restrictions of the Posse Comitatus Act...."); Hayes v. Hawes, 921 F.2d 100, 102-103 (7th Cir. 1990)("10 U.S.C. § 375 and the regulations promulgated there under at 32 C.F.R. §§ 213.1-213.11 make the proscriptions of [18 U.S.C.] § 1385 applicable to the Navy and serve to limit its involvement with civilian law enforcement officials"); State v. Short, 113 Wash.2d 35, 39, 775 P.2d 458, 460 (1989)("[b]ecause the limitations on the use of the armed services contained in 10 U.S.C. § 375 correspond closely with those in the posse comitatus act, the same analysis should apply"); United States v. Ahumedo-Avendano, 872 F.2d 367, 372 n.6 (11th Cir. 1989)("[t]he Posse Comitatus Act does not expressly regulate the use of naval forces as a posse comitatus; the courts of appeal that have considered this question, however, have concluded that the prohibition embodied in the Act applies to naval forces, either by implication or by virtue of executive act"); United States v. Roberts, 779 F.2d 565, 568 (9th Cir. 1986)(" the Posse Comitatus Act and sections 371-378 of Title 10 embody similar proscriptions against military involvement in civil law enforcement...."); United States v. Del Prado-Montero, 740 F.2d 113, 116 (1st Cir. 1984)("18 U.S.C. § 1385 prohibits the use of the Army and the Air Force to enforce the laws of the United States, a proscription that has been extended by executive act to the Navy"); United States v. Chaparro-Almeida, 679 F.2d 423, 425 (5th Cir. 1982)(dicta in case involving the Coast Guard); United States v. Walden, 490 F.2d 372, 373-74 (4th Cir. 1974)("[t]he use of Marines as undercover investigators by the Treasury Department is counter to a Navy military regulation proscribing the use of military personnel to enforce civilian laws.... Thus, though by its terms the Posse Comitatus Act does not make criminal the use of Marines to enforce federal laws, the Navy has adopted the restriction by self-imposed administrative regulation").

As an examination of the cases listed above and in the previous footnote demonstrate, although in basic agreement subsequent courts have sometime described their views as in conflict. In fact, one camp will cite Walden for the proposition that the Posse Comitatus Act does not apply to the Navy or Marines although its requirements have been adopted by administrative and/or legislative supplements, while the other camp will cite Walden for the assertedly contrary proposition that the Posse Comitatus Act requirements apply to the Navy and Marines by way of regulation and/or legislative supplement. A third group takes an abbreviate route to the same destination by simply citing Walden for the principle that the Posse Comitatus Act applies to Navy and the Marines, *see e.g.*, People v. Caviano, 148 Misc.2d 426, 560 N.Y.S.2d 932, 936 n.1 (1990); State v. Presgraves, 328 S.E.2d 699, 701 n.3 (W.Va. 1985); State v. Maxwell, 328 S.E.2d 506, 509 n.4 (W.Va. 1985); People v. Wells, 175 Cal.App.3d 876, 879, 221 Cal.Rprt. 273, 275 (1985); People v. Blend, 121 Cal.App.3d 215, 222, 175 Cal.Rprt. 263, 267 (1981).

[333] DOD Directive No. 5525.5 (Jan. 15, 1986) applies to the Office of the Secretary of Defense (OSD), the Military Departments, the Organization of the Joint Chiefs of Staff (OJS), the Unified and Specified Commands, and the Defense Agencies. The term 'Military Service' refers to the Army, Navy, Air Force, and Marine Corps.

[334] *See* 46 Stat. 316 (1878), directing the Secretary of the Treasury to issue three months extra pay to those who had engaged in the military service of the United States during the war with Mexico and listing the cutter service as one source of possibly qualifying service.

[335] 14 U.S.C. § 1.

[336] 14 U.S.C. § 3.

[337] United States v. Chaparro-Almedia, 679 F.2d 423, 425 (5th Cir. 1982)(Posse Comitatus Act inapplicable to Coast Guard operating under the Department of Transportation); Jackson v. State, 572 P.2d 87, 93 (Alaska 1977)(same).

[338] 14 U.S.C. § 3.

[339] 14 U.S.C. § 2.

[340] *See* Panagacos v. Towery, 782 F. Supp. 2d 1183 (W.D. Wash. 2011)(Coast Guard member not covered by Posse Comitatus Act).

[341] *See* Maryland v. United States, 381 U.S. 41, 46 (1965).

[342] *See* Meeks, *supra* footnote 284, at 96-99; Furman, *supra* footnote 147, at 101.

[343] *See supra* footnote 112, and accompanying text.

[344] The status of the District of Columbia National Guard is somewhat different since it is a creature entirely of federal creation. This being the case it might be thought that the D.C. National Guard should be considered perpetually "in federal service" or that the Posse Comitatus Act would apply to it at all times even though the treatment of the National Guard in the various states might be different. This, however, is not the view of the Department of Justice, which has concluded the Posse Comitatus Act applies to the D.C. National Guard only when it is called into federal service as a state National Guard might be. The Department has also determined that even if this were not the case, the Posse Comitatus Act permits the D.C. National Guard "to support the drug law enforcement efforts" of the D.C. police because of the authority granted by Congress in D.C. Code 39-104 (declaring that the D.C. National Guard shall not be subject to any duty except when called into federal service or to "aid civil authorities in the execution of the laws or suppression of riots" [D.C. Code § 39-603 authorizes D.C. officials, in times of tumult, riot, or mob violence, to request the President to call out the D.C. National Guard to aid "in suppressing such violence and enforcing the laws"]) and D.C. Code § 39-602 (authorizing the Commanding General of the D.C. National Guard to order "such drills, inspections, parades, escort, *or other duties*, as he may deem proper")(emphasis added), *Use of the National Guard to Support Drug Interdiction Efforts in the District of Columbia*, 13 Op. Off. Legal Counsel 110 (1989).

[345] Gilbert v. United States, 165 F.3d 470, 473 (6th Cir. 1999); United States v. Hutchings, 127 F.3d 1255, 1258 (10th Cir. 1997); United States v. Benish, 5 F.3d 20, 25-6 (3rd Cir. 1993); United States v. Kyllo, 809 F. Supp. 787, 792-93 (D. Ore. 1992), *aff'd* 190 F.3d 1041 (9th Cir. 1999), *rev'd on other grounds* 533 U.S. 27 (2001); Wallace v. State, 933 P.2d 1157, 1160 (Alaska App. 1997); *accord*, Steven B. Rich, *The National Guard, Drug Interdiction and Counterdrug Activities, and the Posse Comitatus Act: The Meaning and Implications of 'In Federal Service'*, 1994 ARMY LAW. 35, 42-3 (June,1994). However, in two of the Wounded Knee cases, in which National Guard involvement in the civilian law enforcement efforts helped doom federal prosecution, the courts made no effort to determine whether the Guard had been called into federal service, suggesting to some that the Guard was covered in any event. United States v. Banks, 383 F. Supp. 368, 376 (D.S.D. 1974); United States v. Jaramillo, 380 F. Supp. 1375, 1380-381 (D.Neb. 1974); *see also*, United States v. McArthur, 419 F. Supp. 186, 193 n.3 (D.N.D. 1976)(a third Wounded Knee case listing "use by federal civil law enforcement officers of material and equipment furnished by ... the South Dakota National Guard ...aerial photographic reconnaissance provided by ... the Nebraska National Guard ... and the maintenance of military vehicles performed by members of the Nebraska National Guard" as "evidence of military involvement"); Meeks, *supra* footnote 284, at 96-98.

A federal district court in *United States v. Kyllo* suggested that 32 U.S.C. §112 (which permits the Secretary of Defense to provide funds for the drug interdiction activities conducted by various state National Guards when not in federal service) authorizes such Guards to assist in civilian law enforcement efforts, 809 F. Supp. at 793; *see also* People v. Marolda, 394 N.J. Super. 430, 927 A.2d 154 (2007)(without discussing status of members of Coast Guard and of National Guard who aided state officials in aerial search for drugs, regarding Posse Comitatus Act as inapplicable).

The legislative history of earlier efforts to involve the National Guard (while in state service) in drug interdiction indicates that the Congress believed that "[w]hen not in federal service, the National Guard is not subject to the Posse Comitatus Act," H.R. REP. NO.100-989, 455, *reprinted in* 1988 U.S.C.C.A.N. 2503, 2583.

[346] "The restrictions of section A. above [the Directive's posse comitatus proscriptions], do not apply to the following persons.... 2. A member of the National Guard when not in Federal Service," DOD Directive No. 5525.5.b.2. Proposed32 C.F.R. pt. 182 applies to the National Guard "when under Federal command and control" or when they activated in "title 32, U.S. Code status to fulfill a request for defense support of civil authorities" as approved by the respective governors of affected states. Proposed 32 C.F.R. § 182.2(c).

[347] "If a soldier sees a man assaulting me with a view to take my life, he is not going to stand by and see him do it, he comes to my relief not as a soldier, but as a human being, a man with a soul in his body, and as a citizen.... The soldier standing by would have interposed if he had been a man, but not as a soldier. He could not have gone down in pursuance of an order from a colonel or a captain, but he would have done it as a man." 7 CONG. REC. 4245 (1878)(remarks of Sen. Merriman). The weight afforded remarks in the Senate should perhaps reflect the fact that the act was the work of a Democratic House, forced upon a reluctant Republican Senate.

[348] People v. Taliferro, 116 Ill.App.3d 861, 520 N.E.2d 1047, 1051 (1988)(an airman acted as an undercover agent for local drug enforcement officers; "Ferguson participated in a controlled drug purchase in exactly the same manner as any other citizen would participate in such transaction"); Burkhart v. State, 727 P.2d 971, 972 (Okla.Crim.App. 1986)(military undercover agent investigating drugs sold to military personnel purchased some from the defendant and testified against him; "the agent 'did not assume any greater authority than that of a private citizen in purchasing the marijuana'"); People v. Burden, 411 Mich. 56, 303 N.W.2d 444, 446-47 (1981)(airman agreed to serve undercover after being charged with drug sales by civilian authorities; "[i]n cooperating with and assisting the civilian police agency, Hall was not acting as a member of the military. He was acting only as a civilian. His military status was merely incidental to and not essential to his involvement with the civilian authorities. He was not in military uniform. He was not acting under military orders. He did not exercise either explicitly or implicitly any military authority. Moreover, Hall was not a regular law enforcement agent of the military, * * * nor does the record suggest that Hall's usefulness to civilian authorities was in any way enhanced by virtue of his being a military man.... [T]he assistance rendered by Hall was in no way different from the cooperation which would have been given by a private citizen offered the same opportunity to avoid criminal prosecution"); People v. Blend, 121 Cal.App.3d 215, 227, 175 Cal.Rptr.263, 270 (1981)(a Navy Wave caught by civilian authorities in violating the drug laws, agreed to serve undercover for the civilian police; "the [posse comitatus] act does not apply to military personnel who are acting clearly on their own initiative as private citizens"); Lee v. State, 513 P.2d 125, 126 (Okla.Crim.App. 1973)(military undercover agent in cooperation with local police purchases drugs off-base from a civilian; "agent Smith did not assume any greater authority than that of a private citizen in purchasing the marijuana in the instant case"); Hildebrandt v. State, 507 P.2d1323, 1325 (Okla.Crim.App. 1973)(military undercover investigators traced the source of drugs sold to military personnel to the defendant; the "soldier led the agents to a location outside the scope of their military jurisdiction, at which time the agents assumed no greater authority than that of a private citizen"); Hubert v. State, 504 P.2d 1245,1246-247 (Okla.Crim.App. 1972)(same).

[349] Meeks, *supra* footnote 284, at 126-27 ("Military personnel are all private citizens as well as members of the federal military. The prohibitions of the Posse Comitatus Act do not apply to military personnel who are performing the normal duties of a citizen such as reporting crimes and suspicious activities, making citizens' arrests where allowed by local law and otherwise cooperating with civil police. It is not sufficient for military personnel to be 'volunteers,' they must clearly be acting on their own initiative and in a purely unofficial and individual capacity. Commanders must be careful to insure that activities which are in violation of the act are not being carried on under the labels of 'individual' or 'unofficial' assistance. Some factors which may signal a violation of the Act include aid given during duty hours, aid prompted or suggested by a military superior or aid given with the knowledge or acquiescence of a military superior. Other considerations include the manner in which the civil authorities contacted the military person, whether that person regularly performs military law enforcement functions, and whether or not the individual's usefulness to civil authorities is related to his military status"); Rice, *supra* footnote 284, at 128-33 (also noting that the catalyst for some of the difficulties stemmed from the holding in O'Callahan v. Parker, 395 U.S. 258 (1969)(since overturned) limiting military jurisdiction over crimes committed by military personnel to those which were service connected).

[350] Fox v. State, 908 P.2d 1053, 1057 (Alaska App. 1995)("In civilian prosecutions stemming from joint military-civilian investigations into off-base drug sales, courts have interpreted these regulations to require the government to demonstrate a military purpose – that is a nexus between the targeted off-base sales and military personnel; this purpose must be shown to have been the primary purpose of the military's participation. In the absence of a nexus between the targeted off-base drug sales and military personnel, courts have condemned joint investigations as violations of the Posse Comitatus Act "); State v. Gunter, 902 S.W.2d 172, 175 (Tex. App. 1995)(after quoting the private citizen language in *Burkhardt*, *supra*, the court declared, "[a] majority of courts have also noted that where military involvement is limited and where there is an independent military purpose of preventing illicit drug transactions to support the military involvement, the

coordination of military police efforts with those of civilian law enforcement does not violate the Act. Where the military participation in an investigation odes not pervade the activities of civilian officials, and does not subject the citizenry to the regulatory exercise of military power, it doe snot violate the Act"); State v. Pattioay, 78 Haw. 455, 466, 896 P.2d 911, 922 (1995)("Absent evidence to support the prosecution's claim of a primary military purpose, we must uphold the circuit court's conclusion that the joint civilian-military [undercover drug] investigation violated the PCA, 10 U.S.C. § 375, and relevant federal regulations"); Taylor v. State, 640 So.2d1127, 1136 (Fla.App. 1994) ("[m]ilitary participation in civilian law enforcement activities is restricted by the federal Posse Comitatus Act and by 10 U.S.C. §375. Cases addressing this issue have ruled that where military involvement is limited and there is an independent military purpose, 'the coordination of military police efforts with those of civilian law enforcement officials does not violate either section 1385 or section 375.' Hayes v. Hawes, 921 F.2d 100, 103 (7th Cir. 1990). The test for violation of the federal law is (1) whether civilian law enforcement officials made a direct active use of military investigators to execute the laws; (2) whether the use of the military pervaded the activities of the civilian officials; or (3) whether the military was used so as to subject citizens to the exercise of military power which was regulatory, proscriptive, or compulsory in nature").

[351] State v. Short, 113 Wash.2d 35, 39-40, 775 P.2d 458, 460 (1989); State v. Morris, 522 A.2d 220, 221 (R.I. 1987); People v. Hayes, 144 Ill.App. 3d 696, 494 N.E.2d 1238, 1240 (1986); *see also*, Furman, *supra* footnote 147, at 101.

[352] *See e.g.*, Hayes v. Hawes, 921 F.2d 100 (7th Cir. 1990); People v. Wells, 175 Cal.App.3d 878, 221 Cal.Rprt. 273 (1988); State v. Maxwell, 328 S.E.2d 506 (W.Va. 1985); State v. Presgraves, 328 S.E.2d 699 (W.Va. 1985); United States v. Hartley, 486 F. Supp. 1348, 1356 (M.D.Fla. 1980), *aff'd*, 678 F.2d 961 (11th Cir. 1982); Meeks, *supra* footnote 284, at 83 ("civilian investigators operate under the immediate supervision of military officers who are prohibited by the Act from aiding local authorities. Holding that the civilian subordinates are not also prohibited allows a principal to accomplish things through his agent that he could not otherwise lawfully do himself. It is foolhardy to assume that it is only the sight of the man in military uniform aiding the sheriff that tends to offend the civilian community").

[353] DOD Dir. No. 5525.5 (Encl.4) E4.2.3, a comparable provision appeared in 32 C.F.R. §213.10(b)(3)(July 1, 1992 ed.). Proposed 32 C.F.R. pt. 182 does not list comparable "exceptions based on status," but suggests that the restrictions apply to all DOD personnel as a matter of policy. Proposed 32 C.F.R. §182.4(b)(1).

[354] *Effect of Posse Comitatus Act on Proposed Detail Of Civilian Employee to the National Infrastructure Protection Center*, 22 U.S. Op. Off. Legal Counsel 103 (1993).

[355] *Assignment of Army Lawyers to the Department of Justice*, 10 U.S. Op. Off. Legal Counsel 115, 121 (1986).

[356] *Extraterritorial Effect of the Posse Comitatus Act*, 13 Op. Off. Legal Counsel 387 (1989); Deanne C. Siemer & Andrew S. Effron, *Military Participation in United States Law Enforcement Activities Overseas: The Extraterritorial Effect of the Posse Comitatus Act*, 54 ST. JOHN'S L. REV. 1 (1979).

[357] United States v. Bowman, 260 U.S. 94, 98 (1922); Blackmer v. United States, 284 U.S. 421 (1932); United States v.Yunis, 924 F.2d 1086, 1090-91 (D.C. Cir. 1991).

[358] Chandler v. United States, 171 F.2d 921, 936 (1st Cir. 1948).

[359] Gillars v. United States, 182 F.2d 962, 973 (D.C. Cir. 1950); D'Aquino v. United States, 192 F.2d 338, 351 (9th Cir. 1951); United States v. Cotton, 471 F.2d 744, 748-49 (9th Cir. 1973).

[360] 10 U.S.C. § 379.

[361] *Cf.*, United States v. Klimavicius-Viloria, 144 F.3d 1249, 1259 (9th Cir. 1998); United States v. Khan, 35 F.3d 426, 431-32 (9th Cir. 1994)(both determining that the particular activities of Navy personnel on the high seas in aid of law enforcement officials did not violate 10 U.S.C. § 375).

[362] "The Committee considered and narrowly rejected a suggestion that the assistance permitted by this section be made available only outside the United States," H.R. REP.NO. 97-71, pt.2, 12 n.3, *reprinted in* 1981 U.S.C.C.A.N. 1785, 1795.

[363] DOD Dir. No. 5525.5, § 2.2.

[364] Proposed 32 C.F.R. Part 182 is inapplicable to assistance to law enforcement officials in foreign governments, 32 C.F.R. § 182.2(d)(2), while § 182.4(b)(2) provides that "the restrictions in [the Posse Comitatus Act and 10 U.S.C. § 375] shall apply to all actions of DoD personnel within and without the territorial boundaries of the United States," unless an exception is granted by the Secretary or Deputy Secretary of Defense, § 182.4(c).

[365] 22 U.S.C. § 2291.

[366] 22 U.S.C. § 2291(c) prohibits U.S. officers and employees who are participating in foreign police actions from directly effecting a narcotics arrest except under exigent circumstances to protect life or safety, or from participating in or observing the interrogation of a U.S. person arrested in a foreign country for a narcotics offense unless the person consents in writing.

In the course of its opinion concerning the extraterritorial application of the Posse Comitatus Act, the Office of Legal Counsel characterized an earlier version of the Mansfield Amendment as applicable only in the case of American involvement "in the internal enforcement activities of foreign countries" and not applicable to the overseas enforcement of American law, *Extraterritorial Effect of the Posse Comitatus Act*, 13 Op. Off. Legal Counsel 387, 410-11 n.16 (1989)(citing dicta in *United States v. Green*, 671 F.2d 46, 53 n.9 (1st Cir. 1982), for the proposition that the Mansfield Amendment "was only intended to 'insure that U.S. personnel do not become involved in sensitive, internal law enforcement operations which could adversely affect U.S. relations with that country'" and inferring that U.S. enforcement of its laws within the territory of another nation for misconduct within that nation would not similarly adversely affect relations and was intended to be covered). However tenable that position may once have been, it seems to have been undermined by the inclusion of subparagraph (4) making the Amendment inapplicable in cases where the foreign country has agreed to the application of American drug laws within its territorial waters.

367 Matthew Gilligan, *Opening the Gate? An Analysis of Military Law Enforcement Authority Over Civilian Lawbreakers On and Off the Federal Installation*, 161 MIL.L.REV. 1, 11 (1999); State v. Pattioay, 78 Haw. 455, 467, 896 P.2d 911, 923 (1995); Moon v. State, 785 P.2d 45, 48 (Alaska App. 1990).

368 *See* LIEBER, *supra* footnote 155, at 28 n. 2 (noting indictment in 1879 of two Army officers for providing troops to federal marshal to assist in arresting suspected violators of federal revenue laws). The incident involved a stand-off of sorts between federal and state law enforcement officers, in which U.S. Deputy Marshal Walter Johnson was himself arrested by state officials for having arrested, on blank warrants which he filled in at the time of arrest, citizens suspected of running illicit stills. He then secured the help of soldiers from the 10th Cavalry to arrest the original suspects again as well as the state officials who had freed them. *See Conflict of Authority in Texas*, N.Y. HERALD-TRIB., December 13, 1879, at 2; *Frontier Jurisdiction,*26 TEX. B. J. 391 (1963) (reporting state case against the deputy marshal). Despite the notoriety of the incident, the two officers were eventually acquitted. *See Acquittal of Captain Nolan and Lieutenant Flipper*, DALLAS WKLY HERALD, December 15, 1881, at 1 (explaining that charges were dropped against the Lieutenant after the jury acquitted the Captain); *Army Officers Acquitted*, CINCINNATI COM. TRIB., December 16, 1881, at 3 (opining that "[c]harity alone prevented a rigid prosecution"). One of those officers later described a similar incident in which the same two officers were indicted for assisting the same federal deputy marshal, this time by holding prisoners overnight at Fort Elliott, two men who were suspected of stealing ammunition from the camp and selling it to local cowboys. HENRY O. FLIPPER, NEGRO FRONTIERSMAN 11-12 (1963)(autobiographical account). In that case, he reported Captain Nolan entered a guilty plea for the both of them, and each was fined one dollar. *Id.* However, that story appears to be uncorroborated by contemporary accounts, and Flipper's autobiography does not mention the first incident. It seems probable that there was only a single set of indictments. Lieutenant Flipper was already well-known as the first black cadet to have graduated from West Point.

369 Smith v. United States, 293 F.3d 984, 988 (7th Cir. 2002); Robinson v. Overseas Military Sales Corp., 21 F.3d 502, 511 (2d Cir. 1994); Lamont v. Haig, 539 F. Supp. 552, 558–59 (D.S.D. 1982).

370 490 F.2d 372 (4th Cir. 1974).

371 490 F.2d at 376.

372 490 F.2d at 377.

373 *E.g.*, United States v. Wolffs, 594 F.2d 77, 85 (5th Cir. 1979)("We pretermit discussion of whether there was a violation of the statute or regulation. We need not decide that complex and difficult issue because assuming without deciding that there was a violation application of an exclusionary rule is not warranted."); People v. Hayes, 144 Ill.App.3d 696, 699, 494 N.E.2d 1238, 1240 (1986)("numerous decisions with facts similar to those presented here have found that no violation of the Act occurs if the aid is not characterized as military and the investigation merely coordinates with civilian police. More importantly, with few exceptions, the courts have uniformly held that the exclusionary rule does not apply to evidence seized in violation the Posse Comitatus Act"); other cases include, United States v. Johnson, 410 F.3d 137 (4th Cir. 2005); United States v. Mullin, 178 F.3d 334, 342-43 (5th Cir. 1999); United States v. Al-Talib, 55 F.3d 923, 930 (4th Cir. 1995); State v. Gonzales, 247 P.3d 1111, 1115, 149 N.M. 226, 230, 2011-NMCA-007, 007 (N.M.App. 2010); State v. Gunter, 902 S.W.2d 172 (Tex.App. 1995); Taylor v. State, 640 So.2d 1127 (Fla.App. 1994)(finding a violation but declining to exclude evidence); State v. Valdobinos, 122 Wash.2d 270, 858 P.2d 199 (1993); United States v. Mendoza-Cecelia, 963 F.2d 1467 (11th Cir. 1992); McPherson v. State 800 P.2d 928 (Alaska App. 1990); People v. Caviano, 148 Misc.2d 426, 560 N.Y.S.2d 932 (N.Y.S.Ct. 1990); Moon v. State, 785 P.2d 45, 46-48 (Alaska App. 1990); Badoino v. State, 785 P.2d 39, 42-43 (Alaska App. 1990); Hayes v. Hawes, 921 F.2d 100 (7th Cir. 1990); State v. Short, 113 Wash.2d 35, 40, 775 P.2d 458, 460 (1989); State v. Poe, 755 S.W.2d 41, 44-45 (Tenn. 1988); United States v. Bacon, 851 F.2d 1312 (11th Cir. 1988); United States v. Griley, 814 F.2d 967 (4th Cir. 1987); State v. Morris, 522 A.2d 220 (R.I. 1987); United States v. Hartley, 796 F.2d 112 (5th Cir. 1986); United States v. Roberts, 779 F.2d 565 (9th Cir. 1986)(found violation but declined to find application of the exclusionary rule appropriate); Burkhart v. State, 727 P.2d 971 (Okla.Crim.App. 1986); People v. Wells, 175 Cal.App.3d 876, 221 Cal.Rptr. 273 (1985); State v. Maxwell, 328 S.E.2d 506 (W.Va. 1985); Unites States v. Chaparro-Almeida, 679 F.2d 423 (5th Cir. 1982); People v. Burden, 411 Mich.56, 303 N.W.2d 444 (1981); State v. Sanders, 303 N.C. 608, 281 S.E.2d 7 (N.C. 1981); State v. Trueblood, 46 N.C.App. 541, 265 S.E.2d 662 (N.C.App. 1980); State v. Nelson, 298 N.C. 573, 260 S.E.2d 629 (1979); State v. Danko, 219 Kan. 490, 548 P.2d 819 (9176); Hubert v. State, 504 P.2d 1245 (Okla.Crim.App. 1972); United States v. Vick, __ F. Supp. 2d __, 2012 WL 263661 (E.D. Va. Jan. 27, 2012); Aviles v. Department of the Army, 666 F. Supp. 2d 224, 234 (D.P.R. 2009).

[374] State v. Pattioay, 78 Haw. 455, 896 P.2d 911 (1995); People v. Tyler, 854 P.2d 1366 (Colo.App. 1993), *rev'd on other grounds*, 874 P.2d 1037 (Colo. 1994); Taylor v. State, 645 P.2d 522 (Okla.Crim.App. 1982).

[375] United States v. Lewis, 824 F. Supp. 2d 169 (D.D.C. 2011).

[376] Ker v. Illinois 119 U.S. 436, 444 (1886); Frisbie v. Collins, 342 U.S. 519, 522 (1952); United States v. Alvarez-Machain, 504 U.S. 655, 661-62 (1992).

[377] Chandler v. United States 171 F.2d 921 (1st Cir. 1949); Gillars v. United States, 182 F.2d 962 (D.C. Cir. 1950); D'Aquino v. United States, 192 F.2d 338 (9th Cir. 1951).

[378] United States v. Wooten, 377 F.3d 1134, 1140 (10th Cir. 2004); United States v. Mendoza-Cecelia, 963 F.2d 1467, 1478 n.9 (11th Cir. 1992); United States v. Yunis, 924 F.2d 1086, 1093-94 (D.C. Cir. 1991); State v. Morris, 522 A.2d 220, 221 (R.I. 1987); United States v. Roberts, 779 F.2d 565, 568 (9th Cir. 1986), United States v. Cotton, 471 F.2d744, 749 (9th Cir. 1973).

[379] *See supra* footnote 258 and accompanying text.

[380] United States v. Banks, 383 F. Supp. 368, 374-77 (D.S.D. 1974); United States v. Jaramillo, 380 F. Supp. 1375, 1378-381 (D.Neb. 1974).

[381] Bissonette v. Haig, 800 F.2d 812, 814-16 (8th Cir. 1986), *aff'd as if by an equally divided court for want of a quorum*, 485 U.S. 264 (1988); *see also*, Applewhite v. United States, 995 F.2d 997 (10th Cir. 1993). Bivens v. Six Unknown Named Agents of the Federal Bureau of Narcotics, 403 U.S. 388 (1971), recognized a private cause of action in tort for injuries suffered as a result of a constitutional violation.

[382] Wrynn v. United States, 200 F. Supp. 457, 464-65 (E.D.N.Y. 1961); Rice, *supra* footnote 284, at 115.

[383] *See* Riley v. Newton, 94 F.3d 632 (11th Cir. 1996)(county investigator not liable for excessive force on the part of military policeman assisting in an arrest).

[384] Furman, *supra* footnote 147, at 85-86; Meeks, *supra* footnote 284, at 83 (both citing extensively to internal instructions, directives and opinions advising members of the military to refrain from conduct understood to be contrary to the Posse Comitatus Act); Peterson, *supra* footnote 262, at 145 n.165 ("when the Army believes the Posse Comitatus Act actually applies, the Army interprets the prohibitions of the Act broadly"); *cf.*, Rice, *supra* footnote 284, at 118 & 118 n.55)("Unexpected decisions cause ripples in the steady flow of jurisprudence. Consequently, the notoriety of the *Banks* case [one of the Wounded Knee quartet of cases] should not be surprising. It also caused hesitancy on the part of the Department of Defense.* *During the Hanafi Muslem hostage situation in Washington, D.C., the Justice Department had requested grenades in case the gunmen began to kill their hostages. There was a delay in responding to the request")(footnote 55 of the article is quoted following the asterisks).

In: A Selection of Federal Acts
Editors: P. Brown and K. M. Mitchell

ISBN: 978-1-62417-047-8

Chapter 2

FOREIGN CORRUPT PRACTICES ACT (FCPA): CONGRESSIONAL INTEREST AND EXECUTIVE ENFORCEMENT*

Michael V. Seitzinger

SUMMARY

The Foreign Corrupt Practices Act of 1977 (FCPA) was enacted principally to prevent corporate bribery of foreign officials. This act had three major parts: (1) it required the keeping by corporations of accurate books, records, and accounts; (2) it required issuers registered with the Securities and Exchange Commission to maintain a responsible internal accounting control system; and (3) it prohibited bribery by American corporations of foreign officials.

For a number of years after passage of the act, Congress debated amending it in response to numerous criticisms. On August 23, 1988, the President signed into law the Omnibus Trade and Competitiveness Act of 1988, of which Title V is known as the Foreign Corrupt Practices Act Amendments of 1988.

The amendments maintained the three major parts of the 1977 Act, but significant changes were made. One of these changes enacted a "knowing" standard in order to find violations of the act. This standard was intended to encompass "conscious disregard" and "willful blindness." The amendments provided certain defenses against finding violations of the act, such as that the gift is lawful under the laws of the foreign country and that the gift is a bona fide and reasonable expenditure or for the performance or execution of a contract with the foreign government.

In 1998 the act was further amended in order to implement the Organization of Economic Cooperation and Development Convention on Combating Bribery of Foreign Public Officials in International Business Transactions. These amendments expanded the scope of coverage to

---

* This is an edited, reformatted and augmented version of the Congressional Research Service Publication, CRS Report for Congress R41466, dated February 7, 2012.

include some foreign persons and extended jurisdiction beyond the borders of the United States.

Criticisms of the act have continued. Especially prominent recently have been suggestions that businesses convicted of violating the Foreign Corrupt Practices Act should be debarred from receiving federal government contracts. Bills were introduced in the 111th Congress to address this issue.

In addition to congressional scrutiny of the act, the executive branch appears to have increased oversight of suspected American businesses for alleged violations. There have been a number of settlements and indictments concerning violations of the act. In early 2012 the federal government had both successes and losses resulting from its FCPA charges.

INTRODUCTION

During the mid-1970s investigations and administrative and legal actions against numerous domestic corporations revealed that the practice of making questionable or illegal payments by United States corporations to foreign government officials existed to some extent within the American business community. The legal and regulatory mechanisms for dealing with these payments had involved actions by the Securities and Exchange Commission (SEC) against public corporations for concealing from required public disclosure substantial payments made by the firm and the potential for an antitrust action for restraints of trade or fraud prosecutions by the Department of Justice.

Government officials and administrators contended that more direct prohibitions on foreign bribery and more detailed requirements concerning corporate recordkeeping and accountability were needed to deal effectively with the problem. The revelations of slush funds and secret payments by American corporations were stated to have affected adversely American foreign policy, damaged abroad the image of American democracy, and impaired public confidence in the financial integrity of American corporations.[1]

FOREIGN CORRUPT PRACTICES ACT OF 1977

Congress responded with the passage of the Foreign Corrupt Practices Act (FCPA) of 1977.[2] The principal purpose of the 1977 Act was to prevent corporate bribery of foreign officials. It has three major provisions to attempt to accomplish this purpose.

The first major provision amended Section 13(b)[3] of the Securities Exchange Act of 1934[4] to require issuers which must register their securities with the SEC to keep detailed books, records, and accounts which accurately record corporate payments and transactions.

The second major provision required SEC registered issuers to institute and maintain an internal accounting control system to assure management's control, authority, and responsibility over the firm's assets.[5]

The third major provision of the original 1977 Foreign Corrupt Practices Act prohibited domestic corporations, whether or not registered with the SEC, from corruptly bribing a foreign official, a foreign political party, party official, or candidate for the purpose of obtaining or maintaining business. Two provisions of the 1977 Act[6] made it a crime for any

American business to use the mails or interstate commerce to offer or pay money or anything of value to a foreign official or to a foreign political party, party official, or candidate for foreign political office in order to influence the person in his decision making or to use his influence to assist the firm in obtaining or retaining business.

The 1977 Act also prohibited the payment of money to any person by a business if the business knew or had reason to know that the payment was to be used to bribe a foreign official for his influence in obtaining or retaining business. Congressional intent appeared to place an affirmative responsibility on the corporation to exercise control over its officers, directors, and employees, and to take steps to assure that its foreign agents did not use corporate assets or payments made to them to bribe foreign officials.[7]

Under the 1977 Act not all payments to employees of foreign governments were intended by Congress to be considered illegal bribes. For example, the definition of "foreign official" excluded employees of a foreign government "whose duties are essentially ministerial or clerical." Also, the legislative history of the act specifically stated that it was not intended to cover "grease payments" to foreign officials, explained as payments for expediting shipments through customs or placing a transatlantic telephone call, securing required permits, or obtaining adequate police protection, transactions which may involve even the proper performance of duties.[8] The legislative history also suggested that extortions of money by foreign officials might be used as a defense against bribery charges by a business if its property or lives of its employees were threatened. An example used to illustrate acceptable payments was the payment to a foreign official to prevent the dynamiting of an oil rig.[9]

Criticisms of the Foreign Corrupt Practices Act of 1977

Almost since passage of the 1977 Act, frequent criticism of the operation of the act occurred. Opponents argued that the act had a chilling effect upon United States export trade and that many companies ceased foreign operations rather than face the uncertainties and the burdens of the act.

Critics of the 1977 Act also argued for removal of the "reason to know" standard concerning liability for actions of a firm's agent in a foreign country. This would eliminate the legal responsibility of the management of a domestic firm over the unauthorized and undirected actions of an agent without the necessity of management's also showing that it had no "reason to know" that the agent was using corporate funds, payments, or commissions to bribe foreign officials. These critics argued that American firms should not have to bear the responsibility of playing detective concerning the independent actions of persons that they retained as agents in foreign countries.

Critics also contended that the internal accounting controls required by the 1977 Act were too costly and burdensome upon domestic firms, especially when potential criminal penalties within the act for failure to institute adequate controls arguably made officials of firms overly and unnecessarily cautious in implementing costly accounting controls. The public recordkeeping requirements were also criticized as unduly burdensome. Critics of the act argued for a materiality standard for public recordkeeping in which a firm would be required to report only expenditures and outlays deemed material to the profits and revenues of the firm.

Another frequent criticism of the 1977 Act was that the United States was more interested in exporting its cultural biases than its products. It was argued that, in nations in which acceptance of a fee or payment by a government official from one doing business with the government is customary and not unlawful under the laws of that nation, no violation of a United States law should occur. Critics also argued that an international agreement among the world's industrialized nations prohibiting businesses of all those countries from bribing foreign officials was necessary to prevent businesses of other countries from gaining an unfair and harmful competitive advantage over American businesses.

Foreign Corrupt Practices Act Amendments of 1988

In response to these criticisms, Congress for a number of years considered amending the 1977 Foreign Corrupt Practices Act. After considerable debate through at least three Congresses, the Foreign Corrupt Practices Act Amendments of 1988 were signed into law as Title V of the Omnibus Trade and Competitiveness Act of 1988[10] on August 23, 1988. Although the amendments maintained the three major parts of the 1977 Act discussed above—the accounting standards, the requirements of SEC registered issuers, and the anti-bribery provisions—the 1988 amendments made some significant changes to the 1977 Act.

Section 5002 of the Trade Act amended Section 13(b) of the Securities Exchange Act to provide that no criminal liability shall be imposed for violation of the accounting standards unless a person knowingly circumvents or knowingly fails to implement a system of accurate and reasonable accounting controls. According to the legislative history, this provision was intended to ensure that criminal penalties would be imposed where acts of commission or omission in keeping books or records or administering accounting controls have the purpose of falsifying books, records, or accounts or of circumventing accounting controls. This was also intended to include the deliberate falsification of books and records and other conduct calculated to evade the internal accounting controls requirement.[11]

Section 5002 of the Trade Act also added to Section 13(b) of the Securities Exchange Act a provision that an issuer holding 50% or less of the voting power of a domestic or foreign firm is required to use its influence only in good faith to cause the domestic or foreign firm to devise and maintain a system of acceptable accounting controls. The House Report stated that this amendment was intended to recognize that it was unrealistic to expect a minority owner to exert a disproportionate degree of influence over the accounting practices of a subsidiary.[12]

For purposes of the accounting standards, "reasonable assurances" and "reasonable detail" mean such level of detail and degree of assurance as would satisfy prudent officials in the conduct of their own affairs. Thus, the prudent man qualification was adopted to clarify that the current standard does not require an unrealistic degree of exactitude or precision.

Section 5003 of the Trade Act amended the provisions of the Foreign Corrupt Practices Act concerning the anti-bribery prohibitions by issuers and domestic concerns. The Foreign Corrupt Practices Act continued to prohibit any issuer having a class of securities registered with the SEC or any officer, director, employee, or agent of the issuer or any stockholder acting on behalf of the issuer or any United States concern to offer, pay, promise to give, or authorize the giving of anything of value to a foreign official, a foreign political party, party official, candidate, or any person for the purpose of obtaining or maintaining business. Section 5003 amended the 1977 Act to prohibit payments to any foreign official for the purpose of "influencing any act or decision of such foreign official in his official capacity, or inducing such foreign official to do or omit to do any act in violation of the lawful duty of such official." This language was inserted so that the foreign bribery standard would conform to the domestic bribery standard found in 18 U.S.C. Section 201.[13]

The "knowing" requirement was retained, and the "recklessly disregarding" standard was abandoned in conference. However, the "knowing" requirement was intended to encompass the "conscious disregard" and "willful blindness" standards, including a conscious purpose to avoid learning the truth.

> [T]he Conferees agreed that "simple negligence" or "mere foolishness" should not be the basis for liability. However, the Conferees also agreed that the so-called "head-in-the-sand" problem—variously described in the pertinent authorities as "conscious disregard," "willful blindness" or "deliberate ignorance"—should be covered so that management officials could not take refuge from the act's prohibitions by their unwarranted obliviousness to any action (or inaction), language or other "signalling device" that should reasonably alert them of the "high probability" of an FCPA violation.[14]

The major changes which Section 5003 of the Trade Act made in the 1977 Foreign Corrupt Practices Act had to do with when the bribery provisions apply to an American business or person acting on behalf of an American business. For example, the anti-bribery provisions under the 1988 Amendments did not apply to any facilitating or expediting payment to a foreign official, political party, or party official.

Further, an American business or individual may use one of the "affirmative defenses" in urging that no violation of the FCPA occurred. The first of these enumerated affirmative defenses is that the payment, gift, offer, or promise of anything of value that was made was lawful under the written laws and regulations of the foreign official's, political party's, party official's, or candidate's country. Another affirmative defense is that the payment, gift, offer, or promise of anything of value that was made was a reasonable and bona fide expenditure, such as travel and lodging expenses which were incurred by or on behalf of a foreign official, party, party official, or candidate, and was directly related to the promotion, demonstration, or explanation of products or services or the execution or performance of a contract with a foreign government or agency. This defense does not apply, however, if a payment or gift is corruptly made in return for an official act or omission because it is then not considered a bona fide, good faith payment.

In the definitional sections of the 1988 Amendments, the terms "knowing" and "routine governmental action" are especially important. A person's state of mind is "knowing" with respect to conduct, a circumstance, or a result if the person is aware of engaging in the conduct, that the circumstance exists, or that the result is substantially certain to occur or if the person has a firm belief that the circumstance exists or that the result is substantially certain to occur. When knowledge of the existence of a particular circumstance is required for an offense, the knowledge is established if a person is aware of a high probability of the existence of the circumstance, unless the person actually believes that the circumstance does not exist.

"Routine governmental action" is only ordinarily and commonly performed by a foreign official in obtaining permits, licenses, or other official documents to qualify a person to do business in a foreign country; processing governmental papers, providing police protection, mail pickup and delivery, or scheduling inspections associated with contract performance or inspections related to transit of goods across country; or providing phone service, power and water supply, loading and unloading cargo, or protecting perishable commodities or products from deterioration. The term does not include any decision by a foreign official whether or on what terms to award new business to or to continue business with a particular firm.

Criminal penalties for violations of the Foreign Corrupt Practices Act were increased. The anti-bribery fine for a firm or domestic concern was raised from $1 million to $2 million and for individuals from $10,000 to $100,000. The maximum imprisonment for bribery for an individual remained five years.[15] For willful violations of the accounting provisions the fine for a corporation may not exceed $25 million and for an individual not more than $5 million and/or imprisonment of up to 20 years.[16] The act also provides for civil penalties of up to $10,000 for violations of the bribery provisions.[17]

Foreign Corrupt Practices Act Amendments of 1998

In 1998 the Foreign Corrupt Practices Act was again amended in order to implement the Organization of Economic Cooperation and Development (OECD) Convention on Combating Bribery of Foreign Officials in International Business Transactions.[18] The 1998 Amendments expanded the scope of persons covered to include certain foreign nationals, such as any officer of a public international organization.[19] The 1998 Amendments also extended the act's jurisdiction beyond the borders of the United States.[20]

Continuing Congressional Concerns

Criticisms of the Foreign Corrupt Practices Act have continued over the years, ranging from its putting American businesses at a competitive disadvantage in the global marketplace to its permitting unethical forms of payment tantamount to bribery. Especially prominent recently has been a call that businesses convicted of violating the act should be barred from or strictly limited in receiving government contracts. Bills in the 111th Congress were introduced to address this issue. For example, H.R. 5366 would, unless waived by the head of a federal agency, permit any person found to have violated the Foreign Corrupt Practices Act to be proposed for debarment from any contract or grant awarded by the federal government. This bill was introduced on May 20, 2010, and reported by the Committee on Oversight and Government Reform on September 14, 2010, accompanied by H.Rept. 111-588. On September 15, 2010, the House passed the bill. On September 16, 2010, it was referred to the Senate Committee on Homeland Security and Governmental Affairs. The House report states the following need for the legislation: "Federal government contractors have used bribes in the past to influence the actions of foreign governments. The source of these bribes in part is American tax dollars paid by the federal government to contractors. This bill seeks to root out companies which tarnish the image of the United States of America by engaging in illegal activities."[21]

H.R. 5837 would prohibit an executive agency from entering into a contract for goods or services unless that person or entity has certified that it and each of its officers, employees, and agents have not violated the Foreign Corrupt Practices Act or any comparable law of any other country. A contractor awarded a contract by a federal agency would be prohibited from entering into any subcontract at any tier with any person or entity which has not made this certification.

Another bill would address the criticism that the act does not allow a private right of action. H.R. 2152 would amend the Foreign Corrupt Practices Act to authorize a private right of action against a company for violation of the act. Lawsuits have been brought to urge allowing a private right of action, but the Sixth Circuit in 1990 found that the act does not allow a private right of action.[22]

Executive Branch Oversight

In addition to congressional scrutiny of the act, the executive branch appears to have increased oversight of suspected American businesses for alleged violations of the act. On January 19, 2010, the U.S. Department of Justice (DOJ) announced that it had indicted 22 executives and employees in the military and law enforcement products industry for engaging in schemes to bribe foreign government officials to obtain and retain business.[23] According to Assistant Attorney General Lanny A. Breuer, "This ongoing investigation is the first large-scale use of undercover law enforcement techniques to uncover FCPA violations and the largest action ever undertaken by the Justice Department against individuals for FCPA violations."[24]

Several other events indicate executive branch concerns with Foreign Corrupt Practices Act violations. On August 6, 2010, Mercator Corporation pled guilty to charges that it had made an illegal payment to a senior government official in Kazakhstan in violation of the act.[25] It has been reported that the Department of Justice and the Securities and Exchange Commission are looking into whether Merck has violated the act in multiple foreign countries.[26]

On July 27, 2010, General Electric agreed to pay $23.4 million to settle a complaint brought by the Securities and Exchange Commission that it had bribed Iraqi government officials to win contracts for supplying medical and water purification equipment under the United Nations oil-for-food program. It has been reported that the General Electric case is the fourth biggest such anti-bribery case brought in the oil-for-food program, after the cases filed against Siemens, Chevron, and Innospec.[27]

There have been reports that federal investigators have been looking into the possibility that Blackwater (renamed Xe) may have violated the Foreign Corrupt Practices Act. An indictment in April 2010 by a federal grand jury in North Carolina contained the following allegation:

> Another means [of circumventing the possession and disposition of arms] consisted of Blackwater/Xe's efforts to gain favor with the Government of the Kingdom of Jordan. When the King of Jordan came to examine Blackwater/Xe's training facility at Moyock, North Carolina, the defendants arranged to present the King and/or his entourage with several firearms as gifts. When the defendants subsequently realized they were unable to account for the disposition of the firearms, they falsified four separate Alcohol, Tobacco, and Firearms (ATF) Form 4473s for submission to federal authorities. The defendants falsely completed the forms to give the appearance that the weapons had been purchased by them as individuals.[28]

In October 2010 Assistant Attorney General Breuer emphasized that the United States takes seriously the enforcement of the Foreign Corrupt Practices Act. He is reported as stating that companies and individuals can expect to see "more and more prosecutions [under the 1977 Foreign Corrupt Practices Act] by the United States and more and more [joint] prosecutions with members of the OECD and throughout the world."[29]

In early 2012 the federal government had both successes and losses resulting from FCPA charges. For example, it was reported that the Justice Department's Criminal Division announced on January 17, 2012, that Marubeni Corporation had agreed to pay a $54.6 million criminal penalty to resolve charges for violating the FCPA during a 10-year-long scheme of bribing the Nigerian government for engineering, procurement, and construction contracts.[30] On January 30, 2012, however, a jury acquitted two businessmen charged by the Department of Justice with violating the FCPA involving a fake deal for the sale of goods to Gabon.[31] On January 31, 2012, a judge declared a mistrial involving three other businessmen in the same FBI sting case involving a military equipment contract for Gabon.[32]

End Notes

[1] S. REPT. 95-114, at 3 (1977).
[2] P.L. 95-213, Title I; 91 Stat. 1494 (1977).
[3] 15 U.S.C. §78m(b).
[4] 15 U.S.C. §§78a *et seq.*
[5] 15 U.S.C. §78m(b)(2)(B).
[6] 15 U.S.C. §§78dd-1 and 78dd-2.
[7] S. REPT. 95-114, at 1 (1977).
[8] S. REPT. 95-114, at 10 (1977).
[9] S. REPT. 95-114, at 10-11 (1977).
[10] P.L. 100-418, Title V; 102 Stat. 1107 (1988).
[11] H. REPT. 100-576, at 916-917 (1988).
[12] H. REPT. 100-576, at 917 (1988).
[13] H. REPT. 100-576, at 918 (1988).
[14] H. REPT. 100-576, at 920.
[15] 15 U.S.C. §78dd-2(g).
[16] 15 U.S.C. §78ff(a).
[17] 15 U.S.C. §78dd-2(g).
[18] P.L. 105-366; 112 Stat. 3302 (1998).
[19] 15 U.S.C. §78dd-1(f).
[20] 15 U.S.C. §§78dd-1(g) and 78dd-2(i). United States businesses and persons are prohibited from acting corruptly outside the United States "in furtherance of" a bribe whether or not using the "mails or any means or instrumentality of interstate commerce."
[21] H.REPT. 111-588, at 2 (2010).
[22] *Lamb v. Phillip Morris, Inc.*, 915 F.2d 1024, 1029-1030 (6th Cir. 1990).
[23] http://www.justice.gov/opa/pr/2010/January/10-crm-048.html.
[24] *Id.*

[25] *United States v. Mercator Corporation*, S3-03-CR (S.D.N.Y. Aug. 6, 2010).

[26] Linda A. Johnson, *Merck Being Probed for Possibly Violating Anti-Bribery Laws*, WASHINGTON POST, August 10, 2010, at A14.

[27] Zachary A. Goldfarb, *GE Agrees to Settle with SEC on Charges of Foreign Bribery*, WASHINGTON POST, July 28, 2010, at A11.

[28] http://www.fcpablog.com/blog/2010/4/19/blackwater-and-bribery.html.

[29] Breuer Says U.S. Expects High Marks for Foreign Corruption, Bribery Efforts, DAILY REPORT FOR EXECUTIVES, 197 DER EE-18 (BNA October 14, 2010).

[30] http://online.wsj.com/article/BT-CO-20120117-713964.html.

[31] http://legaltimes.typepad.com/blt/2012/01/jury-acquits-two-businessmen-in-fcpa-sting-case-.html

[32] http://blogs.wsj.com/law/2012/01/31/judge-declares-mistrial-in-sting-bribery-case/.

In: A Selection of Federal Acts
Editors: P. Brown and K. M. Mitchell
ISBN: 978-1-62417-047-8

Chapter 3

THE ARSENAL ACT: CONTEXT AND LEGISLATIVE HISTORY*

Daniel H. Else

SUMMARY

The Arsenal Act (10 U.S.C. §4532) requires the Secretary of the Army to have all supplies needed by the Army to be made in government-owned factories or arsenals if this can be accomplished "on an economical basis." It also grants the Secretary the authority to "abolish any United States arsenal that he considers unnecessary." This broad mandate, and even broader authority, has lead some observers to question whether the Department of the Army is abiding by either the spirit or the letter of the law in awarding development and procurement contracts. Others have expressed concern that the seeming unilateral authority to abolish arsenals could place them at a disadvantage should the Department of Defense (DOD) seek to close military installations.

Federal arsenals, those government-owned industrial sites that have produced the engines of war for the United States Army virtually since the birth of the nation, exist and operate under the jurisdiction of the Secretary of the Army. They, along with their naval counterparts in the form of federally owned shipyards, have sustained the military services for more than two centuries.

The two sections of the act were written approximately seven decades apart and are grounded in the events of their time. The authority to abolish dates to the era just prior to the Civil War, when the arsenals functioned not only as the nation's principal source of military arms, but also helped to nurture and sustain the country's early commercial industrialization. It was a period when the arsenals were beginning to experience competition in satisfying the Army's needs.

The requirement to have Army supplies made in U.S.-owned factories or arsenals dates to the years immediately following the conclusion of World War I, when Congress, realizing

---

* This is an edited, reformatted and augmented version of the Congressional Research Service Publication, CRS Report for Congress R42062, dated October 28, 2011.

that the United States faced increasing global responsibilities at a time of much-reduced defense appropriations, moved to ensure the continued existence of this "in-house" industrial base. Nevertheless, the statute does not define "supplies," nor does it spell out what is meant by making supplies "on an economical basis."

The Department of the Army has promulgated policy for the implementation of the authority to produce supplies, embodying it in Army Regulation (AR) 700-94, *Army Industrial Base Policy*, of December 2004. AR 700-94 assigns the responsibility for deciding whether a given article is to be manufactured at a government-owned facility or contracted to a commercial vendor to the Assistant Secretary of the Army for Acquisition, Technology, and Logistics (ASA(ATL)). It also requires the Commanding General of Army Materiel Command (AMC) and the individual Program Executive Officers (PEOs) and Program Managers (PMs) to provide the Assistant Secretary with the analyses needed to make that decision.

This report describes the roles of the federal manufacturing arsenals during the years surrounding the enactment of the two sections of the Arsenal Act, one as part of the Army Appropriations Act for 1854, and the other within the Defense Act of 1920, also known as the Army Reorganization Act of 1920, and provides historical context. The report also shows the change in language between the sections' original enactment and today, and it provides details on the Army's policy in implementing the manufacturing sourcing portion of the statute.

INTRODUCTION

In 1794, Congress granted President George Washington the authority to establish national arsenals to arm of the new United States Army with domestically produced weapons. In 1853, Congress gave the Secretary of War (the predecessor to the Secretary of the Army) the authority to abolish any arsenal that he deemed to be unnecessary. In 1920, Congress again stepped into the operation of the nation's weapons factories by requiring the Secretary of War to have all of the supplies needed by the Army to be produced in government-owned factories or arsenals, so long as it could be done on an "economical basis." These latter two provisions still exist in today's United States Code in the form of what is called the Arsenal Act.

The great bulk of materiel used by today's Army is manufactured by private corporations, encouraging some to question the statute's efficacy. Others have expressed concern that the act could place the arsenals at a disadvantage should DOD to look to base closures as a means to reduce defense spending.

The terms "arsenal" and "armory" have often been interchangeable through the decades since the nation was founded. Both have been used to describe manufacturing sites, supply centers, repair depots, and other military facilities. Nevertheless, this report will focus on those industrial arsenals that have been instrumental in providing the materials of war for the Army since the last years of the 18th century. It is to these installations that the Arsenal Act (10 U.S.C. §4532) is directed.

The Role of Arsenals in Supplying the Army

Unlike England, France, and Germany, the United States has never sponsored private manufacturing establishments that specialized in the design and production of heavy munitions. Instead of relying upon a Vickers-Armstrong, a Schneider-Creusot, or a Krupp, the country from its beginning followed the policy of assigning responsibility for Army munitions supply to a special government agency, the Ordnance Department of the Army.[1]

Circa 1920

Source: Library of Congress Collection, Prints and Photographs Division, Call No. LC-D4-73083.

Figure 1. Springfield, MA, Arsenal.

During the Revolutionary War and through the first few years of the country's existence, the Army depended almost exclusively on foreign manufacturers for arms. Desiring to break this reliance on foreign supply, Congress authorized President George Washington in 1794 to establish a federal manufacturing arsenal at Springfield, MA. By the end of 1795, the arsenal had produced its first 295 muskets.[2] Within a few years of the end of the War of 1812, five federal arsenals, specializing in particular products they offered, were in operation. Springfield and Harpers Ferry, VA, manufactured small arms (primarily muskets and pistols). Watervliet, NY, produced artillery equipment and ammunition. Watertown, MA, fashioned artillery gun carriages and small arms. Frankford, PA, fabricated ammunition. Two more facilities were built after the mid-nineteenth century, Rock Island, IL, specializing in artillery recoil mechanisms, and Picatinny, NJ, mixing artillery ammunition, propellants, and explosives, while Harpers Ferry was destroyed at the beginning of the Civil War and never rebuilt.

The six surviving factories, along with a Harpers number of Department of the Navy shipyards, formed the core of a federally owned and operated 19th century military production complex.[3]

Source: Library of Congress Collection, Prints and Photographs Division, Call No. LC-USZ62-134477.

Figure 2. Burning the Arsenal at Ferry, VA, April 18, 1862.

These Army arsenals, under the command of Ordnance Department officers or, for some periods prior to the Civil War, civilian superintendants, were typically manned by a small cadre of military personnel and a large number of skilled civilian "artificers." Production, not innovation, was the strength of the arsenal system. Although the Ordnance Department was officially tasked with responsibility to design weaponry after 1834, new models of all types were normally brought to the Department by entrepreneurs or commercial companies for testing and evaluation. If the evaluators found the prototype worthy, it would be adapted for military use, standardized for manufacture, and placed into production either at an arsenal or on contract at a commercial firm under the close supervision of Ordnance officers. During the decades immediately prior to the Civil War, the arsenals collaborated closely with small arms manufacturers, making the technical expertise of arsenal artificers available to help nurture the nation's fledgling precision gauge and machine tool industries.

As industry evolved in the United States during the mid-19th century, competition between commercial enterprise and the government arsenals to supply the Army's needs became more intense. Several attempts to privatize arms production were made prior to the Civil War, culminating in a provision written into the Army Appropriations Act for 1854, addressed below, that gave the Secretary of War the explicit statutory authority to abolish any arsenal that he deemed unnecessary or useless. Nevertheless, both the Chief of Ordnance at the time, Colonel Henry K. Craig, and the Pierce Administration's Secretary of War, Jefferson Davis, resisted any further move toward commercialization, arguing that the continued use of government manufacturing facilities "guaranteed constant improvement in models and enabled the Ordnance Department to check not only on the quality of contractors output but also on their prices."[4] Federal arsenal production was not again seriously threatened until the late 1960s.[5]

The War Department relied on a steady stream of military equipment, principally manufactured in its arsenals, to satisfy the needs of a very small peacetime Army. During war, the Department resorted to contracting with private enterprise to supply a "surge" capacity for the duration of the emergency. Even after industrialization took hold, the peacetime Army of the 19th century did not present a market of sufficient size to attract the attention of the manufacturing concerns that focused on serving a rapidly expanding civilian sector. Growing public confidence in the ability of American industry to adapt quickly to any situation, plus the lengthy tenure of relatively conservative Chiefs of Ordnance, encouraged a complacency in the development of arms for the Army during the latter half of the century.[6]

Secretary of War, 1853-1857

Source: Library of Congress Collection, Prints and Photographs Division, Call No. LC-USZ62-89800.

Figure 3. Jefferson Davis.

Chief of Ordnance, 1901-1918

Source: Library of Congress Collection, Prints and Photographs Division, Call No. LC-DIG-hec-15300.

Figure 4. Brig. Gen.William B. Crozier, USA.

By the first decades of the 20th century, the roles of Congress and the Chief of Ordnance had reversed from those held a half-century earlier. Though appropriations for arms were modest, Congress became a champion of arsenal production. On the other hand, Brigadier

General William B. Crozier, senior Ordnance officer from 1901 through 1918, routinely protested this policy, arguing that concentrating on federal manufacturing, while it might be less costly than contracting to civilian industry, could hamper efforts to expand production rapidly in the event of future emergency.

Though presaged by the experience of an unprecedented mobilization during the Civil War, the first truly industrial war effort for the United States began in April 1917 with the U.S. entry into World War I. The demands of creating and supplying an army of a size sufficient for the fields of France resulted in an industrial mobilization of unprecedented magnitude and speed. Nonetheless, the mobilization effort was so badly orchestrated by the Army's Ordnance Department (weapons manufacturing) and Quartermaster Department (transportation) that by December 1917 the chiefs of both had been sacked and military supply and procurement responsibilities had been vested in a new civilian-managed wartime Division of Purchase, Storage, and Traffic.

The civilian side of the industrial mobilization proved similarly difficult. Too many contracts, concluded too quickly, contributed to the supply logjams that proved the Army departments' undoing. When the Armistice was declared on November 11, 1918, many of those contracts were abruptly cancelled, precipitating litigation that lasted for decades. Private industry returned to civilian production as soon as possible, leaving the task of supplying the postwar Army largely to the traditional arsenal system.

Nevertheless, the immediate post-war period proved to be one of considerable stress at the arsenals within the Ordnance Department. Although the Defense Act of 1920 stipulated that the Secretary of War would have needed Army supplies made by federally owned factories and arsenals, the large stockpiles of munitions and other materials remaining in war's aftermath made procurement almost moot for the foreseeable future.[7] Appropriations and personnel strengths plunged. For Fiscal Year (FY) 1920, Congress appropriated $20.8 million for ordnance. By FY1923, appropriations amounted to $6.9 million.[8] Personnel strengths saw similar contractions, with the number of military personnel assigned to the Ordnance Department dropping from 10,597 in 1919 to 3,087 in 1922. The number of civilians employed by the Department saw a similar decline. Though numbers for 1919 and 1920 are not available, the Department employed more than 14,000 civilians in 1921. By the next year, almost half had been let go, and civilian end strength stood at 8,119. This combined military and civilian workforce continued to shrink over the next several years.[9]

Thus, impacts of both the nation's rapid, mid-19th century industrialization and the post-World War I contraction of the defense industrial base were captured in contemporary legislation and continue to reverberate in what is now the Arsenal Act.

THE ARSENAL ACT

The act itself consists of only two subsections.

> 10 U.S.C. §4532. Factories and arsenals: manufacture at; abolition of
>
> (a) The Secretary of the Army shall have supplies needed for the Department of the Army made in factories or arsenals owned by the United States, so far as those factories or arsenals can make those supplies on an economical basis.
>
> (b) The Secretary may abolish any United States arsenal that he considers unnecessary.

The statute is a combination of two different provisions of law, enacted nearly 70 years apart, that were eventually combined into a single provision during the early 1950s when the United States Code took its current form.

Subsection (a), which requires the Secretary of the Army to have departmental supplies manufactured in government factories and arsenals to the extent that they can be manufactured "on an economical basis," first appeared in statute in the Defense Act of 1920. Subsection (b) originated in the Army Appropriations Act for 1854. The language of both sections has remained essentially unchanged since their enactment.

The Army Appropriations Act for 1854

In 1853, only a few years after the conclusion of the Mexican War, federal arsenals were managed by military superintendents, and congressional debate on arsenals centered on whether or not to revert to civilian management, an arrangement that had been abandoned in 1840. At the time, the federal arsenals were assisting the machine tool and manufacturing industries to refine their skills and enter into competition with foreign manufacturers of both military and civilian goods. Nevertheless, during floor debate in the House on February 1, 1853, Representative Willis Arnold Gorman, chair of the Committee on Military Affairs, proposed an amendment to the Army Appropriation Bill on behalf of the committee stating that "That the Secretary of War be, and he is hereby, authorized to abolish such of the arsenals of the United States as, in his judgment, may be useless or unnecessary." Mr. Gorman offered to explain the amendment to the chamber, but the Members present suggested that no explanation was needed.[10] The amendment was subsequently adopted by the House, survived conference, and was enacted. In slightly altered form, it can be found in 10 U.S.C. §4532(b).[11]

Notwithstanding this new authority, Secretary of War Jefferson Davis, who took office in March 7, 1853, and his Chief of Ordnance expressed a strong desire to preserve the manufacturing capabilities of the arsenals in order to provide competition to the private sector.

The Defense Act of 1920

In 1920, the emphasis was somewhat different. The experience of World War I and its aftermath had led some in Congress to conclude that retention of a certain minimum level of surge manufacturing capacity within the federally owned industrial base would help in wartime mobilization. Given the massive stocks of war material left over from the recent conflict, apparent remoteness of renewed conflict, and the small size of the postwar Army, arsenal managers, the War Department, and Congress expressed concern that arsenals might not be able to generate sufficient work to maintain a core of manufacturing skills and industrial capacity to respond to an emergency. Hence, the reorganization of the Army embodied in the Defense Act of 1920 included the creation of a permanent Assistant Secretary of War and his appointment as the individual charged with responsibility for procurement of all military supplies and for the regulation of the federal arsenals. Emphasis in congressional debate focused on the need to render the arsenals as efficient as possible in the manufacture of high-quality military goods. This is reflected in the language seen in subsection (a) of the current law.[12]

Notwithstanding the language of the statute, the paucity of Army appropriations over the next several years rendered the statute of minimal economic importance. The following section discusses Army policy on implementation of the Arsenal Act in the current operation of its arsenals.

Arsenal Operations

Except for wartime emergency, the War Department (predecessor to the Department of the Army) did not place significant reliance on private industry to provide military arms and ammunition until after World War I. The first decades of the 20th century saw significant military reform as Congress created the General Staff system and reorganized both the Army and the War Department before and after U.S. involvement in World War I. Two of those reforms, included in the act of 1920, had a direct impact on Army supply.

The first of these created a permanent Assistant Secretary of War, designating him as the chief procurement official for the Army. The second stipulated that arsenals and factories be used for the manufacture of Army supplies, as noted above.

The policy for implementing this provision of the Arsenal Act is outlined in detail in the current Army Regulation (AR) 700-94, *Army Industrial Base Process*, dated December 14, 2004. Paragraph 3-7 quotes 10 U.S.C. §4532(a), noting that the statute does not define the term "supplies," but suggesting that the term's definition in 10 U.S.C. §101(a)(14), "'supplies' includes material, equipment, and stores of all kinds," is broad enough to preclude the arsenals, whose production capacity is finite, from being able to provide for all the Army's considerable supply needs. The Assistant Secretary of the Army for Acquisition, Logistics, and Technology (ASA(ALT)), is tasked in the regulation by the Secretary of the Army with determining which supplies the arsenals can and should manufacture. This authority extends to selecting those Army-required items that will be subject to a "make (by the arsenals) or buy (from commercial manufacturers)" analysis.[13]

AR 700-94 goes on to provide policy on the use of the government-owned industrial base. Paragraph 5-1 begins by stating, "The intent of the Army-owned industrial base is to be postured to support the force structure with efficient, economical, practical, responsive, multifunctional, environmentally responsible, and compliant facilities."[14] Nevertheless, paragraph 5-2 states that, "The Army will rely on the private sector for support of defense production to the maximum extent practical. When market research and ICA (independent cost analysis) confirms that the private sector is either inadequate or unavailable to reliably provide critical materiel needs, an essential nucleus of Government-owned facilities may be established or retained."

Chapter 2 of AR 700-94 assigns the following responsibilities:

1. ASA(ALT) is responsible for deciding "whether Army materiel or its components should be made in an arsenal or bought from the private sector in those cases where the PEO [program executive officer] and AMC [Army Materiel Command] disagree (Para. 2-1(j), p. 3).

2. Commanding General, Army Materiel Command (AMC) is responsible for
   a. managing government-owned, government-operated (GOGO) production installations (para. 2-8(d), p. 5);
   b. analyzing whether to make or buy under the authority of 10 U.S.C. §4532, including the preparation of the analysis for AMC managed items and coordination with the applicable PEO/PM [program manager]. For PEO/PM managed items, he is responsible for providing the "make" estimate for Army materiel and/or its component that is potentially more economically manufactured at an arsenal and providing this analysis to the applicable PEO/PM early in the acquisition life cycle to avoid disruption of program milestones (para. 2-8(d)(4), p. 5).
   c. exercising command and control over Army government-owned, contractor-operated (GOCO) production installations (para. 2-8(e), p. 5).
   d. Develop and implement a phase down of ownership plan for Army-owned production installations in coordination with applicable PEOs/PMs (para. 2-8(f), p. 5).
3. Program Executive Officers (PEOs) and Program Managers (PMs) are tasked with
   a. assessing the ability of the industrial base to support the life cycle requirements for assigned programs and ensuring that an independent cost analysis is conducted when a potential problem exists. PEOs and PMs are to rely on the private sector to the maximum extent possible unless core depot-level maintenance and repair or Army-owned factories are more economical (para. 2-11(a), p. 6).
   b. performing the "make or buy" analysis under the authority of 10 U.S.C. §4532. PEOs and PMs are to prepare the analysis for PEO/PM managed items in coordination with AMC early in the acquisition life cycle so as not to disrupt program milestones (AMC is to furnish the "make" estimates). PEOs and PMs review "make or buy" analyses for AMC managed items that are part of the PEO's/PM's life cycle management responsibility. They are responsible for submitting these analyses to ASA(ALT) for a decision when they and AMC disagree on whether to manufacture items at arsenals or source procurement to a commercial vendor (para. 2-11(e), p. 6).

CONCLUSION

Federal manufacturing arsenals have supported the Army and the nation virtually since their births. Among other functions, the arsenals have designed and manufactured military arms and supplies, nurtured the country's early industrialization, and provided competition to private enterprise. The sophistication evident in arsenal facilities has evolved along with the nation's industrial base, sometimes leading, often trailing commercial industry in technological development, particularly during the years prior to World War I.[15]

Congress has provided statutory guidance for the operation and continued existence of the arsenals in legislation now consolidated in 10 U.S.C. §4532. The statute gives the Secretary of the Army the authority to "abolish" any arsenal that he considers unnecessary.

It also requires the Secretary of the Army to have the supplies needed by the Department of the Army made at factories and arsenals owned by the United States, so long as this production can be carried out "on an economical basis." Yet, this section fails to define "supplies," or to explain what is meant by an "economical basis."

The Department of the Army interprets the Arsenal Act in AR 700-94, *Army Industrial Base Process*, and lays out policy for its implementation. The ASA(ALT) retains the authority to decide whether a given article shall be manufactured in a federal facility or by a commercial supplier. To make that decision, he relies on AMC and the individual PEOs/PMs to assess the relative merits of the two choices and perform the analyses necessary to provide a basis for the decision. While the statute appears to emphasize the use of arsenals for supplying the Army, AR 700-94 directs PEOs/PMs "to rely on the private sector to the maximum extent possible unless ... Army-owned factories are more economical."

End Notes

[1] Constance McLaughlin Greene, Harry C. Thomson, and Peter C. Roots, *United States Army in World War II, The Technical Services: The Ordnance Department: Planning Munitions for War* (Washington, DC: Office of the Chief of Military History, Department of the Army, 1955), p. 3.

[2] *Planning Munitions for War* contains a detailed history of federal arms manufacturing through World War II.

[3] The Department of the Navy established its own industrial complex in the form of six shipyards constructed at about the same time. These were located, running from north to south along the Atlantic seaboard, at Portsmouth (Kittery, ME), Charlestown (Boston, MA), Brooklyn (New York City, NY), Philadelphia (Philadelphia, PA), Washington (Washington, DC), and Norfolk (Portsmouth, VA).

[4] *Planning Munitions for War*, p. 19.

[5] Among the original manufacturing arsenals, the Springfield and Watertown Arsenals in MA were closed in 1968, and the Frankford, PA, Arsenal closed in 1977. The arsenals in Watervliet, NY, Rock Island, IL, and Picatinny, NJ, remain open.

[6] In the 54 years between 1864 and 1918, only five Army officers served as Chief of Ordnance, averaging almost 11 years in office. Two chiefs, Brigadier General Steven Vincent Benet, Sr. (1874 – 1891), and Major General William Crozier (1901 – 1918), each held the post for 17 years.

[7] The specific provision regarding federal production of war materials was introduced during debate on March 10, 1920, as a committee amendment to the bill. As agreed to by the House, the language read in part, "He [the Secretary of War] shall cause to be manufactured or produced at the Government arsenals and Government-owned factories of the United States all such supplies or articles needed by the War Department as said arsenals and Government-owned factories are capable of manufacturing or producing: *Provided*, That the cost of manufacturing or producing such articles or supplies at said arsenals and Government-owned factories shall not exceed the cost if purchased in the open market ... ." "Army Reorganization Bill," House debate, *Congressional Record*, March 10, 1920, p. 4156.

[8] Appropriations are stated in current, or then-year, dollars. Figures are taken from *Planning Munitions for War*, Table 1, p. 41.

[9] Ibid., Table 3, p. 44.

[10] Rep. Willis Arnold Gorman, "Army Appropriations Bill," House debate, *The Congressional Globe*, February 1, 1853, p. 460.

[11] The Secretary of War and the Department of War were reconstituted as the Secretary of the Army and Department of the Army when the National Security Act of 1947 (P.L. 80-235) took effect.

[12] The bill, also referred to as the "Army Reorganization Act," was taken up in the 66th Congress, 2nd Session, as H.R.12775.

[13] The regulation also stipulates that the Arsenal Act is not applicable to depot level maintenance and repair activities.

[14] AR 700-94, p. 12.

[15] The authors of Planning Munitions for War discuss at length an inherent technological conservatism within the Ordnance Department that was strong during the latter half of the 19th and the early decades of the 20th centuries. See Chapter 1, "Origins and Growth to 1919."

In: A Selection of Federal Acts
Editors: P. Brown and K. M. Mitchell
ISBN: 978-1-62417-047-8

Chapter 4

THE EMERGENCY PLANNING AND COMMUNITY RIGHT-TO-KNOW ACT (EPCRA): A SUMMARY*

Linda-Jo Schierow

SUMMARY

This report summarizes the Emergency Planning and Community Right-to-Know Act (EPCRA) and the major regulatory programs that mandate reporting by industrial facilities of releases of potentially hazardous chemicals to the environment, as well as local planning to respond in the event of significant, accidental releases.

The Emergency Planning and Community Right-to-Know Act (42 U.S.C. 11001-11050) was enacted in 1986 as Title III of the Superfund Amendments and Reauthorization Act (P.L. 99-499). In Subtitle A, EPCRA established a national framework for the U.S. Environmental Protection Agency (EPA) to mobilize local government officials, businesses, and other citizens to plan ahead for chemical accidents in their communities. EPCRA required each state to create a State Emergency Response Commission (SERC), to designate emergency planning districts, and to establish local emergency planning committees (LEPCs) for each district. EPA is required to list extremely hazardous substances, and to establish threshold planning quantities for each substance. The law directs each facility to notify the LEPC for its district if it stores or uses any "extremely hazardous substance" in excess of its threshold planning quantity. LEPCs are to work with such facilities to develop response procedures, evacuation plans, and training programs for people who will be the first to respond in the event of an accident. EPCRA requires that facilities immediately report a sudden release of any hazardous substance that exceeds the reportable quantity to appropriate state, local, and federal officials.

Subtitle B directs covered facilities annually to submit information about the chemicals that they have present to the LEPC, SERC, and local fire department. In addition, manufacturers and other facilities designated by EPA must estimate and report to EPA

---

* This is an edited, reformatted and augmented version of the Congressional Research Service Publication, CRS Report for Congress RL32683, dated April 5, 2012.

annually on releases from their facilities of certain toxic chemicals to the land, air, or water. EPA must compile that data into a computerized database, known as the Toxics Release Inventory (TRI). Generally, all information about chemicals that is required to be reported to LEPCs, SERCs, or EPA is made available to the general public, but EPCRA authorizes reporting facilities to withhold the identity of a chemical if it is a trade secret. Citizens are given the authority to bring civil action against a facility, EPA, a governor, or an SERC for failure to implement EPCRA requirements.

INTRODUCTION

The Emergency Planning and Community Right-to-Know Act (EPCRA) establishes requirements and a framework to ensure that the U.S. Environmental Protection Agency (EPA), state and local governments, and the private sector will work together to control and, if necessary, respond to releases of hazardous chemicals to the environment. This report describes key provisions of EPCRA. In addition, it provides several references for more detailed information about the act, and a table that cross-references sections of the U.S. Code with corresponding sections of the act. The report highlights key provisions rather than providing a comprehensive inventory of the act's numerous sections, and addresses authorities and limitations imposed by the statute, rather than the status of implementation or other policy issues.

OVERVIEW

The sudden, accidental release in December 1984 of methyl isocyanate in an industrial incident at the Union Carbide plant in Bhopal, India, and the attendant loss of thousands of lives and widespread injuries motivated many in Congress to support legislation to reduce the risk of chemical accidents in the United States. The Emergency Planning and Community Right-to-Know Act (42 U.S.C. 11001-11050) was enacted in 1986 as Title III of the Superfund Amendments and Reauthorization Act (P.L. 99-499). EPCRA established state commissions and local committees to develop and implement procedures for coping with releases of hazardous chemicals, and mandated annual reporting to government officials on environmental releases of such chemicals by the facilities that manufacture or use them in significant amounts. EPA facilitates planning, enforces compliance when necessary, and provides public access to information about environmental releases of toxic chemicals.

SUBTITLE A. EMERGENCY PLANNING AND NOTIFICATION

EPCRA established a national framework for EPA to mobilize local government officials, businesses, and other citizens to plan ahead for possible chemical accidents in their communities. Subtitle A requires local planning to respond to sudden releases of chemicals that might occur in the event of a spill, explosion, or fire. It is intended to ensure that responsible officials will know what hazardous chemicals are used or stored by local businesses and will be notified quickly in the event of an accident.

Under Section 301, each state is required to create a State Emergency Response Commission (SERC), to designate emergency planning districts, and to establish local emergency planning committees (LEPCs) for each district. Section 302 requires EPA to list extremely hazardous substances and to establish threshold planning quantities for each substance. Originally, Congress defined chemicals as "extremely hazardous substances" if they appeared on a list EPA published in November 1985 as Appendix A in "Chemical Emergency Preparedness Program Interim Guidance." However, EPA has authority to revise the list, and the threshold quantities of chemicals. Based on listing criteria, the intent appears to be to include only chemicals in quantities that could harm people exposed to them for only a short period of time. The law directs each facility to notify the LEPC for its district if it stores or uses any "extremely hazardous substance" in excess of its threshold planning quantity.

Section 303 directs LEPCs to work with facilities handling specified "extremely hazardous substances" to develop response procedures, evacuation plans, and training programs for people who will be the first to respond in the event of an accident. Upon request, facility owners and operators are required to provide an LEPC with any additional information that it finds necessary to develop or implement an emergency plan.

Section 304 requires that facilities immediately report a release of any "extremely hazardous substance" or any "hazardous substance" (a much broader category of chemicals defined under the Comprehensive Environmental Response, Compensation, and Liability Act (CERCLA) Section 102(a)) that exceeds the reportable quantity to appropriate state, local, and federal officials.[1] Releases of a reportable quantity of a "hazardous substance" also must be reported to the National Response Center under CERCLA Section 103(a).

SUBTITLE B. REPORTING REQUIREMENTS

Subtitle B establishes various reporting requirements for facilities. The information collected may be used to develop and implement emergency plans, as well as to provide the public with general information about chemicals to which they may be exposed.

The Occupational Health and Safety Act of 1970 (OSHAct) requires most employers to provide employees with access to a material safety data sheet (MSDS) for any "hazardous chemical." This "right-to-know" law for workers aims to ensure that people potentially exposed to such chemicals have access to information about the potential health effects of exposure and how to avoid them. EPCRA, Section 311, requires facilities covered by OSHAct to submit an MSDS for each "hazardous chemical" or a list of such chemicals to the LEPC, the SERC, and the local fire department. EPA has authority to establish categories of health and physical hazards and to require facilities to list hazardous chemicals grouped by such categories in their reports. An MSDS need only be submitted once, unless there is a significant change in the information it contains. An MSDS must be provided in response to a request by an LEPC or a member of the public. "Hazardous chemicals" are defined by the *Code of Federal Regulations*, Title 29, at Section 1910.1200(c).[2]

EPCRA, Section 312, requires the same employers to submit annually an emergency and hazardous chemical inventory form to the LEPC, SERC, and local fire department. These forms must provide estimates of the maximum amount of the chemicals present at the facility at any time during the preceding year; estimates of the average daily amount of chemicals present; and the general location of the chemicals in the facility.[3] Information must be provided to the public in response to a written request. EPA is authorized to establish threshold quantities for chemicals below which facilities are not required to report.

Section 313 mandates development of the Toxic Release Inventory (TRI), a computerized EPA database of "toxic chemical" releases to the environment by manufacturing facilities.[4] It requires manufacturing facilities that manufacture, use, or process "toxic chemicals" to report annually to EPA on the amounts of each chemical released to each environmental medium (air, land, or water) or transferred off-site. EPA makes TRI data available in "raw" and summarized forms to the general public. The public may obtain specific information (e.g., about a particular manufacturing facility) by submitting a request in writing to EPA. EPA distributes written and electronic, nationwide and state-by-state summaries of annual data. Raw data and summaries also are available over the Internet.[5]

EPCRA, Section 313, generally requires a report to EPA and the state from each manufacturer with 10 or more employees and who either uses 10,000 pounds or manufactures or processes 25,000 pounds of any "toxic chemical" during the reporting year. However, EPA may adjust (and has adjusted in the past) these thresholds for classes of chemicals or categories of facilities.

EPCRA enumerates the following data reporting requirements for each covered chemical present at each covered facility:[6]

- whether it is manufactured, processed, or otherwise used, and the general category of use;
- the maximum amount present at each location during the previous year;
- treatment or disposal methods used; and
- the amount released to the environment or transferred off-site for treatment or disposal.

EPCRA requires reporting by manufacturers, which the law defines as facilities in Standard Industrial Classification codes 20 through 39.[7] The law authorized EPA to expand reporting requirements to additional industries. EPA promulgated a rule May 1, 1997, requiring reports on toxic releases from seven additional industrial categories, including some metal mining, coal mining, commercial electric utilities, petroleum bulk terminals, chemical wholesalers, and solvent recovery facilities (62 *Federal Register* 23834).[8]

The original statute specified 313 "toxic chemicals" or categories of chemicals for which reporting was required, but EPCRA gave EPA authority to add or delete chemicals from the list either on its own initiative, or in response to citizen petitions. EPA has removed more than 15 and added a few hundred so that the current list includes 666 individual chemicals.[9] The listing criteria specified in Section 313(d)(2) authorize EPA to add a chemical when it is "known to cause or can reasonably be anticipated to cause" the following:

- "significant adverse acute human health effects at concentration levels that are reasonably likely to exist beyond facility site boundaries as a result of continuous, or frequently recurring, releases";
- in humans—cancer, birth defects, or serious or irreversible chronic health effects; or
- "because of—i) its toxicity, ii) its toxicity and persistence in the environment, or iii) its toxicity and tendency to bioaccumulate in the environment, a significant adverse effect on the environment of sufficient seriousness, in the judgment of the Administrator, to warrant reporting under this Section."

SUBTITLE C. GENERAL PROVISIONS

Subtitle C contains various general provisions, definitions, and authorizations.

Trade Secrets

Section 322 authorizes reporting facilities to withhold the identity of a chemical if it is a trade secret, and they follow procedures established by EPA.

Information for Health Professionals

Special provisions are made in Section 323 for informing health professionals of a chemical identity that has been withheld to protect confidential business information, if the information is needed to diagnose or treat a person exposed to the chemical.

Right to Know

Section 324 directs EPA, governors, SERCs, and LEPCs to make emergency response plans, MSDSs, lists of chemicals, inventory forms, toxic chemical release forms, and follow-up emergency notices available to the general public.

Enforcement

Section 325 establishes civil, administrative, and criminal penalties for noncompliance with mandatory provisions of the act. Citizens are given the authority to bring civil action against a facility, EPA, a governor, or an SERC by Section 326.

Chemical Transport

Chemicals being transported or stored incident to transport are not subject to EPCRA requirements, according to Section 327.

Other Provisions

Section 328 authorizes EPA to issue regulations. Definitions are provided in Section 329. Section 330 authorizes to be appropriated "such sums as may be necessary" to carry out this title.

Table 1. Major U.S. Code Sections: Emergency Planning and Community Right-to-Know Act (42 U.S.C. 11001-11050)

42 U.S.C.	Section Title	EPCRA, P.L. 99-499, Title III
Subchapter I -	Emergency Planning and Notification	Subtitle A
11001	Establishment of state commissions, planning districts, and local committees	Sec. 301
11002	Substances and facilities covered and notification	Sec. 302
11003	Comprehensive emergency response plans	Sec. 303
11004	Emergency notification	Sec. 304
11005	Emergency training and review of emergency systems	Sec. 305
Subchapter II -	Reporting Requirements	Subtitle B
11021	Material safety data sheets	Sec. 311
11022	Emergency and hazardous chemical Inventory forms	Sec. 312
11023	Toxic chemical release forms	Sec. 313
Subchapter III-	General Provisions	Subtitle C
11041	Relationship to other law	Sec. 321
11042	Trade secrets	Sec. 322
11043	Provision of information to health professions, doctors and nurses	Sec. 323
11044	Public availability of plans, data sheets, forms, and follow up notices	Sec. 324
11045	Enforcement	Sec. 325
11046	Civil actions	Sec. 326
11047	Exemption	Sec. 327
11048	Regulations	Sec. 328
11049	Definitions	Sec. 329
11050	Authorizations	Sec. 330

SELECTED REFERENCES

[1] Gray, Peter L. (2002). *EPCRA: Emergency Planning and Community Right-to-Know Act.* Basic Practice Series. Chicago, IL, ABA Publishing, 156 p.

[2] U.S. Environmental Protection Agency, Office of Pollution Prevention and Toxics. *2010 TRI National Analysis*. Available at http://www.epa. gov/tri/tridata/tri10 /nationalanalysis/index.htm, visited April 5, 2012.

[3] Wolf, Sidney M. (1996). "Fear and Loathing about the Public Right To Know: The Surprising Success of the Emergency Planning and Community Right-to-Know Act." *Journal of Land Use & Environmental Law*, v. *11*, n. 2, pp. 217-325.

End Notes

[1] Under CERCLA Section 102(a), a "hazardous substance" includes any "elements, compounds, mixtures, solutions, and substances which, when released into the environment may present a substantial danger to the public health or welfare or the environment." Included in this definition are substances listed under the authority of any of the major environmental statutes (see CERCLA Section 101(14)).

[2] EPCRA does not cover foods, food additives, or other substances regulated by the Food and Drug Administration; solids in a manufactured item to the extent exposure to people or the environment does not occur; substances used for personal or household purposes; substances used in research or hospitals; or substances used in routine agricultural operations.

[3] EPCRA allows facilities to report aggregate amounts of chemicals with similar health and environmental effects. This is called "Tier I" information. However, chemical-specific information ("Tier II") must be provided on request (under certain conditions) to an SERC, LEPC, fire department, or the public.

[4] "Toxic chemicals" are substances that may sicken people who are exposed to them in relatively small amounts by eating, drinking, or breathing, or through skin absorption. The term "hazardous substance" is broader, including toxic chemicals, but also substances that are explosive, flammable, corrosive, or otherwise harmful.

[5] See, for example, EPA's Envirofacts, TOXNET operated by the National Library of Medicine, or Right-to-Know Net, provided by OMB Watch: respectively, http://www.epa.gov/enviro/ html/toxic_releases.html, visited April 5, 2012; http://toxnet.nlm.nih.gov/cgi-bin/sis/ htmlgen?TRI, visited April 5, 2012; and http://www.rtknet.org/, visited April 5, 2012.

[6] Congress added data submission requirements for manufacturers and processors of toxic substances when it enacted the Pollution Prevention Act of 1990.

[7] Standard Industrial Codes were changed to North American Industry Classification System codes on March 21, 2003 (66 *Federal Register* 13872-13887).

[8] Current regulations promulgated under EPCRA may be found at Title 40 in the *Code of Federal Regulations*, Part 372.

[9] EPA, Toxics Release Inventory (TRI) Program, TRI Chemicals List, http://www.epa.gov/tri/ trichemicals /index.htm.

In: A Selection of Federal Acts
Editors: P. Brown and K. M. Mitchell
ISBN: 978-1-62417-047-8

Chapter 5

THE TOXIC SUBSTANCES CONTROL ACT (TSCA): A SUMMARY OF THE ACT AND ITS MAJOR REQUIREMENTS*

Linda-Jo Schierow

SUMMARY

This report summarizes the Toxic Substances Control Act (TSCA) and the major regulatory programs dealing with chemical production and distribution in U.S. commerce.

The President's Council on Environmental Quality proposed comprehensive federal legislation in 1971 to identify and control potentially dangerous chemicals in U.S. commerce that were not adequately regulated under other environmental statutes. President Ford signed TSCA into law on October 11, 1976. Subsequently, five titles were added to address specific concerns—asbestos in 1986 (Title II, P.L. 99-519), radon in 1988 (Title III, P.L. 100-551), lead in 1992 (Title IV, P.L. 102-550), environmental and energy issues in schools in 2007 (Title V, P.L. 110-140), and formaldehyde emissions from composite wood products in 2010 (Title VI, P.L. 111-199). In 2008, Congress added provisions to Title I, Section 6 and Section 12, banning certain activities with respect to elemental mercury (P.L. 110-414).

TSCA authorizes EPA to identify potentially dangerous chemicals in U.S. commerce that should be subject to federal control. The act authorizes EPA to gather and disseminate information about production, use, and possible adverse effects to human health and the environment of existing chemicals, and to issue "test rules" that require manufacturers and processors of potentially dangerous chemicals to conduct and report the results of scientific studies to fill information gaps. For chemicals new to U.S. commerce, TSCA requires pre-market screening and regulatory tracking of new chemical products.

If EPA identifies unreasonable risks associated with existing or new chemicals, TSCA requires the agency to initiate rulemaking to reduce risks to a reasonable level. EPA may regulate the manufacture, importation, processing, distribution, use, and/or disposal of

---

* This is an edited, reformatted and augmented version of the Congressional Research Service Publication, CRS Report for Congress RL31905, dated December 5, 2011.

chemicals. TSCA provides a variety of regulatory tools to EPA, ranging in severity from a total ban on production, import, and use to a requirement that a product must bear a warning label at the point of sale. However, TSCA directs EPA to use the least burdensome option that can reduce risk to a level that is reasonable, given the benefits provided by the chemical product or process.

Title I of the original statute establishes the core program, directs EPA to control risks from polychlorinated biphenyls (PCBs), and bans certain activities with respect to elemental mercury. Title II directs EPA to set standards for asbestos mitigation in schools and requires asbestos contractors to be trained and certified. Title III directs EPA to provide technical assistance to states that choose to support radon monitoring and control. Title IV provides similar assistance with respect to abatement of lead-based paint hazards. Title V addresses environmental issues at schools, including energy efficiency. Finally, Title VI directs EPA to set standards for emissions of formaldehyde from composite wood products.

INTRODUCTION

The Environmental Protection Agency (EPA) is responsible for identifying and regulating toxic substances in U.S. commerce under the authority of the Toxic Substances Control Act (TSCA). This report defines key terms, provides a brief history of toxic substances control law, and describes key provisions of TSCA. In addition, this report lists several references for more detailed information about the act and provides a table that cross references sections of the *U.S. Code* with corresponding sections of the act. The report is descriptive rather than analytic, highlights key provisions rather than providing a comprehensive inventory of the act's numerous sections, and addresses authorities and limitations imposed by statute, rather than the status of EPA implementation or other policy issues.

OVERVIEW

The Toxic Substances Control Act (15 U.S.C. 2601 *et seq.*) authorizes the EPA to screen existing and new chemicals used in manufacturing and commerce to identify potentially dangerous products or uses that should be subject to federal control. Both naturally occurring and synthetic chemicals are subject to TSCA, with the exception of chemicals regulated under other federal laws concerning food, drugs, cosmetics, firearms, ammunition, pesticides, tobacco, or mixtures. EPA may require manufacturers and processors of chemicals to conduct and report the results of tests to determine the effects of potentially dangerous chemicals on living things. Based on test results and other information, EPA must regulate the manufacture, importation, processing, distribution, use, and/or disposal of any chemical that presents an unreasonable risk of injury to human health or the environment. A variety of regulatory tools is available to EPA under TSCA, ranging in severity from a total ban on production, import, and use to a requirement that a product bears a warning label at the point of sale. TSCA directs EPA to use the least burdensome option that can reduce risk to a level that is reasonable, given the benefits provided by the chemical product or process.

Federal legislation to control toxic substances was originally proposed in 1971 by the President's Council on Environmental Quality. Its report, "Toxic Substances," defined a need for comprehensive legislation to identify and control chemicals whose manufacture, processing, distribution, use, and/or disposal was potentially dangerous and not adequately regulated under other environmental statutes. The House and Senate each passed bills in both the 92nd and 93rd Congresses (in 1972 and 1973, respectively), but controversies over the scope of chemical screening prior to commercial production and distribution, level of costs, and the relationship to other regulatory laws stalled final action. Episodes of environmental contamination—including contamination of the Hudson River and other waterways by PCBs, the threat of stratospheric ozone depletion from chlorofluorocarbon (CFC) emissions, and contamination of agricultural produce by polybrominated biphenyls (PBBs) in the state of Michigan—together with more exact estimates of the costs of imposing toxic substances controls, opened the way for final passage of the legislation. President Ford signed the TSCA into law on October 11, 1976. The original legislation included a single title, which has since been designated Title I.

TSCA (Title I) directs EPA to

- require manufacturers and processors to conduct tests for existing chemicals if (1) their manufacture, distribution, processing, use, or disposal may present an unreasonable risk of injury to health or the environment; or they are to be produced in substantial quantities and the potential for environmental release or human exposure is substantial or significant; (2) existing data are insufficient to predict the effects of human exposure and environmental releases; and (3) testing is necessary to develop such data (§4);
- prevent future risks through pre-manufacture screening and regulatory tracking of new chemical products (§5);
- control unreasonable risks already known, including risks from polychlorinated biphenyls (PCBs), as well as risks for existing chemicals that may be discovered in the future (§6); and
- gather and disseminate information about chemical production, use, and possible adverse effects to human health and the environment (§8).

Table 1. Toxic Substances Control Act and Major Amendments (codified as 15 U.S.C. 2601-2671)

Year	Act	Public Law Number
1976	Toxic Substances Control Act	P.L. 94-469
1986	Asbestos Hazard Emergency Response Act	P.L. 99-519
1988	Radon Program Development Act	P.L. 100-551
1990	Radon Measurement	P.L. 101-508, §10202
1990	Asbestos School Hazard Abatement Reauthorization Act	P.L. 101-637
1992	Residential Lead-Based Paint Hazard Reduction Act of 1992	P.L. 102-550
2007	Energy Independence and Security Act of 2007, subtitle E - Healthy High-Performance Schools	P.L. 110-140
2008	Mercury Export Ban Act of 2008	P.L. 110-414
2010	Formaldehyde Standards for Composite Wood Products Act	P.L. 111-199

Authorization for appropriations for these activities and a state grant program for control of toxic substances in the environment expired on September 30, 1983, although appropriations for these programs have continued.

In October 2008, Congress amended TSCA Title I when it enacted the Mercury Export Ban Act of 2008 (P.L. 110-414). It prohibits certain activities with respect to elemental mercury.

Subsequently, five titles have been added to TSCA to address specific concerns—asbestos in 1986 (Title II, P.L. 99-519), radon in 1988 (Title III, P.L. 100-551), lead in 1992 (Title IV, P.L. 102-550), schools in 2007 (Title V, P.L. 110-140), and formaldehyde in 2010 (Title VI, P.L. 111-199). Title II directs EPA to set standards for asbestos mitigation in schools, and requires asbestos contractors to be trained and certified. Title III directs EPA to provide technical assistance to states that choose to support radon monitoring and control. Title IV provides similar assistance with respect to abatement of lead-based paint hazards. Title V addresses environmental issues at schools, including energy efficiency. Finally, Title VI establishes limits on emissions of formaldehyde from composite wood products.

Title I

Testing of Chemicals

Many chemicals, even some in widespread use, are not well characterized in terms of their potential health and environmental effects. One of the major goals of TSCA was to induce the development of test data by producers (i.e., manufacturers, importers, and processors) of chemicals in commerce. Section 4 of TSCA directs EPA to require the development of test data on existing chemicals when certain conditions prevail: (1) the manufacture, processing, distribution, use, or disposal of the chemical "may present an unreasonable risk;" or (2) the chemical is produced in very large volume and there is a potential for a substantial quantity to be released into the environment or for substantial or significant human exposure. Under either condition, EPA must issue a rule requiring tests if (a) existing data are insufficient to resolve the question of safety, and (b) testing is necessary to develop the data.

Because there were more than 55,000 chemicals in U.S. commerce at the time EPA was to begin developing test rules, Congress established a special interagency committee to help EPA determine which chemicals should be considered first, and to coordinate testing needs and efforts among government agencies. At least every six months the Interagency Testing Committee (ITC) must consider candidate chemicals for inclusion on a list of substances that the ITC recommends to EPA for development and promulgation of test rules. TSCA directs the ITC to "designate" a subset of chemicals on the list for EPA action within 12 months. The list can contain no more than 50 "designated" chemicals at any time. When a chemical is designated, EPA has one year to respond by issuing a proposed test rule or a notice explaining why no testing is needed.

TSCA requires the ITC to consider the following factors when it makes listing decisions: (1) quantity of the substance to be manufactured, (2) quantity of the chemical in environmental releases, (3) number of people who will be exposed occupationally and the duration of exposure, (4) extent of non-occupational human exposure, (5) similarity of the chemical to any other chemical known to present an unreasonable risk, (6) existence of data concerning environmental or health effects of the chemical, (7) the quantity of information to be gained by testing, and (8) the availability of facilities and personnel for performing testing. Chemicals known or suspected to cause or contribute to cancer, gene mutations, or birth defects are to be assigned a higher priority. In response to information that indicates "there may be a reasonable basis to conclude that a chemical ... presents or will present a significant risk of serious or widespread harm to human beings from cancer, gene mutations, or birth defects," TSCA requires EPA action to prevent or reduce that risk or publication of a finding that the risk is not unreasonable.

Pre-manufacture Notification for New Chemicals or Uses

TSCA (§5) requires manufacturers, importers, and processors to notify EPA at least 90 days prior to producing or otherwise introducing a new chemical product into the United States. Any information or test data that is known to, reasonably ascertainable by, or in possession of the notifier, and that might be useful to EPA in evaluating the chemical's potential adverse effects on human health or the environment, must be submitted to EPA at the same time. TSCA also requires EPA to be notified when there are plans to produce, process, or use an existing chemical in a way that differs from previously permitted uses, if the Administrator has determined by rule that new uses of the chemical may produce significant changes in human and environmental exposures and therefore require notification. The 90-day notice provides EPA with the opportunity to evaluate the chemical use and, if necessary, to prohibit or limit such activity before it occurs to prevent unreasonable risk of injury to human health or the environment.

EPA has 45 days after notification (or up to 90 days if it extends the period for good cause) to evaluate the potential risk posed by the chemical. If EPA determines that there is a reasonable basis to conclude that the substance presents or will present an unreasonable risk, the Administrator must promulgate requirements to protect adequately against such risk. Alternatively, EPA may determine that the proposed activity related to a chemical does not present an unreasonable risk; this decision may be based on the available data, or, when no data exist to document the effects of exposure, on what is known about the effects of chemicals in commerce with similar chemical structures and used in similar ways.

The purpose of EPA's screening procedure is to identify potential hazards, and control them before use of a chemical becomes widespread. If data are inadequate to make an informed judgment and (1) manufacture, processing, distribution in commerce, use, or disposal may present an unreasonable risk; or (2) a chemical is to be produced in substantial quantities, and the potential for environmental release or human exposure is substantial or significant, EPA may issue a proposed order to prohibit or limit such activities until sufficient data are submitted.

Although the legislative history of TSCA includes a presumption that testing of new products would take place before they were widely used, either as the chemical was developed, or as its markets grew, TSCA also forbids promulgation of blanket testing requirements for all new chemicals. This reflects concern that uniform testing requirements might stifle innovation in the chemical industry. Thus, EPA must decide which chemicals, or which categories of chemicals, warrant the costs of pre-market testing. EPA reviews approximately 1,000 new chemical manufacturing notices annually.

Regulatory Controls for Hazardous Chemicals

TSCA requires EPA to regulate manufacturing, processing, distribution in commerce, use, or disposal of a chemical if it will present an unreasonable risk of injury to health or the environment, and the risk cannot be reduced to a sufficient degree under another federal law administered by EPA. The alternative means available to EPA for controlling chemical hazards that present unreasonable risks are specified in Section 6 of TSCA. EPA has the authority to

- prohibit or limit the amount of production or distribution of a substance in commerce;
- prohibit or limit the production or distribution of a substance for a particular use;
- limit the volume or concentration of the chemical produced;
- prohibit or regulate the manner or method of commercial use;
- require warning labels and/or instructions on containers or products;
- require notification of the risk of injury to distributors and, to the extent possible, consumers;
- require record-keeping by producers;
- specify disposal methods; and
- require replacement or repurchase of products already distributed.

EPA also may impose any of these requirements in combination or for a specific geographical region. However, EPA is required by TSCA to regulate only "to the extent necessary to protect adequately" against a risk, and to use the "least burdensome" regulatory approach, even in controlling unreasonable risks.

Two chemical substances are directly addressed in Title I: PCBs and elemental mercury. TSCA directs EPA to regulate PCBs and to ban most uses. In addition, TSCA prohibits the sale, distribution, or transfer of elemental mercury by federal agencies.

Information Gathering

Section 8 of TSCA requires EPA to develop and maintain an inventory of all chemicals, or categories of chemicals, manufactured or processed in the United States. The first version of this inventory identified approximately 55,000 chemicals in commerce in 1979. All chemicals not on the inventory are, by definition, "new" and subject to the notification provisions of Section 5. These chemicals must be added to the inventory if they enter U.S. commerce. Chemicals need not be listed if they are only produced in very small quantities for purposes of experimentation or research.

To aid EPA in its duties under TSCA, the agency was granted considerable authority to collect information from industries. EPA may require maintenance of records and reporting of chemical identities, names, and molecular structures; categories of use; amounts manufactured and processed for each category of use; descriptions of byproducts resulting from manufacture, processing, use, and disposal; environmental and health effects; number of individuals exposed; number of employees exposed and the duration of exposure; and manner or method of chemical disposal.

Manufacturers, processors, and distributors of chemicals are required to maintain records of significant adverse reactions to health or the environment alleged to have been caused by a substance or mixture. Records of adverse effects on the health of employees must be retained for 30 years from the date of reporting. Industry also must submit lists and copies of health and safety studies. Studies showing adverse effects previously unknown must be submitted to EPA as soon as they are completed or discovered.

Imminent Hazards

Section 7 provides EPA authority to take emergency action through the district courts to control a chemical substance or mixture which presents an imminent and unreasonable risk of serious widespread injury to health or the environment.

Relation to other Laws

Section 9 requires EPA to report cases of chemical risk to other federal agencies with the authority to prevent or reduce the risk. If the other agency determines that the activity does not present the risk described by EPA in its report, or initiates action under the law to protect against the risk, TSCA prohibits EPA from taking regulatory action with respect to such risk. For statutes under EPA's jurisdiction, TSCA gives the Administrator discretion to decide if a risk can best be handled under the authority of TSCA.

Enforcement and Judicial Review

Section 11 authorizes EPA to inspect any facilities subject to TSCA requirements and to issue subpoenas requiring attendance and testimony of witnesses, production of reports and documents, answers to questions and other necessary information. Section 13 mandates TSCA enforcement at the national borders by the Treasury Department.

Section 15 identifies acts prohibited under TSCA, while Section 16 describes penalties for acts violating these prohibitions, as well as recourse available to anyone accused of such violations. Section 16 authorizes civil penalties, not to exceed $25,000 per violation per day, and affords the defendant an opportunity to request a hearing before an order is issued and to petition for judicial review of an order after it is issued. Criminal penalties also are authorized for willful violations. Section 17 provides jurisdiction to U.S. district courts in civil actions to enforce TSCA Section 15 by restraining or compelling actions that violate or comply with it, respectively. Chemicals may be seized and condemned if their manufacture, processing, or distribution violated the act.

Section 19 authorizes any person to file a petition for judicial review of specified rules within 60 days of issuance under TSCA. The court is directed to set aside specified rules if they are not supported by substantial evidence in the rulemaking record taken as a whole.

Section 20 authorizes civil suits by any person against any person in violation of the act. It also authorizes suits against EPA to compel performance of nondiscretionary actions under TSCA. Section 21 provides the public with the right to petition for the issuance, amendment, or repeal of a rule requiring toxicity testing of a chemical, regulation of the chemical, or reporting.

Confidential Business Information

Section 14 provides broad protection of proprietary confidential information about chemicals in commerce. Disclosure by EPA employees of such information generally is not permitted, except to other federal employees, or when necessary to protect health or the environment. Data from health and safety studies of chemicals are not protected unless their disclosure would reveal a chemical process or chemical proportion in a mixture. Wrongful disclosure of confidential data by federal employees is prohibited, and may result in criminal penalties.

Chemical Categories

Section 26 allows EPA to impose regulatory controls on categories of chemicals, rather than on a case-by-case basis. However, EPA cannot regulate a group merely because it is composed of new chemical substances.

State Preemption

TSCA Section 18 preempts state actions that establish or continue in effect requirements applicable to a chemical substance or mixture that is regulated under TSCA Section 5 or 6, unless the state requirement is identical to the federal requirement, implements another federal law, or prohibits use of the substance or mixture within the state. However, a state may ask EPA to allow a state requirement that provides a significantly higher degree of protection from risk than does the federal requirement.

Other Provisions

TSCA Section 10 directs EPA to conduct and coordinate among federal agencies research, development, and monitoring that is necessary to the purposes of the act.

Section 12 excludes chemical products manufactured for export from TSCA requirements except for reporting and record keeping requirements in Section 8. In 2008, Congress excluded elemental mercury from this exemption, banning its export beginning in 2013, with the exception of mercury contained in coal. Other exemptions for essential uses may be granted by rule.

Section 22 waives compliance when in the interest of national defense.

Section 23 provides protection of employees who assist in carrying out the provisions of the act (i.e., "whistle-blowers").

The potential effects of TSCA rules on employment must be monitored by EPA, according to Section 24.

Section 25 mandates study of the need for indemnification of people affected by federal laws administered by EPA and of the feasibility of establishing a standard classification system for chemical substances and of storing and retrieving information about them.

Section 26 authorizes data sharing and cooperative action to facilitate TSCA implementation between EPA and other federal agencies. It also authorizes collection of fees for EPA processing of data submitted in response to an order under Section 4 or 5. EPA is directed to establish an office to assist the regulated community. The agency also must establish a procedure to ensure disclosure of financial interests in the regulated community by EPA employees. Final orders issued under TSCA must contain a statement of basis and purpose. Finally, Section 26 established within EPA a new Assistant Administrator for Toxic Substances.

TSCA Section 27 authorizes research and development of test methods for chemicals by the Public Health Service in cooperation with EPA.

Grants to states are authorized by Section 28 to establish and operate programs to prevent or eliminate unreasonable risks to health or the environment.

Section 29 authorized appropriations through 1983.

An annual report is mandated by Section 30.

TITLE II (ASBESTOS IN BUILDINGS)

Growing public concern about the presence of potentially hazardous asbestos in buildings, especially in schools, led to congressional efforts to address this problem. Title II of TSCA, the Asbestos Hazard Emergency Response Act (AHERA), was enacted in 1986 (P.L. 99-519) and amended in July 1988 (P.L. 100-368). It required EPA to set standards by October 1987, for responding to the presence of asbestos in schools. The standards, set at levels adequate to protect public health and the environment, identify appropriate response actions that depend on the physical condition of asbestos. Schools, in turn, were required to inspect for asbestos-containing material, and to develop and implement a plan for managing any such material. Plans for managing asbestos were to be submitted by schools before May 1989, and implementation was to begin by July 1989. The law contains no deadlines for schools to complete implementation.

Title II requires asbestos contractors and analytical laboratories to be certified, and schools to use certified persons for abatement work. Training and accreditation requirements also apply to inspectors, contractors, and workers performing asbestos abatement work in all public and commercial buildings. EPA may award training grants to nonprofit organizations for asbestos health and safety programs. However, authorization of appropriations for this grant program expired September 30, 1995. Other Title II requirements (such as mandates that buildings be inspected for asbestos) have not been extended to non-school buildings.

To enforce requirements, TSCA authorizes EPA to take emergency action with respect to schools if school officials do not act to protect children. The act also authorizes citizen action with respect to asbestos-containing material in a school and to compel action by EPA, either through administrative petition or judicial action. Civil penalties not to exceed $5,000 are authorized for violations such as failing to conduct an inspection or to develop a school management plan.

Concern about how schools would pay for required actions was addressed in separate legislation (the Asbestos School Hazard Abatement Act of 1984, or ASHAA, P.L. 98-377). It established a program offering grants and interest-free loans to schools with serious asbestos problems and demonstrated financial need. Although EPA for several years did not request funding for this program, Congress appropriated funds. Authorization of appropriations for this program expired September 30, 1995, and Congress has not appropriated funds since FY1993; a total of $382 million in grant and loan funds were appropriated from FY1984 through FY1993. Repaid ASHAA loans are returned to an Asbestos Trust Fund, established in TSCA Title II, to become a dedicated source of revenues for future asbestos control projects.

TITLE III (RADON PROGRAMS)

In October 1988, Congress amended TSCA by adding Title III—Indoor Radon Abatement (15 U.S.C. 2661 *et seq.,* P.L. 100-551). The basic purpose of Title III is to provide financial and technical assistance to the states that choose to support radon monitoring and control; neither monitoring nor abatement of radon is required by the act.

Title III required EPA to update its pamphlet "A Citizen's Guide to Radon," to develop model construction standards and techniques for controlling radon levels within new buildings, and to provide technical assistance to states. EPA is to provide technical assistance by establishing an information clearinghouse; publishing public information materials; establishing a national database of radon levels detected, organized by state; providing information to professional organizations representing private firms involved in building design and construction; submitting to Congress a plan for providing financial and technical assistance to states; operating cooperative projects with states; conducting research to develop, test, and evaluate radon measurement methods and protocols; developing and demonstrating new methods of radon measurement and mitigation, including methods that are suitable for use in nonresidential child care facilities; operating a voluntary program to rate radon measurement and mitigation devices and methods and the effectiveness of private firms and individuals offering radon-related services; and designing and implementing training seminars. The proficiency rating program and certification for training programs collect fees for service, and therefore are meant to be self-supporting, but Congress authorized $1.5 million to be appropriated to establish these programs. Congress authorized $3 million to be appropriated for each of three years beginning in 1989 for the other provisions of Sections 303, 304, and 305.

A matching grant program was established for the purpose of assisting states in developing and implementing programs for radon assessment and mitigation. For this program, $30 million was authorized to be appropriated over three years, with funds targeted to states or projects that made efforts to ensure adoption of EPA's model construction standards and techniques for new buildings; gave preference to low-income persons; or addressed serious and extensive radon contamination problems or had the potential to reduce risk or to develop innovative assessment techniques, mitigation measures, or management approaches.

Other sections of Title III require EPA to conduct a study to determine the extent of radon contamination in schools; identify and list areas of the United States with a high probability of having high levels of indoor radon; make grants or cooperative agreements to establish and operate at least three regional radon training centers; and provide guidance to federal agencies on radon measurement, risk assessment, and remedial measures.

All authorizations for appropriations specific to this title expired September 30, 1991, although appropriations have continued.

TITLE IV (LEAD EXPOSURE REDUCTION)

The 102nd Congress added Title IV to TSCA when it enacted the Residential Lead-Based Paint Hazard Reduction Act of 1992 as Title X in the Housing and Community Development Act of 1992 (P.L. 102-550). TSCA Title IV aims to accelerate federal efforts to reduce risks to young children who daily are exposed to lead-based paint in their homes. In addition, it was intended to stimulate development of lead inspection and hazard abatement services in the private sector, while ensuring that the services provided and any products employed are reliable and effective in reducing risk. To these ends, Title IV directs EPA to

- promulgate definitions of lead-contaminated dust, lead-contaminated soil, and lead-based paint hazards;
- ensure that people engaged in detection and control of lead hazards are properly trained and that contractors are certified;
- publish requirements for the accreditation of training programs for workers;
- develop criteria to evaluate the effectiveness of commercial products used to detect or reduce risks associated with lead-based paint;
- establish protocols, criteria, and minimum performance standards for laboratory analysis of lead in paint films, soil, and dust;
- establish a program to certify laboratories as qualified to test substances for lead content; and
- publish and distribute to the public a list of certified or accredited environmental sampling laboratories.

Title IV explicitly applies these requirements to federal facilities and activities that may create a lead hazard.

In addition, Congress directed EPA to conduct a study of lead hazards due to renovation and remodeling activities that may incidentally disturb lead-based paint. EPA is required to promulgate guidelines for the renovation and remodeling of buildings or other structures when these activities might create a hazard.

Title IV directs EPA to establish a clearinghouse and hotline to distribute information about the hazards of lead-based paint, how to avoid exposure and reduce risk, and new technologies for removing or immobilizing lead-based paint. In addition, Congress mandated development of a lead hazard information pamphlet; public education and outreach activities for health professionals, the general public, homeowners, landlords, tenants, consumers of home improvement products, the residential real estate industry, and the home renovation industry; and information to be distributed by retailers of home improvement products to provide consumers with practical information related to the hazards of renovation where lead-based paint may be present.

Title IV authorizes states to propose programs to train and certify inspectors and contractors engaged in the detection or control of lead-based paint hazards. States also may develop the required informational pamphlets. TSCA requires EPA to promulgate a model state program that may be adopted by any state. Congress gave EPA the authority to approve or disapprove authorization for state proposals and to provide grants for states to develop and implement authorized programs. A federal program must be established, administered, and enforced by EPA in each state without an authorized program.

The Department of Health and Human Services also has responsibilities under Title IV of TSCA. It mandates a study by the Centers for Disease Prevention and Control (CDC) and the National Institute for Environmental Health Sciences to determine the sources of lead exposure to children who have elevated lead levels in their bodies. The National Institute for Occupational Safety and Health is directed to study ways of reducing occupational exposure to lead during abatement activities.

The act established a rule-making docket to ensure the availability to the general public of all documents submitted to agencies that are relevant to regulatory decisions pursuant to this legislation. The docket is required to include the drafts of all proposed rules submitted by EPA to the President's Office of Management and Budget (OMB), written comments on the drafts, and written responses to comments. In addition, the agency must provide an explanation for any major change to a proposed rule that appears in the final rule, and such changes may not be made based on information not filed in the docket. Dockets are required to be established in each EPA regional office.

Congress authorized to be appropriated "such sums as may be necessary" for TSCA Title IV.

In addition to amending TSCA, Title X of the Housing and Community Development Act of 1992 authorized grants to states for risk assessments and lead-based paint removal and immobilization in private housing for low-income residents; establishing state training, certification, or accreditation programs for inspectors and abatement contractors; and research at the Department of Housing and Urban Development (HUD). Authorization for appropriations for these grants expired September 30, 1994, but appropriations have continued. Title X directed HUD to establish guidelines for federally supported work involving risk assessments, inspections, interim controls, and abatement of lead-based paint hazards. In addition, the National Institute for Occupational Safety and Health (NIOSH) was provided $10 million for training people who remove or immobilize paint.

TITLE V (REDUCING RISKS IN SCHOOLS)

At the end of 2007, the 110th Congress added a fifth title to TSCA, subtitled Healthy High-Performance Schools. Enacted as Title IV, Subtitle E (§461) of P.L. 110-140, the Energy Independence and Security Act of 2007, TSCA Title V authorizes EPA to establish a state grant program to provide technical assistance for EPA programs to schools and develop and implement state school environmental health programs. State programs must include standards for school building design, construction, and renovation, and identify ongoing school building environmental problems and recommended solutions. Environmental problems specifically mentioned in the law include "contaminants, hazardous substances, and pollutant emissions." EPA's authority to provide grants expires five years after the date of enactment.

Title V requires the EPA Administrator, in consultation with the Secretary of Education and the Secretary of Health and Human Services, to issue voluntary guidelines within 18 months of Title V enactment for selecting sites for schools (presumably new schools). The guidelines are to account for the "special vulnerability of children to hazardous substances or pollution exposures in any case in which the potential for contamination at a potential school site exists," modes of transportation available to students and staff, efficient use of energy, and potential use of a school at the site as an emergency shelter.

Title V also requires the EPA Administrator, in consultation with the Secretary of Education and the Secretary of Health and Human Services, to issue voluntary guidelines within two years of enactment for developing and implementing state environmental health programs for schools. These guidelines must take into account the findings of federal initiatives established under "relevant federal law with respect to school facilities," including initiatives related to water and energy conservation authorized by Sections 431 through 441, and work related to high-performance green buildings authorized by Section 492 of P.L. 110-140. In particular, the guidelines must take into account "environmental problems, contaminants, hazardous substances, and pollutant emissions"; natural day lighting; ventilation; heating and cooling; moisture control and mold; maintenance, cleaning, and pest control; acoustics; and "other issues relating to the health, comfort, productivity, and performance of occupants of the school facilities." In addition, Title V requires that the guidelines provide "technical assistance on siting, design, management, and operation of school facilities"; collaborate with children's environmental health centers in school environmental investigations"; assist states and the public to better understand and improve the environmental health of children; and take into account "the special vulnerability of children in low-income and minority communities to exposures from contaminants, hazardous substances, and pollutant emissions."

Several provisions in Title V refer to entities established under other sections of the Energy Independence and Security Act of 2007 (P.L. 110-140). For example, Title V contains directives for the Federal Director of the Office of Federal High-Performance Green Buildings in the General Services Administration, which was created by Section 436(a). In addition, there is reference to the national high-performance green building clearinghouse established in Section 423(1) "to carry out public outreach to inform individuals and entities of the information and services [related to high-performance green buildings] available governmentwide." Title V requires the Federal Director to ensure, "to the maximum extent practicable," that the public clearinghouse "receives and makes available information on the exposure of children to environmental hazards in school facilities." The EPA Administrator is directed to prepare an annual report to Congress on activities carried out under Title V authority, and this report also must be made available to the public through the clearinghouse.

For the purposes of carrying out the provisions of Title V, Congress authorized appropriations of $1.5 million annually through 2013.

TITLE VI (LIMITING FORMALDEHYDE EMISSIONS)

In July 2010, Congress enacted the Formaldehyde Standards for Composite Wood Products Act (P.L. 111-199), adding a new Title VI to TSCA. The new title mandates specific formaldehyde emission standards for hardwood plywood, medium-density fiberboard, and particleboard that is sold, supplied, offered for sale, or manufactured in the United States. The standards are phased in over two years from enactment and are based on the voluntary national formaldehyde emissions standards established by ASTM International (formerly known as the American Society for Testing and Materials), method ASTM E-1333-96 (2002).

Table 2. Major *U.S. Code* Sections, Toxic Substances Control Act (codified as 15 U.S.C. 2601-2692)

15 U.S.C.	Section Title	Toxic Substances Control Act (as amended)
Subchapter I	Control of Toxic Substances	
2601	Findings, policy and intent	§2
2602	Definitions	§3
2603	Testing of chemical substances and mixtures	§4
2604	Manufacturing and processing notices	§5
2605	Regulation of hazardous chemical substances and mixtures	§6
2606	Imminent hazards	§7
2607	Reporting and retention of information	§8
2608	Relationship to other federal laws	§9
2609	Research, development, collection, dissemination, and utilization of data	§10
2610	Inspections and subpoenas	§11
2611	Exports	§12
2612	Entry into customs territory of the United States	§13
2613	Disclosure of data	§14
2614	Prohibited acts	§15
2615	Penalties	§16
2616	Specific enforcement and seizure	§17
2617	Preemption	§18
2618	Judicial	§19
2619	Citizen's civil actions	§20
2620	Citizen's petitions	§21
2621	National defense waiver	§22
2622	Employee protection	§23

15 U.S.C.	Section Title	Toxic Substances Control Act (as amended)
2623	Employment effects	§24
2624	Studies	§25
2625	Administration	§26
2627	Development and evaluation of test methods	§27
2628	Authorization of appropriations	§28
2629	Annual report	§29
Subchapter II	Asbestos Hazard Emergency Response	
2641	Congressional findings and purpose	§201
2642	Definitions	§202
2643	EPA regulations	§203
2644	Requirements if EPA fails to promulgate regulations	§204
2645	Submission to state Governor	§205
2646	Contractor and laboratory accreditation	§206
2647	Enforcement	§207
2648	Emergency authority	§208
2649	State and federal law	§209
2650	Asbestos contractors and local educational agencies	§210
2651	Public protection	§211
2652	Asbestos ombudsman	§212
2653	EPA study of asbestos-containing material in public buildings	§213
2654	Transition rules	§214
2655	Worker protection	§215
Subchapter III	Indoor Radon Abatement	
2661	National goal	§301
2662	Definitions	§302
2663	EPA's citizen guide	§303
2664	Model construction standards and techniques	§304
2665	Technical assistance to states for radon programs	§305
2666	Grant Assistance to states for radon programs	§306
2667	Radon in schools	§307
2668	Regional radon training centers	§308
2669	Study of radon in federal buildings	§309
2670	Regulations	§310
2671	Additional authorizations	§311
Subchapter IV	Lead Exposure Reduction	
2681	Definitions	§401
2682	Lead-based paint activities training and certification	§402
2683	Identification of dangerous levels of lead	§403
2684	Authorized state programs	§404
2685	Lead abatement and measurement	§405
2686	Lead hazard information pamphlet	§406
2687	Regulations	§407
2688	Control of lead-based paint at federal facilities	§408
2689	Prohibited acts	§409
2690	Relationship to other federal law	§410
2691	General provisions relating to administrative proceedings	§411

Table 2. (Continued)

15 U.S.C.	Section Title	Toxic Substances Control Act (as amended)
2692	Authorization of appropriations	§412
Subchapter V	Healthy High-Performance Schools	
2695	Grants for healthy school environments	§501
2695a	Model guidelines for siting of school facilities	§502
2695b	Public outreach	§503
2695c	Environmental health program	§504
2695d	Authorization of appropriations	§505
Subchapter VI	Formaldehyde Standards for Composite Wood Products	
2697	Formaldehyde Standards	§601

Note: This table shows only the major code sections. For more detail and to determine when a section was added, the reader should consult the official printed version of the *U.S. Code*.

The standards apply to plywood, particleboard, and medium-density fiberboard in the form of an unfinished panel or incorporated into a finished good. Certain products are excluded, including many forms of lumber and panels used for outdoor applications, such as structural plywood, prefabricated wood I-joists, most windows, antiques or other previously owned goods, and composite wood products used inside automobiles, trucks, rail cars, boats, and aircraft.

EPA is required to promulgate regulations ensuring compliance with the emission standards and must include provisions relating to labeling, chain of custody requirements, sell-through provisions; ultra low-emitting formaldehyde resins, finished goods, third-party testing and certification; auditing and reporting of third-party certifiers; recordkeeping; enforcement, laminated products; and exceptions for products and components containing "de minimis amounts" of composite wood products. The new law prohibits stockpiling of products manufactured before the effective date of the act for sale after that date. Also prohibited is any requirement for labeling products manufactured prior to the "designated date of manufacture."

P.L. 111-199 requires an annual report to Congress on the status of implementation and the extent to which relevant industries have achieved compliance. Finally, the act directs the Secretary of Housing and Urban Development to update regulations concerning formaldehyde emissions from composite wood in manufactured homes (24 Code of Federal Regulations 3280.308) to ensure that the standards established by TSCA Title VI are implemented.

SELECTED REFERENCES

[4] Bergeson, Lynn L. (2000). *TSCA: Toxic Substances Control Act*. Basic Practice Series. Chicago, IL: Section of Environment, Energy, and Resources, American Bar Association, 151 p.

[5] Bergeson, Lynn L., Campbell, Lisa M. & Lisa Rothenberg. (2000). TSCA and the Future of Chemical Regulation, *EPA Administrative Law Reporter*, v. *15*, n. 4, 23 p.

[6] CRS Report RS21688, *Lead-Based Paint Poisoning Prevention: Summary of Federal Mandates and Financial Assistance for Reducing Hazards in Housing*, by Linda-Jo Schierow.

In: A Selection of Federal Acts
Editors: P. Brown and K. M. Mitchell
ISBN: 978-1-62417-047-8

Chapter 6

FAIR CREDIT REPORTING ACT: RIGHTS AND RESPONSIBILITIES*

Margaret Mikyung Lee

SUMMARY

The purpose of the Fair Credit Reporting Act (FCRA) is "to require that consumer reporting agencies adopt reasonable procedures for meeting the needs of commerce for consumer credit, personnel, insurance, and other information in a manner which is fair and equitable to the consumer, with regard to the confidentiality, accuracy, relevancy, and proper utilization of such information." The FCRA establishes consumers' rights in relation to their credit reports, as well as permissible uses of credit reports. It also imposes certain responsibilities on those who collect, furnish, and use the information contained in consumers' credit reports.

The FCRA has been amended several times over the last decade. The Fair and Accurate Credit Transactions Act of 2003 (FACT Act, P.L. 108-159) amended the FCRA to include a number of provisions aimed at preventing identity theft and assisting victims. The Credit Card Accountability Responsibility and Disclosure Act of 2009 (Credit CARD Act, P.L. 111-24) strengthened protections for young consumers and advertising disclosures regarding free credit reports from consumer reporting agencies. More recently, the Consumer Financial Protection Act of 2010, part of the Dodd-Frank Wall Street Reform and Consumer Protection Act (P.L. 111-203), established the Consumer Financial Protection Bureau and transferred administrative functions, including most rulemaking and reporting, as well as certain enforcement functions, from other federal agencies, such as the Federal Trade Commission and the Federal Reserve Board, to the Bureau.

This report discusses consumers' rights under the FCRA, as well as the type of information included in credit reports, permissible uses of credit reports, disclosure requirements, and requirements for users of consumer credit reports and furnishers of

* This is an edited, reformatted and augmented version of the Congressional Research Service Publication, CRS Report for Congress RL31666, dated February 2, 2012.

information. It also addresses FCRA provisions aimed at preventing identity theft and assisting victims of identity theft.

Introduction

The purpose of the Fair Credit Reporting Act (FCRA)[1] is "to require that consumer reporting agencies adopt reasonable procedures for meeting the needs of commerce for consumer credit, personnel, insurance, and other information in a manner which is fair and equitable to the consumer, with regard to the confidentiality, accuracy, relevancy, and proper utilization of such information."[2] The FCRA establishes consumers' rights in relation to their credit reports, as well as permissible uses of credit reports, disclosure requirements, and requirements for users of consumer credit reports and furnishers of information. The Fair and Accurate Credit Transactions Act of 2003 (FACT Act) amended the FCRA to include a number of provisions aimed at preventing identity theft and assisting victims.[3] The Credit Card Accountability Responsibility and Disclosure Act of 2009 (Credit CARD Act)[4] strengthened protections for young consumers and advertising disclosures regarding free credit reports from consumer reporting agencies. More recently, the Consumer Financial Protection Act of 2010,[5] part of the Dodd-Frank Wall Street Reform and Consumer Protection Act (Dodd-Frank Act),[6] established the Consumer Financial Protection Bureau (CFPB or the Bureau) and transferred administrative functions, including rulemaking and reporting, as well as certain enforcement functions, from other federal agencies such as the Federal Trade Commission and the Federal Reserve Board, to the Bureau.[7]

The FCRA applies to the files maintained by "consumer reporting agencies," a term broadly defined to include anyone in the business of furnishing reports on the creditworthiness of consumers to third parties.[8] Consumer reporting agencies are also commonly known as credit bureaus or credit reporting agencies. A consumer reporting agency "is essentially a clearinghouse for information supplied by credit grantors and collection agencies, and culled by the bureau itself from public records."[9] In addition to several thousand small bureaus that often serve limited geographic areas, there are three major consumer reporting agencies that operate on a nationwide basis—Experian, Equifax, and Trans Union. Information on a particular consumer may be maintained by any one or all of the consumer reporting agencies serving a particular geographic area.

Information Included in Consumer Credit Reports

Consumer credit reports generally include information about consumers' "credit worthiness [sic], credit standing, credit capacity, character, general reputation, personal characteristics, or mode of living."[10] The FCRA explicitly excludes certain types of financial reports from the definition of a consumer report. For example, "any report containing information solely as to transactions or experiences between the consumer and the person making the report" is excluded from the definition of consumer report, as are communications of that information among persons related by common ownership or affiliated by corporate control.[11] Authorizations or approvals of specific extensions of credit by the issuer of a credit card are also excluded from the definition of consumer report.[12]

With relatively few exceptions, there appears to be a consensus among the consumer reporting agencies as to the types of information that should be included in a report.[13] Information reported by a credit bureau commonly includes "identifying information, usually the individual's full name, Social Security number, address, telephone number, and spouse's name; financial status and employment information, including income, spouse's income, place, position, and tenure of employment, other sources of income, duration, and income in former employment; credit history, including types of credit previously obtained, names of previous credit grantors, extent of previous credit, and complete payment history; existing lines of credit, including payment habits and all outstanding obligations; public record information, including pertinent newspaper clippings, arrest and conviction records,[14] bankruptcies, tax liens, and lawsuits; and finally a listing of bureau subscribers that have previously asked for a credit report on the individual."[15]

The Fair Credit Reporting Act limits the amount of time that adverse or negative information can be included in a consumer's credit report. Generally, a credit reporting agency is prohibited from reporting adverse information that is more than seven years old, or in the case of bankruptcies, more than ten years old.[16] If a bankruptcy filed under title 11 of the United States Code is included on a consumer's report, the report shall also identify the chapter under which the case arose, if such information is provided by the source of the information.[17] If a bankruptcy case or filing under title 11 of the United States Code is withdrawn by the consumer before a final judgment, the report must include the fact that the case or filing was withdrawn.[18]

In addition to adverse credit information, consumer reporting agencies are also allowed to include information on a consumer's failure to pay overdue child support, if such information has been provided to the agency by a state or local child support enforcement agency or verified by any state or federal government agency. This information remains on the consumer report for up to seven years.[19]

Medical information may be included in consumer reports under certain circumstances and if consumer reporting agencies and creditors follow statutory and regulatory procedures and conditions to protect the confidentiality of such information.[20]

PERMISSIBLE USES OF CONSUMER CREDIT REPORTS

The Fair Credit Reporting Act outlines the purposes for which a consumer credit report may be furnished to a requester.[21] In general, a consumer reporting agency may furnish a copy of a consumer's report to a person the agency has reason to believe intends to use the information for the purpose of extending credit to the consumer or for reviewing or collecting of the consumer's credit account.[22] Consumer credit reports may also be issued where there is another "legitimate business need" for the information contained in the report in connection with a business transaction initiated by the consumer, or for purposes of reviewing an existing account to determine whether the consumer continues to meet the terms of the account.[23] Reports may be furnished to executive branch departments and agencies in connection with the issuance of government-sponsored travel charge cards that are billed to employees.[24] An insurer may receive a report in connection with the underwriting of an insurance policy involving the consumer for which the consumer has applied.[25] Various other uses are permitted, including, among others, a response to a court order, a decision regarding a consumer's employment, and determination by a government agency of a consumer's ability to make child support payments.[26]

Reports may be issued in connection with transactions not initiated by the consumer only if authorized by the consumer, or if the transaction is a firm offer for credit or insurance and the consumer has not elected to have his name removed from lists provided by the agency for this purpose.[27] A consumer may elect to have his name removed from such lists by notifying the reporting agency that he does not consent to the release of reports for this purpose.[28] If the consumer has not authorized the release of such reports and has not elected to have his name removed from the lists, the agency may release only certain information about the consumer. Information released in connection with transactions not initiated by the consumer is limited to the name and address of the consumer, an identifier that is not unique to the consumer and that is used solely for the purpose of verifying the consumer's identity, and other information pertaining to the consumer that does not identify his/her relationship or experience with respect to a particular creditor or other entity.[29] The Credit CARD Act of 2009 added protections from prescreened offers for persons under 21 years of age. Credit reports for such consumers cannot be issued in connection with such offers unless the consumer has consented.[30]

In addition to reports issued for the commercial purposes discussed above, a consumer reporting agency may also issue a report to a person it has reason to believe "intends to use the information in connection with a determination of the consumer's eligibility for a license or other benefit granted by a governmental entity required by law to consider an applicant's financial responsibility or status."[31]

The FCRA also authorizes consumer credit reports to be released for certain legal purposes. Specifically, the act authorizes consumer credit reports to be released "in response to the order of a court having jurisdiction to issue such an order," or in response to "a subpoena issued in connection with proceedings before a Federal grand jury."[32] Reports may also be issued to state or local child support enforcement agencies if needed to establish the consumer's capacity to pay child support or to determine the amount of such payments.[33]

If certain requirements are met, reports may also be issued for employment purposes.[34] In order to obtain a report for employment purposes, the requester must certify that the report will not be used in violation of any state or federal law.[35] The consumer must be told by the prospective employer that a report may be obtained and must consent to the procurement of a report by the employer.[36] If the employer intends to take adverse action based in whole or in part on the report, the consumer must be provided with a copy of the report and a description of the rights afforded to consumers under the FCRA.[37]

A consumer report may also be issued to the Federal Deposit Insurance Corporation or the National Credit Union Administration as part of its powers, as conservator, receiver, or liquidating agent for an insured depository institution or insured credit union or in connection with the resolution or liquidation of a failed or failing insured depository institution or insured credit union.[38]

CONSUMER RIGHTS

The Fair Credit Reporting Act outlines consumers' rights in relation to their credit reports. Under the FCRA, consumers have the right to access all information in their credit reports, including the sources of the information, and the right to disclosure of their credit scores.[39] A consumer may request one free credit report, not including a free credit score, each year from each of the nationwide consumer reporting agencies.[40] Pursuant to an amendment by the Credit CARD Act of 2009,[41] advertisements for a free credit report in any medium, including television, radio, and the internet, must include a disclosure to the effect that free annual reports are available under federal law at "AnnualCreditReport.com" or other sources authorized by federal law and that the privately advertised service is not the free report required by law. Free reports may also be obtained under certain circumstances, such as notice of an adverse action based on information in a credit report or a consumer's request for a credit report in conjunction with a fraud alert.[42] Absent one of these circumstances, a consumer may be charged up to $11.00 for additional copies of his or her credit report.[43] Except in certain circumstances, a consumer reporting agency may charge a fair and reasonable fee, as determined by the Bureau ($11.00 maximum), for providing a consumer's current credit score or the one most recently calculated for an extension of credit.[44] This paid disclosure must include a notice that the credit score purchased by the consumer may differ from a score purchased and used by a lender or other user of credit reports and scores.[45] As required by the Dodd-Frank Act, the Bureau issued a report in 2011 on the nature, range, and size of variations between credit scores sold to creditors and those sold to consumers by consumer reporting agencies and whether such variations disadvantage consumers.[46]

In addition to the disclosure of information contained in the consumer's credit report, a consumer is also entitled to receive information identifying each person who obtained a consumer credit report for employment purposes during the previous two years, or for any other purpose during the previous year.[47] Additional information that must be disclosed to the consumer upon request includes "the dates, original payees, and amounts of any checks upon which is based any adverse characterization of the consumer, included in the file at the time of the disclosure;" and "a record of all inquiries received by the agency during the one-year period preceding the request that identified the consumer in connection with a credit or insurance transaction that was not initiated by the consumer."[48]

Consumers have the right to dispute the completeness or accuracy of information contained in their files.[49] Once a consumer notifies the consumer reporting agency of the dispute, the agency must reinvestigate and record the current status of the disputed information, or delete it from the consumer's file within 30 days.[50] The consumer reporting agency must also notify the furnisher of the disputed information of the consumer's dispute and provide the furnisher with all relevant information the agency has received from the consumer regarding the dispute.[51]

In conducting the reinvestigation, the consumer reporting agency must review and consider all relevant information submitted by the consumer.[52] The agency may terminate the reinvestigation if it reasonably determines that the dispute is frivolous or irrelevant, or if the consumer fails to provide sufficient information to investigate the disputed information.[53] Should the agency determine that the dispute is frivolous or irrelevant, it must notify the consumer of the determination not later than five business days after making such determination.[54] If the reinvestigation leads to a determination that the disputed information is in fact inaccurate, incomplete, or unverifiable, the consumer reporting agency must delete that item of information from the consumer's credit file.[55]

The consumer reporting agency must provide written notice of the results of the reinvestigation to the consumer within five days of completing the reinvestigation.[56] The notice must include a statement that the reinvestigation is completed; a copy of the consumer report reflecting the information in the consumer's file revised during the reinvestigation; a notice that, if requested by the consumer, a description of the procedure used to determine the accuracy and completeness of the information can be provided; a notice that the consumer has the right to add a statement to his/her file disputing the accuracy or completeness of the information contained therein; and a notice that the consumer has the right to request that the consumer reporting agency send notices regarding deleted information to specified parties.[57]

RESPONSIBILITIES OF CONSUMER REPORTING AGENCIES

Certain provisions of the Fair Credit Reporting Act are aimed at ensuring that the information in consumers' credit files is accurate and complete. As discussed above, under the FCRA, consumer reporting agencies must conduct a reasonable reinvestigation if a consumer disputes the accuracy of any information in his/her file.[58] The agencies also must notify requesters of consumer reports of any substantial discrepancies between the address the agency has on file for a consumer and the consumer's address included in the request.[59]

In addition to their responsibilities related to the accuracy of information in consumers' files, credit reporting agencies must also ensure that consumer credit reports are released only for the purposes discussed above.[60] In order to ensure that the reports are used for permissible purposes, the credit reporting agencies must require that the prospective users of the information identify themselves, certify the purposes for which the information is sought, and certify that the information will be used for no other purpose.[61]

Consumer reporting agencies also have a duty to notify furnishers of information in the files and users of consumer reports of their responsibilities under the FCRA.[62]

In addition to the general responsibilities discussed above, a consumer reporting agency has responsibilities with regard to investigative consumer reports and reports provided for employment purposes. Prior to collecting information for or preparing an investigative consumer report, the agency must disclose to the consumer the nature and scope of the requested investigation and the fact that such a report may be made.[63] A consumer reporting agency may not prepare or furnish an investigative consumer report unless it has received certification from the requesting party that the required disclosures have been made to the consumer.[64] With regard to reports prepared for employment purposes, a consumer reporting agency must take precautions to insure the accuracy of public record information that may be included in the report.[65] The consumer must be notified that such information is being reported and be given the name and address of the person to whom the information is being reported; or the agency must "maintain strict procedures designed to insure that whenever public information which is likely to have an adverse effect on the consumer's ability to obtain employment is reported it is complete and up to date."[66]

RESPONSIBILITIES OF FURNISHERS OF INFORMATION

Many types of businesses and organizations contribute information to consumers' credit files. The major credit reporting agencies classify contributors of information into the following categories: "automobile dealers; banks, clothing, department, and variety stores; finance agencies; grocery and home furnishing dealers; insurers; jewelry and camera stores; contractors; lumber, building materials, and hardware suppliers; medical-care providers; national credit card companies and airlines; oil companies (credit card divisions); personal services other than medical; mail-order houses; real estate agents; hotel keepers; sporting goods and farm and garden supply dealers; utilities; fuel distributors; government agencies (e.g. the Federal Housing Administration and the Veterans Administration); wholesalers; advertisers; and collection agencies."[67]

Generally, any person who has information related to a consumer's financial activities can report information about that person's transactions and experiences with the consumer to a consumer reporting agency. However, a person or business with information about a consumer is not required to report that information to a consumer reporting agency. If negative information is reported, the furnisher must notify the consumer in writing.[68]

Persons who furnish information to consumer reporting agencies have a duty to provide accurate information. Under the FCRA, a furnisher may not provide any information relating to a consumer to a consumer reporting agency if the person knows or has reasonable cause to believe that the information is inaccurate.[69] Furnishers of information are also prohibited from furnishing information if they have been notified by the consumer that the information they are reporting is inaccurate.[70] Furnishers are also prohibited from furnishing information identified by the consumer as resulting from identity theft, unless the furnisher subsequently knows or is informed by the consumer that the information is correct.[71] The FCRA requires furnishers of information to have in place reasonable procedures to prevent information resulting from identity theft from being refurnished after notification from a consumer reporting agency that such information is being blocked because it resulted from identity theft.[72]

In addition to the reinvestigation requirements imposed on consumer reporting agencies, furnishers of information are also required to investigate disputed information. After a furnisher of information receives notice from a consumer reporting agency regarding disputed information in a consumer report, the person furnishing the information must investigate and report the results to the consumer reporting agency.[73] If the furnisher finds that the information is incomplete or inaccurate, the furnisher must report those results to all other consumer reporting agencies to which the incomplete or inaccurate information was furnished.[74] Furnishers of information must also notify consumer reporting agencies when an account is closed by the consumer, and when delinquent accounts are being placed for collection, charged to profit or loss, or subjected to any other similar action.[75]

The FCRA also allows consumers to dispute the accuracy of information directly with the furnisher. Furnishers must investigate the disputed information and report the results to the consumer within a specified period of time.[76] If the information is found to be inaccurate, the furnisher must notify each consumer reporting agency to which the information was originally furnished and provide the correct information.[77]

Requirements for Users of Consumer Reports

As noted above, consumer credit reports can be used only for the purposes specified in the Fair Credit Reporting Act. Despite these limitations, users of consumer credit reports vary widely. The most common users of consumer reports are credit grantors, such as credit card companies. Other common users include insurers, employers, collection agencies, and government agencies.[78] The FCRA imposes specific requirements on persons who use the information contained in consumer reports.

Users of consumer reports must follow the requirements set forth in the Fair Credit Reporting Act if they take any adverse action with respect to any consumer that is based in whole or in part on any information contained in the consumer's report.[79] If such action is taken, the user must provide the consumer with oral, written, or electronic notice of the adverse action.[80] The notice must include the name, address, and telephone number of the consumer reporting agency that furnished the report to the user; and a statement that the consumer reporting agency did not take the adverse action and is unable to provide the consumer with specific reasons why the adverse action was taken.[81] The consumer must also be notified of his or her right to obtain a free copy of the consumer report from the consumer reporting agency that furnished the report and of the consumer's right to dispute the accuracy or completeness of that report.[82] The consumer must also be given written or electronic disclosure of a credit score used in any adverse action based in whole or in part on any information in the consumer report, including the range of credit scores, the factors adversely affecting the score, the date the score was created, and the provider of the credit score.[83]

A notice must also be provided by users who grant, extend, or otherwise provide credit on material terms that are materially less favorable than the most favorable terms available to a substantial proportion of consumers from or through that user.[84] The notice must inform the consumer that the terms offered to the consumer were set based on information from a consumer report; identify the consumer reporting agency that furnished the report; inform the consumer that he or she may obtain a free copy of the consumer report from that agency; provide the contact information specified by the agency for obtaining such reports; and provide the credit score used in deciding the credit terms, the range of credit scores, the factors adversely affecting the score, the date the score was created, and the provider of the credit score.[85]

The FCRA also imposes duties on users of consumer reports when reports are used in connection with a credit or insurance transaction not initiated by the consumer. Written solicitations made to consumers regarding credit or insurance transactions not initiated by the consumer must include a "clear and conspicuous statement" that information from the consumer's credit report was used in connection with the transaction; the consumer received the offer for credit or insurance because he or she satisfied specified criteria; and the credit or insurance may not be extended if, after the consumer responds to the offer, the consumer does not meet additional criteria used to determine creditworthiness or insurability.[86] The statement must also inform the consumer of his/her right to prohibit information contained in his/her file from being used in connection with any transaction he/she did not initiate and how he/she may exercise this right.[87]

IDENTITY THEFT PROVISIONS

The FCRA includes a number of provisions aimed at preventing identity theft and assisting victims of identity theft.[88] These provisions mirror laws passed by state legislatures and create a national standard for addressing consumer concerns with regard to identity theft and other types of fraud.[89] They impose responsibilities on consumer reporting agencies, furnishers of information, and users of consumer credit reports, and provide consumers with rights for protecting the information in their files and insuring that the information contained in them is accurate.

Credit card issuers are required to follow certain procedures when they receive a request for an additional or replacement card within a short period of time following notification of a change of address for the same account.[90] In a further effort to prevent identity theft, credit card account numbers must be truncated on electronically printed receipts,[91] and, upon request, social security numbers must be truncated on credit reports provided to a consumer.[92] Because hundreds of apparently frivolous lawsuits were being brought for willful noncompliance where the expiration date of a credit card was on a receipt although the number was truncated and there was no allegation of injury to consumers, a 2008 amendment to the FCRA clarified that the mere printing of the expiration date did not constitute willful noncompliance if the receipt otherwise complied with the FCRA.[93]

Consumers who have been victims of identity theft, or expect that they may become victims, can have fraud alerts placed in their files.[94] A consumer may request a fraud alert from one consumer reporting agency and that agency is required to notify the other nationwide consumer reporting agencies of the alert.[95] In general, fraud alerts are to be maintained in the file for 90 days, but a consumer may request an extended alert which is maintained for up to seven years. The fraud alert becomes a part of the consumer's credit file and is thus passed along to all users of the report. The alert must also be included with any credit score generated using the consumer's file.[96]

In addition to the fraud alert, victims of identity theft may have information resulting from the crime blocked from their credit reports.[97] After receiving proof of the consumer's identity, a copy of an identity theft report, the identification of the alleged fraudulent information, and a statement by the consumer that this particular information does not relate to any transaction he/she conducted, a consumer reporting agency must block this particular information from being reported and must notify the furnisher of the information in question that it may be the result of identity theft. Requests to block information must also be referred to other consumer reporting agencies.[98]

Victims of identity theft may request information about the alleged crime. A business entity is required, upon request and subject to verification of the victim's identity, to provide copies of application and business transaction records evidencing any transaction alleged to be a result of identity theft to the victim without charge or to any law enforcement agency investigating the theft and authorized by the victim to receive the records in question.[99]

Pursuant to FACT Act amendments in 2003,[100] the federal agencies regulating the financial services industry promulgated guidelines and regulations, known as the Red Flags Rule, requiring financial institutions and creditors to establish reasonable policies and procedures to prevent identity theft.[101] The Red Flags Rule had an effective date of January 1, 2008, and a mandatory compliance date of November 1, 2008, but the mandatory compliance date was delayed several times due in part to controversy over the scope of entities covered by the rule as creditors.[102] The final mandatory compliance date was December 31, 2010, permitting time for Congress to enact the Red Flag Program Clarification Act of 2010,[103] clarifying that creditors covered by the rule do not include businesses that advance funds for expenses incidental to the services they offer, such as lawyers, doctors, dentists, etc. Creditors subject to the rule are entities that "regularly and in the ordinary course of business" obtain credit reports in connection with credit transactions, furnish information to consumer reporting agencies in connection with credit transactions, and extend credit based on an obligation to repay.

End Notes

[1] P.L. 91-508, Title VI, §601, 84 Stat. 1128 (1970), codified as amended at 15 U.S.C. §§1681–1681x.

[2] 15 U.S.C. §1681(b).

[3] P.L. 108-159, 117 Stat. 1952. These provisions are discussed in detail *infra* at Identity Theft Provisions. More information on these provisions and other issues related to identity theft can be found in CRS Report R40599, *Identity Theft: Trends and Issues*, by Kristin M. Finklea; CRS Report RL31919, *Federal Laws Related to Identity Theft*, by Gina Stevens. For information on data security generally and related legislative proposals, see CRS Report RL34120,*Federal Information Security and Data Breach Notification Laws*, by Gina Stevens, and CRS Report RL33273, *Data Security: Federal Legislative Approaches*, by Gina Stevens.

[4] P.L. 111-24, 123 Stat. 1734 (2009).

[5] P.L. 111-203, Title X, §§1001–1100H, 124 Stat. 1376–2113 (2010).

[6] P.L. 111-203, 124 Stat. 1376 (2010).

[7] *Id.*, §§1024-1027, 1029, and 1061 provide for the certain functions of the CFPB and the transfer of functions from the other federal financial services agencies and the Federal Trade Commission to the CFPB. The changes to administrative enforcement authority for the FCRA made by §1088 of the Dodd-Frank Act are codified at 15 U.S.C.§1681s. The Dodd-Frank Act did not transfer to the Bureau the rulemaking authority for the Red Flag guidelines and regulations pursuant to 15 U.S.C. §1681m(e) and for the disposal of records pursuant to 15 U.S.C. §1681w. Also, the Federal Trade Commission retained rulemaking authority over auto dealers pursuant to §1029 of the Dodd-Frank Act. Pursuant to §1024(c)(3) of the Dodd-Frank Act, the CFPB and the FTC recently concluded a Memorandum of Understanding to establish a framework for coordinating enforcement and regulatory efforts, available at http://www.ftc.gov/os/2012/01/120123ftc-cfpb-mou.pdf, press release available at http://www.ftc.gov/opa/2012/01/ftccfpb.shtm. Regulation V, the Fair Credit Reporting regulations, are now at 12 C.F.R. part 1022, part of the CFPB regulations, promulgated at 76 Fed. Reg. 79308 (2011).
For more information on the transfer of functions to the CFPB, see CFPB, *Streamlining Inherited Regulations*, 76 Fed. Reg. 75825 (2011); CFPB, *Identification of Enforceable Rules and Orders*, 76 Fed. Reg. 43569 (2011); CFPB, *Agencies Issue Statement to Clarify Supervisory and Enforcement Responsibilities For Federal Consumer Financial Laws,* at http://www.consumerfinance.gov/pressrelease/agencies-issue-statement-to-clarify-supervisory-and-enforcement-responsibilities-for-federal-consumer-financial-laws; and CRS Report R41338, *The Dodd-Frank Wall Street Reform and Consumer Protection Act: Title X, The Consumer Financial Protection Bureau*, by David H. Carpenter. The Federal Trade Commission issued a report on its experiences administering and enforcing the FCRA, *Forty Years of Experience with the Fair Credit Reporting Act: An FTC Staff Report and Summary of Interpretations* (2011), while simultaneously rescinding its official staff interpretations in the Code of Federal Regulations, in anticipation of the transfer of certain regulatory functions to the CFPB, report and rescission available at http://www.ftc.gov/opa/ 2011/07/fcra.shtm.

[8] 15 U.S.C. §1681a(f). The FCRA defines a consumer reporting agency as "any person which, for monetary fees, dues, or on a cooperative nonprofit basis, regularly engages in whole or in part in the practice of assembling or evaluating consumer credit information or other information on consumers for the purpose of furnishing consumer reports to third parties, and which uses any means or facility of interstate commerce for the purpose of preparing or furnishing consumer reports."

[9] Frederick H. Miller, et al., *Consumer Law: Cases, Problems, and Materials*, p. 296.

[10] 15 U.S.C. §1681a(d)(1).

[11] 15 U.S.C. §1681a(d)(2)(A). "The first type of excluded information [among persons related by common ownership] is information based on first hand experience of one of the affiliates. The second type [among persons affiliated by corporate control] is any other information shared by affiliates, provided that the sharing

is disclosed to the consumer and the consumer is given the opportunity to direct that the information not be shared among related entities." Debtor-Creditor Law §16.02[3] (Matthew Bender & Co. 2011).

[12] 15 U.S.C. §1681a(d)(2)(B).

[13] Miller, *supra* note 9.

[14] Experian does not maintain information concerning criminal records; see http://www.experian. com/credit-education/credit-report-faqs.html.

[15] Miller, *supra* note 9.

[16] 15 U.S.C. §1681c(a). The seven- and ten-year reporting limitations do not apply to transactions involving, or which may be expected to involve, an amount greater than $150,000; the underwriting of life insurance involving, or which may involve, an amount of $150,000 or more; or to the employment of any individual at an annual salary which equals, or may be expected to equal, more than $75,000. 15 U.S.C. 1681c(b). Information regarding certain types of student loans may be reported until the loan is paid in full. 20 U.S.C. §1087cc(c)(3).

[17] 15 U.S.C. §1681c(d).

[18] *Id.*

[19] 15 U.S.C. §1681s-1.

[20] FACT Act of 2003, P.L. 108-159, §§411 and 412, 117 Stat. 1999-2003, amending 15 U.S.C. §§1681a(d)(3) and (i), 1681b(g), 1681c(a)(6), and 1681s-2(a)(9).

[21] 15 U.S.C. §1681b.

[22] 15 U.S.C. §1681b(a)(3)(A).

[23] 15 U.S.C. §1681b(a)(3)(F).

[24] 15 U.S.C. §1681b(a)(3)(G).

[25] 15 U.S.C. §1681b(a)(3)(C). For more information on the use of consumer credit information by the insurance industry, see CRS Report RS21341, *Credit Scores: Credit-Based Insurance Scores*, by Baird Webel.

[26] 15 U.S.C. §1681b(a).

[27] 15 U.S.C. 1681b(c)(1). This provision allows "prescreening" by a consumer reporting agency. "Prescreening" is the process "whereby a consumer reporting agency compiles or edits a list of consumers who meet specific criteria and provides this list to the client or third party on behalf of the client for use in soliciting these consumers for the client's products or services." Prescreening is permissible under the Fair Credit Reporting Act if the client agrees in advance that each consumer on the list will receive an offer of credit. See CCH Consumer Credit Guide, ¶ 25,050.

[28] 15 U.S.C. §1681b(e). Pursuant to the 2003 amendment to the FCRA, persons who use consumer reports for prescreening purposes must provide the consumer with a statement including the address and telephone number where the consumer may request to be excluded from prescreened lists. The consumer's election to be excluded from such lists is effective for five years. FACT Act of 2003, P.L. 108-159, §213, 117 Stat. 1978, codified as amended at 15 U.S.C. §1681m(d)(2).

[29] 15 U.S.C. §1681b(c)(2).

[30] 15 U.S.C. §1681b(c)(1)(B)(iv); subparagraph (iv) was added by the Credit CARD Act of 2009, P.L. 111-24, §302, 123 Stat. 1748.

[31] 15 U.S.C. §1681b(a)(3)(D).

[32] 15 U.S.C. §1681b(a)(1).

[33] 15 U.S.C. §1681b(a)(4). In order for reports to be released for this purpose, the paternity of the consumer must have been established or acknowledged by the consumer; the consumer must be given notice of the request; and the report must be kept confidential and used only for this purpose. Id.

[34] 15 U.S.C. §1681b(a)(3)(B). Under the FCRA, "employment purposes" mean "a report used for the purpose of evaluating a consumer for employment, promotion, reassignment or retention as an employee." 15 U.S.C. §1681a(h).

[35] 15 U.S.C. §1681b(b)(1).

[36] 15 U.S.C. §1681b(b)(2).

[37] 15 U.S.C. §1681b(b)(3).

[38] 15 U.S.C. §1681b(a)(6).

[39] 15 U.S.C. §1681g(a). Credit scores must be made available to consumers pursuant to an amendment in the FACT Act of 2003, P.L. 108-159, §212(a), (b), 117 Stat. 1973, codified as amended at 15 U.S.C. §1681g(a), (f). Prior to this amendment, consumer reporting agencies were under no obligation to release credit scores. For a discussion of how credit scores are used, see CRS Report RS21298, *Credit Scores: Development, Use, and Policy Issues*, by Pauline Smale.

[40] 15 U.S.C. §1681j(a), as amended by the FACT Act of 2003, P.L. 108-159, §211(a), 117 Stat. 1968. For more information on free credit reports, see CRS Report RL32008, *A Consumer's Access to a Free Credit Report: A Legal and Economic Analysis*, by Loretta Nott and Angie A. Welborn. The free credit report is not required to include the consumer's credit score. The credit score must be disclosed upon request, but a reasonable fee may be imposed for the disclosure. P.L. 108-159, §212(b), 117 Stat. 1973-1975, codified as amended at 15 U.S.C. §1681g(f)(8).

[41] Section 205 of the Credit CARD Act of 2009, *supra* note 4, codified as amended at 15 U.S.C. §1681j(g); this requirement responded to consumer confusion about whether certain free credit reports, offered by consumer reporting agencies in conjunction with the sale of other credit information or monitoring services, were the statutorily required free annual reports. See also the related rule at 12 C.F.R. §1022.138.
[42] See 15 U.S.C. §1681j(b), (c), and (d).
[43] 15 U.S.C. §1681j(f) and Federal Trade Commission, *Charges for Certain Disclosures*, 75 Fed. Reg. 80817 (2010)(notice of the annual adjustment, based on the Consumer Price Index, of the maximum reasonable fee that can be charged for disclosures under 15 U.S.C. §1681g, other than the free annual credit report and notices and disclosures required by the FCRA). Section 1088 of the Dodd-Frank Act, *supra* note 6, transferred the responsibility for the annual fee adjustment to the CFPB (see 15 U.S.C. §1681j(f)(2)), but it has not yet adjusted the fee for 2012.
[44] *Id.* and 15 U.S.C. §1681g(f)(8). Certain mortgage lenders must disclose to a consumer the credit score used for the purpose of the loan; 15 U.S.C. §1681g(g). Also, as discussed *infra* notes 83 and 85, when users of credit reports take an adverse action or offer credit on terms less favorable than usual, they must disclose the credit score on which such actions were based.
[45] 15 U.S.C. §1681g(f)(1).
[46] Section 1078 of the Dodd-Frank Act, *supra* note 6, required the study and report by the Bureau, *Report to Congress: The impact of differences between consumer- and creditor-purchased credit scores*, available at http://www.consumerfinance.gov/report/the-impact-of-differences-between-consumer-and-creditor-purchased-credit-scores.
[47] 15 U.S.C. §1681g(a)(3).
[48] 15 U.S.C. §1681g(a)(4), (5).
[49] 15 U.S.C. §1681i.
[50] 15 U.S.C. §1681i(a)(1)(A).
[51] 15 U.S.C. §1681i(a)(2)(A).
[52] 15 U.S.C. §1681i(a)(4).
[53] 15 U.S.C. §1681i(a)(3)(A).
[54] 15 U.S.C. §1681i(a)(3)(B).
[55] 15 U.S.C. §1681i(a)(5).
[56] 15 U.S.C. §1681i(a)(6)(A).
[57] 15 U.S.C. §1681i(a)(6)(B).
[58] 15 U.S.C. §1681i(a)(1)(A).
[59] 15 U.S.C. §1681c(h).
[60] 15 U.S.C. §1681e(a)
[61] *Id.*
[62] 15 U.S.C. §1681e(d). For discussions of the responsibilities of furnishers of information and users of credit reports, see relevant sections following in this report.
[63] 15 U.S.C. §1681d(a), (b).
[64] 15 U.S.C. §1681d(d).
[65] 15 U.S.C. §1681k.
[66] 15 U.S.C. §1681k(a)(1), (2).
[67] Miller, *supra* note 9, p. 298.
[68] 15 U.S.C. §1681s–2(a)(7).
[69] 15 U.S.C. §1681s–2(a)(1).
[70] *Id.*
[71] 15 U.S.C. §1681s–2(a)(6).
[72] *Id.*
[73] 15 U.S.C. §1681s-2(b)(1).
[74] *Id.*
[75] 15 U.S.C. §1681s-2(a)(4), (5).
[76] 15 U.S.C. §1681s-2(a)(8(E).
[77] *Id.*
[78] For descriptions of how each uses the information contained in consumer reports, see Miller, *supra* note 9, pp. 300–301.
[79] In general, an adverse action is any negative action, such as a denial or termination, taken with respect to the consumer's application or continued coverage for credit, insurance, or employment. The FCRA provides a detailed definition of adverse action at 15 U.S.C. §1681a(k).
[80] 15 U.S.C. §1681m(a)(1).
[81] 15 U.S.C. §1681m(a)(3). Particular requirements relate to adverse actions based on information received from third parties other than consumer reporting agencies. These requirements generally impose a duty on the user to disclose the reasons for the adverse action and the nature of the information received from the third party. See 15 U.S.C. 1681m(b).

[82] 15 U.S.C. §1681m(a)(4).
[83] 15 U.S.C. §1681m(a)(2); the requirement for credit score disclosure was added by §1100F of the Dodd-Frank Act, *supra* notes 5 and 6.
[84] 15 U.S.C. §1681m(h)(1).
[85] 15 U.S.C. §1681m(h)(5). The subparagraph requiring credit score disclosure (15 U.S.C. §1681m(h)(5)(E)) was added by §1100F of the Dodd-Frank Act, *supra* notes 5 and 6.
[86] 15 U.S.C. §1681m(d)(1).
[87] Id. See also 15 U.S.C. §1681b(e).
[88] For more information on identity theft issues and the Red Flags Rule, discussed *infra*, see CRS Report R40599, *Identity Theft: Trends and Issues*, by Kristin M. Finklea.
[89] Generally, many of these federal provisions preempt similar state laws. For more information on the preemptive effects of the Fair Credit Reporting Act, see CRS Report RS21449, *Fair Credit Reporting Act: Preemption of State Law*, by Margaret Mikyung Lee.
[90] 15 U.S.C. §1681m(e)(1)(C). These are part of the Red Flag guidelines and rules designed to prevent identity theft.
[91] 15 U.S.C. §1681c(g).
[92] 15 U.S.C. §1681g(a)(1)(A).
[93] Credit and Debit Card Receipt Clarification Act, P.L. 110-241, §3(a), 122 Stat. 1565 (2008) (codified at 15 U.S.C. 1681n(d)). The U.S. Supreme Court recently granted certiorari to United States v. Bornes, No. 11-192 (January 13, 2012), http://www.supremecourt.gov/ orders/courtorders%5C011312zr.pdf, to decide whether the Little Tucker Act, 28 U.S.C. 1346(a)(2), waives the sovereign immunity of the United States with respect to damages actions for violations of the FCRA. The federal government allegedly violated the FCRA prohibition against printing the expiration date of a consumer's credit card on a receipt provided at the point of sale or transaction. The plaintiff/respondent had received electronic internet and email receipts displaying the expiration date of the personal credit card he used to pay government filing fees for a client's lawsuit.
[94] 15 U.S.C. §1681c-1.
[95] 15 U.S.C. §§1681c-1(a)(1)(B) and 1681s(f)(1).
[96] 15 U.S.C. §1681c-1(a)(1)(A).
[97] 15 U.S.C. §1681c-2.
[98] 15 U.S.C. §1681s(f)(1).
[99] 15 U.S.C. §1681g(e).
[100] Section 114 of the FACT Act, *supra* note 3, made amendments codified at 15 U.S.C. §1681m(e).
[101] 72 Fed. Reg. 63718 (2007). The Dodd-Frank Act did not transfer authority to prescribe regulations with regard to the Red Flags requirements to the CFPB; such authority is retained by the federal banking agencies as well as the National Credit Union Administration, the Federal Trade Commission, the Commodity Futures Trading Commission, and the Securities and Exchange Commission.
[102] See 156 Cong. Rec. H8059-60 (daily ed. December 7, 2010); 156 Cong. Rec. S8288-89 (daily ed. November 30, 2010); Federal Trade Commission, *FTC Extends Enforcement Deadline for Identity Theft Red Flags Rule* (2010), at http://www.ftc.gov/opa/2010/05/redflags.shtm; Federal Trade Commission, *FTC Extends Enforcement Deadline for Identity Theft Red Flags Rule* (2009), at http://www.ftc.gov/opa/2009/10 /redflags.shtm.
[103] P.L. 111-319, 124 Stat. 3457 (2010), codified at 15 U.S.C. §1681m(e)(4).

In: A Selection of Federal Acts
Editors: P. Brown and K. M. Mitchell
ISBN: 978-1-62417-047-8

Chapter 7

THE COMBATING AUTISM ACT: OVERVIEW AND FUNDING*

Amalia K. Corby-Edwards

SUMMARY

Autism spectrum disorder (ASD) and autism are general terms for a group of developmental disabilities that cause impairments in social skills and communication, and are often characterized by certain atypical behaviors. The federal government has a role in the financing (through Medicaid and State Children's Health Insurance Programs) and delivery (through funding of developmental disabilities programming in schools, Title V Maternal and Child Health funding, and other sources) of treatment for ASD. The number of autism cases and their appropriate diagnosis and treatment affect federal and state expenditures. As such, Congress has shown interest in financing research on ASD prevalence, causes, and optimal treatment for individuals with ASD.

On September 26, 2011, the 112th Congress passed the Combating Autism Reauthorization Act (CARA, P.L. 112-32), which reauthorized funding for autism research authorized under the Combating Autism Act of 2006 (CAA, P.L. 109-416). The CAA was enacted to address public and congressional concern with growing rates of autism; to increase existing autism research funding authorizations; and to stimulate state-level coordination of health, education, and disability programs. The CAA authorizes funding for ASD surveillance, research, and education at the Department of Health and Human Services (HHS), at the Centers for Disease Control and Prevention (CDC), the Health Resources and Services Administration (HRSA), and the National Institutes of Health (NIH).

The CAA authorizes funding for the CDC to administer a grant program for states and other entities to conduct surveillance on ASD and developmental disabilities, and to establish regional centers of excellence in ASD epidemiology. These funds have been used to develop

* This is an edited, reformatted and augmented version of the Congressional Research Service Publication, CRS Report for Congress R42369, dated February 22, 2012.

a multi-state network for the collection, analysis, and reporting multiple years of state and local data on ASD prevalence to the CDC.

The CAA authorizes funding for the HRSA to support autism education, intervention, and early detection. These activities are designed to increase ASD awareness, to reduce barriers to screening and diagnosis, and to promote evidence-based interventions.

NIH is authorized under the CAA to conduct and fund basic scientific research on autism and other developmental disabilities. In addition, NIH is tasked with the coordination of all research, screening, intervention, and education efforts through the Interagency Autism Coordinating Committee.

The Combating Autism Act authorized appropriations for these activities from FY2007 through FY2011. The Combating Autism Reauthorization Act of 2011 extends authorizations of appropriations at FY2011 levels for FY2012 through FY2014. This report presents an overview of the CAA and CARA, HHS funding and activities under the CAA and CARA for FY2007 through FY2012 and the FY2013 President's budget request, other federal activities related to autism, and selected issues for Congress.

INTRODUCTION

Autism spectrum disorder (ASD) and autism are general terms for a group of developmental disabilities that cause impairments in social skills and communication, and are often characterized by certain atypical behaviors.[1] Autism spectrum disorders include autistic disorder, Asperger disorder, and pervasive developmental disorder-not otherwise specified.[2] These conditions have overlapping symptoms that differ in terms of onset, severity, and nature. ASDs are referred to as "spectrum disorders" because they encompass a range of behaviorally defined conditions. The complex nature of these conditions creates diagnostic challenges; there are no consistent genetic[3] or biologic markers[4] to facilitate diagnosis.

Autism has been linked to abnormal biology and chemistry in the brain; however, the cause or causes of these abnormalities remain unknown. According to the Centers for Disease Control and Prevention (CDC), as many as 1 in 110 eight-year-olds currently have an autism spectrum disorder, with boys affected more than four times as often as girls.[5] This represents an increase from past autism rates, and has generated public interest in the causes of autism. The increased prevalence has also focused attention on the demand for effective treatment and support services for individuals with these conditions. In addition, some have questioned whether the current rates of ASD reflect increased awareness and diagnosis, a true increase in the incidence of ASD, or a combination of these factors.[6]

For many, autism is a lifelong illness whose symptoms often manifest before age three. Autistic children and adults generally display a unique set of symptoms, but common traits associated with autism include difficulty talking, repeated behaviors, and aversion to loud noises. ASD impedes an individual's communication skills, making it difficult to learn or to integrate socially. There are no medical treatments for autism itself; however, medications and behavioral therapy can help mitigate certain symptoms. While there is currently no known cause or cure for autism, research to determine the cause or causes may identify risk factors, some of which may be modifiable. Other studies may determine optimal methods of screening and diagnosis, identify the most effective mental and behavioral health therapies, and find the best medical treatments for individuals with ASD.

The federal government has a role in the financing (through Medicaid and State Children's Health Insurance Programs) and delivery (through funding of developmental disabilities programming in schools, Title V Maternal and Child Health funding, and other sources) of treatment for ASD.[7]

The number of cases and their appropriate diagnosis and treatment affect federal and state expenditures.[8] As such, Congress has shown interest in financing research on ASD prevalence, causes, and optimal treatment for individuals with ASD. This interest in ASD surveillance and research has been demonstrated through inclusion of autism research provisions in the Children's Health Act (CHA, P.L. 106-310) in 2000, enactment of the Combating Autism Act in 2006 (CAA, P.L. 109-416), and the recent enactment of the Combating Autism Reauthorization Act (CARA, P.L. 112-32) by the 112th Congress.

This report presents an overview of the CAA and CARA, Department of Health and Human Services (HHS) funding and activities under the CAA and CARA, other federal activities related to autism, and selected issues for Congress.

THE COMBATING AUTISM ACT (CAA)

The precursor to the CAA was the Children's Health Act of 2000 (CHA), which addressed a number of child health issues. Title I of the CHA authorized the Secretary of HHS (the Secretary) to conduct certain activities relevant to autism and developmental disabilities. It established funding for autism surveillance at the CDC and established the National Center on Birth Defects and Developmental Disabilities. Under the CHA, the National Institutes of Health (NIH) was authorized to expand and intensify its autism research efforts and to establish Centers of Excellence for autism research. The CHA also established an Autism Coordinating Committee to coordinate research within NIH, and authorized funds for HHS to establish and implement an information and education campaign for health care providers and the general public.

Enacted in 2006 and subsequently reauthorized by the Combating Autism Reauthorization Act of 2011, the CAA is intended to address growing concern about the increasing prevalence of autism spectrum disorders, and to stimulate research into possible autism causes and treatments. It authorized funding from FY2007 through FY2011 for autism research, screening, early intervention, and education. CARA reauthorized this funding through FY2014.

The CAA authorizes the Secretary to expand, intensify, and coordinate existing ASD research activities; to expand surveillance and epidemiological research; to increase awareness of ASD; and to provide access to screening and early intervention services. It authorizes expanded research activities at NIH, and created the Interagency Autism Coordinating Committee (IACC) to coordinate all federal autism research efforts (this expanded the mission of the Autism Coordinating Committee described above). At the CDC, the CAA authorizes surveillance and establishes ASD awareness programs. At the Health Resources and Services Administration (HRSA), the CAA authorizes expanded federal efforts in autism education, early detection, and intervention. The CAA also required a report to Congress on implementation and progress four years after enactment, which was provided to Congress on January 7, 2011.[9] CARA requires a report to Congress two years after enactment.

The following sections summarize the programs and funding authorized under the CAA and subsequently reauthorized by CARA.

Surveillance and Epidemiological Research

The CAA authorizes the CDC to award competitive grants for the collection, analysis, and reporting of state-level epidemiological data on ASD and other developmental disabilities. The CDC must establish guidelines for reporting these data, in collaboration with other public and private entities. The CDC is also required to coordinate the federal response to potential or alleged clusters of ASD or developmental disabilities (DD).

The CAA also requires the CDC to award grants or cooperative agreements for the establishment of regional centers of excellence in the epidemiology of ASD and other developmental disabilities. The purpose of the centers of excellence is to collect and analyze information on the number, incidence, correlates, and causes of ASD and other DD. The centers are required to collect and report data according to the guidelines established by CDC. In addition, centers are required to develop an area of special research expertise (such as genetics, epigenetics, or environmental epidemiology), and to identify suitable cases and controls for research into potential causes or risk factors for ASD.

Autism Education, Early Detection, and Intervention

The CAA authorizes the Secretary to provide grants for projects designed to (1) increase awareness of ASD; (2) reduce barriers to screening and diagnosis; (3) promote evidence-based interventions for individuals with ASD or other developmental disabilities; (4) train health care professionals to use valid, reliable screening tools; and (5) provide early intervention if needed. The Secretary must use an interdisciplinary approach that also focuses on specific issues for children who are not receiving early diagnosis and interventions. These activities are carried out through HRSA.

The Secretary must, subject to funding, provide information and education on ASD to increase public awareness of developmental milestones; promote research into the development and validation of reliable screening tools; promote early screening of high-risk individuals; increase the number of individuals who are able to diagnose or rule out ASD; increase the number of individuals who are able to provide evidence-based interventions; and promote the use of evidence-based interventions for high-risk individuals.

The Secretary must, subject to funding, collaborate with a number of federal programs for low-income individuals to provide culturally competent information regarding ASD and developmental disabilities, in collaboration with the Department of Education and the Department of Agriculture. These programs include Head Start; Early Start; Healthy Start; programs under the Child Care and Development Block Grant Act of 1990; Medicaid, including the Early and Periodic Screening, Diagnosis, and Treatment Program (EPSDT); the State Children's Health Insurance Plan (CHIP); the Maternal and Child Health Block Grant;

Individuals with Disabilities Education Act Parts B and C; and the Special Supplemental Nutrition Program for Women, Infants, and Children (WIC).

The CAA authorizes the Secretary to require states to designate a lead agency responsible for disseminating the information described above available to individuals in the state. This information may be provided through toll-free numbers, Internet websites, mailings, or other means, as determined by the governor of each state. In addition, the Secretary, through the states, must promote and assist the development and use of screening tools. The Secretaries of HHS and the Department of Education must provide for the collection, storage, coordination, and public availability of screening tools and educational materials. The CAA also authorizes the Secretary to fund grants to expand existing interdisciplinary training and leadership programs (authorized in Title V of the Social Security Act). The Secretary must also promote best practices in autism screening and diagnosis.

Centers of Excellence in Autism Research, and Research Coordination

The CAA authorizes the Secretary of HHS to expand, intensify, and coordinate ASD research activities at NIH, and to consolidate existing program activities if necessary. It directs NIH to investigate the cause, diagnosis, early detection, prevention, services, supports, intervention, and treatment of ASD.

The CAA also authorizes the Interagency Autism Coordinating Committee (IACC) at NIH to coordinate all ASD research, screening, intervention, and education efforts within HHS. Members of the IACC are appointed for a term of four years and may be reappointed once. Members must include representatives of the following: Administration for Children and Families (ACF), CDC, Centers for Medicare and Medicaid Services (CMS), HRSA, NIH, HHS Office on Disability, Substance Abuse and Mental Health Services Administration (SAMHSA), and the Department of Education. No fewer than six members, or one-third of the committee (whichever is greater) must be non-federal public members, including people with autism, parents of people with autism, and leaders of national autism organizations.

The IACC is required to meet at least twice per year in public session. It is responsible for formulating and annually updating the strategic plan for ASD research, and presenting those recommendations to the Secretary and to Congress. The IACC must also monitor all federal ASD activities, make recommendations to the Secretary and to NIH regarding changes to these activities, and make recommendations on public participation in decision making to the Secretary.

Combating Autism Reauthorization Act (CARA)

Funding for CAA programs was authorized through FY2011; the Combating Autism Reauthorization Act (CARA), which extends funding at current levels through FY2014, was signed into law on September 30, 2011. CARA authorizes appropriations through FY2014 for CAA activities, but does not include funding or authorizations for an expansion of research and/or other services as some autism advocates had requested.[10]

FUNDING

Table 1 presents authorizations of appropriations for the provisions of the CAA and CARA. The table includes authorizations of appropriations from FY2007 through FY2014. **Table 2** provides details of funding for CAA activities, as reported by HHS.[11] The table also includes proposed funding levels in the President's FY2013 budget for HRSA and CDC.[12] NIH does not have an autism-specific budget line. For CAA activities, FY2011 funding totaled $229 million. Funding for FY2012 activities is estimated at $232 million, a $3 million increase.

CAA authorizations and funding are presented in two separate tables because funding for autism-related activities is not specifically limited to the authorizations shown in **Table 1**, and may be more or less in a given year. In addition, agencies typically do not have disease-specific budget lines. Autism-related activities may also be funded at CDC and NIH through general authorizations. The information on agency level spending in **Table 2** is compiled from the Moyer Report, a report published by the HHS Office of the Assistant Secretary for Financial Resources. The Moyer Report presents information as reported by the agencies on spending for selected diseases and conditions, including autism.

Table 1.AuthorizationsofAppropriations in the Combating Autism Act of 2006 and the Combating Autism Reauthorization Act of 2011
Dollars in millions

	FY2007	FY2008	FY2009	FY2010	FY2011	FY2012	FY2013	FY2014
Developmental Disabilities and Surveillance Program (PHSA 399AA)	15.0	16.5	18.0	19.5	21.0	22.0	22.0	22.0
Autism Education, Early Detection, and Intervention (PHSA 399BB)	32.0	37.0	42.0	47.0	52.0	48.0	48.0	48.0
Interagency Autism Coordina-ting Committee, Autism Centers of Excellence (PHSA 399CC, 409C, and 404H)	100.0	114.5	129.0	143.5	158.0	161.0	161.0	161.0
Total	147.0	168.0	189.0	210.0	231.0	231.0	231.0	231.0

Source: For FY2007 through FY2011, CAA, P.L. 109-416; FY2012 through FYFY2014, CARA, P.L. 112-32.
Notes: Appropriations are authorized in Section 399EE of the PHSA.

Federally funded autism research not authorized under the CAA, including activities carried out by the Departments of Defense and Education, is discussed below in the section "Other Federal Activities Related to Autism Research."

Table 2. Funding for Activities Related to the Combating Autism Act Dollars in millions

	FY2007	FY2008	FY2009	FY2010	FY2011	FY2012	FY2013 Request
Centers for Disease Control and Prevention[a]	14.8	16.2	20.4	22.1	21.4	21.3	21.3
Health Resources and Services Administration[b]	0	36.4	42.0	47.9	47.9	47.1	47.1
National Institutes of Health[c]	126.8	118.1	254.2	159.6	159.6	163.0	N/A
Total	141.6	170.7	316.6	229.6	228.9	231.4	N/A`

Sources: Compiled by the Congressional Research Service from the FY2011 Moyer Material, Office of the Assistant Secretary for Financial Resources, HHS, February 2010; the FY2012 Moyer Material, Office of the Assistant Secretary for Financial Resources, HHS, March 2011, and the accompanying Conference Report, H.Rept. 112-331, to the FY2012 Consolidated Appropriations Act, P.L. 112-74.

a. For the FY2013 CDC budget request for autism activities, see http://www.cdc.gov/fmo/topic/Budget %20Information/appropriations_budget_form_pdf/FY2013_CDC_CJ_Final.pdf.

b. Prior to FY2008, HRSA autism activities were funded within the Special Projects of Regional and National Significance (SPRANS) set-aside of funds from the Maternal and Child Health Block Grant, and were not provided a separate line of funding. For the FY2013 HRSA budget request for autism activities, see http://www.hrsa.gov/about /budget/budget justification2013.pdf.

c. NIH funding for autism activities is authorized in PHSA Sections 399CC, 409C, and 404H. Autism does not have a specific budget line in the NIH budget; therefore, an autism specific request for FY2013 is unavailable. NIH autism funding for FY2008-2012 is based on NIH's Research, Condition, and Disease Categories (RCDC) tracking system. See http:// report.nih.gov/rcdc/. Funding for FY2007 was reported in the Moyer report, cited above.

AUTISM ACTIVITIES UNDER THE COMBATING AUTISM ACT

The activities carried out by CDC, HRSA, and NIH under the CAA are summarized below. As discussed previously, CDC focuses on surveillance and epidemiological research, NIH on basic science and research coordination, and HRSA on autism education, detection, and early intervention. For further detail on agencies' autism-related activities and publications, refer to the IACC's Report to Congress on Activities Related to Autism Spectrum Disorder and Other Developmental Disabilities Under the Combating Autism Act of 2006.[13]

Centers for Disease Control and Prevention (CDC)

Under the Combating Autism Act, the CDC is responsible for ASD and developmental disabilities surveillance and epidemiological research. Under the CHA and CAA, CDC formed the National Center on Birth Defects and Developmental Disabilities, the Autism and Developmental Disabilities Monitoring Network (ADDM), and the Centers for Autism and

Developmental Disabilities Research and Epidemiology (CADDRE), an ASD education campaign for caregivers and health professionals, and has collaborated on the International Autism Epidemiology Network (IAEN).[14] CDC also coordinates with other agencies, including HRSA and the Department of the Army, on other epidemiologic ASD research.

The National Center on Birth Defects and Developmental Disabilities established the ADDM network for the collection, analysis, and reporting of state-level epidemiological data on ASD and other developmental disabilities. ADDM monitors the prevalence of ASD among eight-year-olds at selected sites. The sites, which are regional or state-based public or private nonprofit entities, collect data on ASD prevalence using uniform surveillance methods, which include screening health and education records at multiple sources. Pilot surveillance sites were established with funding from the Children's Health Act; the program was expanded to additional sites under the CAA. ADDM has published two widely cited reports on ASD prevalence, one in 2007 and another in 2009.[15]

Under the CAA, CDC established a grant program for states or other entities (e.g., private nonprofits institutions, including institutions of higher education and hospitals) to establish regional centers of excellence in ASD. These centers, called the Centers for Autism Developmental Disabilities Research and Epidemiology (CADDRE), are part of a multi-site collaborative study examining the risk factors for ASD and other developmental disabilities.[16] The CADDRE network is currently working on the Study to Explore Early Development (SEED), which seeks to characterize ASD-related traits.[17]

CDC has partnered with the autism advocacy organization Autism Speaks to compile statistics on the global prevalence of autism. This partnership is called the International Autism Epidemiology Network.[18] The IAEN has produced a fact sheet that summarizes global autism prevalence from 2000 to 2008.[19]

In addition to research and surveillance activities, CDC has established a health communication campaign, entitled "Learn the Signs. Act Early," to improve early identification of children with ASD. The campaign is intended to educate parents, health care professionals, and early educators on the developmental milestones of early childhood.

Health Resources and Services Administration (HRSA)

Under the CAA, the Maternal and Child Health Bureau of HRSA must ensure that children with ASD are screened, diagnosed, and receive appropriate treatment. It is also tasked with addressing the shortage of trained professionals who provide autism treatment. HRSA received funding to address the five following objectives: (1) to increase awareness of ASD; (2) to reduce barriers to screening and diagnosis; (3) to promote evidence-based interventions for individuals with ASD or other developmental disabilities; (4) to train health care professionals to use valid, reliable screening tools; and (5) to provide early intervention if needed. To address these objectives, HRSA established or increased support for four programs: Leadership Education in Neurodevelopmental Disabilities (LEND), Developmental Behavioral Pediatric training programs, state implementation programs, and research programs.

HRSA has used CAA funding to support 43 LEND programs and 10 Developmental Behavioral Pediatric training programs by public and private nonprofit agencies in FY2011. The programs focus on the use of screening and diagnostic tools, and continuing education for health care providers that serve women, children, and families. These programs are designed to address the shortage of qualified professionals available to assess and assist autistic individuals.

The governor of each state must designate a lead agency to coordinate the HRSA-funded activities in that state. HRSA state-level grantees have used their funds to implement state autism plans, promote autism awareness, and develop model systems of services for children with ASD and developmental disabilities.[20] The primary focus of state implementation grants is to improve access to ASD and developmental disabilities screening and diagnostic services.

HRSA has established Autism Intervention Research programs, focusing on interventions to improve the health and well-being of children and adolescents with ASD and other developmental disabilities. These grants are provided to develop research networks among public and non-profit private institutions that focus on evidence-based research and the development of best practices in physical health, behavioral health, and the general health and well-being of individuals with ASD. Autism Intervention Research programs develop evidence-based guidelines and test and validate tools for measuring treatment outcomes.

National Institutes of Health (NIH)

CAA funding at NIH supports intramural and extramural research[21] at multiple institutes and centers. Under the CAA, NIH-funded researchers are tasked with studying potential risk factors and causes of autism, and to coordinate and consolidate its research on ASD and other developmental disabilities with other agencies.

NIH supports and coordinates the Autism Centers of Excellence Program, consisting of 11 research centers and networks that focus on identifying the causes of ASD and developing treatments. This includes research on biomarkers, genetic susceptibility, pharmacotherapy, language development, early intervention, and risk and protective factors. Another study, the Early Autism Risk Longitudinal Investigation, is looking into the interaction of environmental and genetic factors in ASD.[22]

NIH has sponsored a number of scientific workshops and symposia on ASD-related research. NIH also supports ASD research infrastructure, including biobanking (storage and archiving of biological samples) support, and the establishment of a common database (the National Database for Autism Research) to warehouse data collected in NIH-funded ASD studies.

The Children's Health Act required NIH to form a committee to coordinate research among the Institutes. The CAA broadened the mission of the coordinating committee to include other entities, both within and outside of HHS. The Interagency Autism Coordinating Committee (IACC), chaired by the director of the National Institute for Mental Health, is intended to facilitate the exchange of information on autism activities among the member agencies, and coordinates HHS autism-related programs and initiatives. The CAA required the IACC to present a strategic plan for ASD research, focusing on gaps, opportunities, and new knowledge in the autism research field. The strategic plan must be updated annually. The

2011 IACC Strategic Plan, released on February 28, 2011, includes a new focus on interventions for non-verbal people with ASD, health promotion efforts, and safety.[23]

Other Federal Activities Related to Autism Research

Federal funding for autism research is not limited to the Combating Autism Act, and is supported by the Department of Defense and the Department of Education in addition to HHS. Many of the stakeholders in the IACC do not receive funding under the CAA, but through their participation in autism research, these stakeholders have an interest and a guiding role. Following is a brief description of the autism-related research activities of the other federal participants in the IACC.

Other HHS Agencies

Certain HHS agencies employ general authorities to direct funds as needed to address public health concerns. For example, CDC may provide funding for autism programs under its general authorities to fund public health activities. Other relevant activities may focus broadly on developmental disabilities and receive funding under different authorities. Within HHS, ACF, CMS, the Office on Disability, and SAMHSA conduct activities that contribute to the growing body of research on ASD. The CAA does not authorize appropriations for these agencies.

ACF is the HHS agency responsible for federal programs that promote the economic and social well-being of families, including Head Start and Temporary Assistance for Needy Families. The agency participates in the IACC and provides services for children with ASD through funds authorized under the Developmental Disabilities Assistance and Bill of Rights Act of 2000 (P.L. 106-402). ACF funds state Developmental Disabilities Councils; Protection and Advocacy Agencies; Centers for Excellence in Developmental Disabilities Education, Research, and Services; and Projects of National Significance.[24]

CMS administers the Medicare, Medicaid, and State Children's Health Insurance Program. The agency participates in the IACC and supports autism education, early detection, and intervention services under the CAA through Medicaid's EPSDT program.[25] CMS has also conducted several studies on best practices in autism treatment, and is planning to issue a report of all state services available to individuals with ASD.

The HHS Office on Disability is primarily a policy office that supports coordination of resources across HHS and federal agencies to support individuals with disabilities, including those with autism.[26]

Finally, SAMHSA is the HHS agency responsible for supporting mental health and substance abuse programs.[27] The agency provides services to children with ASD through the Child Mental Health Initiative, a grant program mandated by Congress to serve children and youth with serious emotional disorders. This program provides grants for the development of coordinated support systems for children who are referred to the program.

Non-HHS Agencies

Federal autism activities are not limited to HHS agencies. Other federal entities use general authorities and previously established programs to address ASD. These entities include the Department of Defense (DOD) and the Department of Education.

The DOD does not receive funds under the CAA. However, it maintains a congressionally directed research program for ASD research, which was first funded in FY2007.[28] The program, which supports a range of scientific and clinical research on autism, received $41 million in total funding from FY2007 to FY2012.[29]

The Department of Education does not receive appropriations under the CAA.[30] However, it funds a number of research programs and collects data on individuals served by special education programs. Programs and services in the Department of Education are geared toward individuals with disabilities in general, and not autism or developmental disabilities specifically.

Coordination of Public and Private Autism Research Funding

In 2010, the IACC conducted an analysis of autism research spending by private and federal entities that are represented on the IACC.[31] Analysts found that private entities funded 24% of autism research in the United States in 2009, while the federal government funded 76%. The report also gauged relevance of the funded projects to the topic areas that were identified in the IACC strategic plan.[32] These objectives for 2009 were (1) When should I be concerned? (2) How can I understand what is happening? (3) What caused this to happen and can it be prevented? (4) Which treatments and interventions will help? (5) Where can I turn for services? (6) What does the future hold, particularly for adults? (7) What other infrastructure and surveillance needs must be met? The vast majority (95%) of ASD research aligned with research questions in the IACC strategic plan, with the largest proportion of research focused on the causes and prevention of ASD. Research on access to ASD-related services and lifespan issues received the least amount of funding.

Issues for Congress

During CAA enactment and reauthorization, several issues were highlighted, some of which are of general interest to Congress when deciding whether to support disease-specific legislation. Specifically, concerns were raised about barriers to data sharing and confidentiality across state and federal government entities; the coordination of surveillance and research, across both agencies and diseases; and the pros and cons of Congress directing funding to specific diseases (or groups of diseases). These concerns apply not only to autism research policy, but can be applied broadly to any disease-specific legislation, and the consequent policy decisions may affect access to care and treatment for individuals with autism.

Coordination of research and sharing of the resulting data is an ongoing interest of Congress. Researchers call for accurate case estimates in order to study common characteristics of autistic individuals and potential risk factors for autism. Federal and state-funded programs provided through health care providers and schools must provide certain services for individuals with ASD, and need accurate estimates to anticipate the need for those services. However, enumerating autism cases for researchers, health care providers, and schools has presented an ongoing challenge at the state, local, and federal levels.[33]

During the reauthorization process, some Members of Congress raised the concern that continuing to pass disease-specific legislation allows Congress to prioritize one disease (or group of diseases, in this case developmental disabilities) over another, and that priority-setting should be left to the agencies that perform the research. The issue of prioritizing one developmental disability over another has also been raised among researchers and families of children with developmental disabilities and other conditions. Advocates for CARA argued that allowing authorization of these programs to lapse would interrupt the progress made under the CAA.

Autism services research, such as the development and adoption of new screening tools and implementation of best practices in autism therapy, has effects on both health care cost and coverage decisions made at the government and individual level. The Patient Protection and Affordable Care Act (ACA, P.L. 111-148) includes provisions that may affect coverage for individuals with autism, including prohibitions on the cancellation of coverage by an insurer due to a preexisting condition, elimination of lifetime caps on insurance benefits and annual limits on coverage, and eligibility for tax subsidies to assist low- and middle-income individuals in the purchase of coverage from state health insurance exchanges. In addition, Medicaid eligibility will be broadened to include single adults. The long-range impact of health reform on individuals with ASD (specifically, the coverage of recommended treatments for ASD) is unknown.

APPENDIX. LIST OF ACRONYMS

ACA	Patient Protection and Affordable Care Act, P.L. 111-148
ACF	Administration for Children and Families
ADDM	Autism and Developmental Disabilities Monitoring Network
ASD	Autism Spectrum Disorder
CAA	Combating Autism Act
CADDRE	Centers for Autism and Developmental Disabilities Research and Epidemiology
CARA	Combating Autism Reauthorization Act
CDC	Centers for Disease Control and Prevention
CHA	Children's Health Act
CHIP	State Children's Health Insurance Program
CMS	Centers for Medicare and Medicaid Services
DD	Developmental Disabilities
DOD	Department of Defense
EPSDT	Early Periodic Screening, Diagnosis, and Treatment Program

HHS	Department of Health and Human Services
HRSA	Health Resources and Services Administration
IACC	Interagency Autism Coordinating Committee
IAEN	International Autism Epidemiology Network
LEND	Leadership Education in Neurodevelopmental Disabilities
NIH	National Institutes of Health
SAMHSA	Substance Abuse and Mental Health Services Administration
WIC	State Supplemental Nutrition Program for Women, Infants, and Children

End Notes

[1] National Institute of Mental Health, *What Are Autism Spectrum Disorders?* http://www.nimh.nih.gov/health/publications/autism/what-are-the-autism-spectrum-disorders.shtml.

[2] As defined by the *Diagnostic and Statistical Manual of Mental Disorders—Fourth Edition*.

[3] A genetic marker is a DNA sequence with a known physical location on a chromosome. Genetic markers can help link an inherited disease with the responsible gene.

[4] A biologic marker is a measurable and quantifiable parameter that serves as an indicator for health and physiology assessments, such as disease risk, environmental exposures, metabolic processes, etc. For example, the presence of antibodies in a blood sample may indicate an infection.

[5] Autism and Developmental Disabilities Monitoring Network, *Prevalence of Autism Spectrum Disorders*, United States, 2006, Atlanta, GA, December 18, 2009, http://www.cdc.gov/ mmwr/preview/mmwrhtml /ss5810a1.htm.

[6] National Institute of Mental Health, "Autism: The Whys of Increased Prevalence," press release, November 23, 2009, http://www.nimh.nih.gov/media/video/bearman.shtml.

[7] See CRS Report RL33202, *Medicaid: A Primer*, by Elicia J. Herz; CRS Report R40444, *State Children's Health Insurance Program (CHIP): A Brief Overview*, by Elicia J. Herz and Evelyne P. Baumrucker; and CRS Report R41833, *The Individuals with Disabilities Education Act (IDEA), Part B: Key Statutory and Regulatory Provisions*, by Ann Lordeman.

[8] Ganz M, "The Lifetime Distribution of the Incremental Societal Costs of Autism," *Arch Pediatr Adolesc Med*, vol. 161, no. 4 (April 2007), pp. 343-349.

[9] Office of Autism Research Coordination, National Institutes of Health, Report to Congress on Activities Related to Autism Spectrum Disorder and Other Developmental Disabilities Under the Combating Autism Act of 2006, U.S. Department of Health and Human Services, December 2010, http://iacc.hhs.gov/reports/reports-to-congress/FY2006-2009/index.shtml.

[10] A number of bills addressing expansion of research, global surveillance, and services for individuals with autism have been introduced in the 112th Congress.

[11] FY2012 Moyer Material, Office of the Assistant Secretary for Financial Resources, HHS, March 2011.

[12] Health Resources and Services Administration, *Justification of Estimates for Appropriations Committees*, Fiscal Year 2013, February 13, 2012, http://www.hrsa.gov/about/budget/ budgetjustification2013.pdf; and Centers for Disease Control and Prevention, *Justification of Estimates for Appropriations Committees*, Fiscal Year 2013, February 13, 2012, http:// www.cdc.gov/fmo/topic/Budget%20Information/appropriations_budget_form_pdf/FY2013_CDC_CJ_Final.pdf.

[13] Office of Autism Research Coordination, National Institutes of Health, *Report to Congress on Activities Related to Autism Spectrum Disorder and Other Developmental Disabilities Under the Combating Autism Act of 2006*, U.S. Department of Health and Human Services, December 2010, http://iacc.hhs.gov/reports/reports-to-congress/FY2006-2009/index.shtml.

[14] See http://www.autismepidemiology.net/.

[15] Prevalence of Autism Spectrum Disorders, Autism and Developmental Disabilities Monitoring Network, Six Sites, United States, 2000, Autism and Developmental Disabilities Monitoring Network, Atlanta, GA, February 9, 2007, http://www.cdc.gov/mmwr/preview/mmwrhtml/ ss5601a1.htm; Prevalence of Autism Spectrum Disorders, Autism and Developmental Disabilities Monitoring Network, United States, 2006, Autism and Developmental Disabilities Monitoring Network, Atlanta, GA, December 18, 2009, http://www.cdc.gov/ mmwr/preview/mmwrhtml/ss5810a1.htm.

[16] See http://www.cdc.gov/ncbddd/autism/caddre.html.

[17] See http://www.cdc.gov/ncbddd/autism/seed.html.

[18] Centers for Disease Control and Prevention and Autism Speaks, "International Autism Epidemiology Network," press release, 2009, http://www.autismepidemiology.net/.

[19] International Autism Epidemiology Network, "Autism Prevalence Around the World (2000-2008)," press release, 2009, http://www.worldautismawarenessday.org/atf/.

[20] See http://mchb.hrsa.gov/programs/autism/statedempolicy.html.

[21] *Extramural research* is performed by non-federal scientists using NIH grant or contract money; *intramural research* is performed by NIH scientists in the NIH laboratories and Clinical Center.

[22] See http://www.earlistudy.org/.

[23] Interagency Autism Coordinating Committee, *2011 Strategic Plan for Autism Spectrum Disorder Research*, January 2011, http://www.iacc.hhs.gov/strategic-plan/2011/IACC_ 2011_Strategic_Plan.pdf.

[24] See the Administration on Developmental Disabilities, ACF: http://www.acf.hhs.gov/ programs/add/.

[25] See CRS Report RL33202, *Medicaid: A Primer*, by Elicia J. Herz.

[26] See the Office on Disability: http://www.hhs.gov/od/index.html.

[27] See SAMHSA: http://www.samhsa.gov/.

[28] U.S. Congress, Senate Committee on Appropriations, *Department of Defense Appropriations Bill, 2007*, report to accompany H.R. 5631, 109th Cong., 2nd sess., July 25, 2006, 109-292 (Washington: GPO, 2006), p. 223.

[29] Congressionally Directed Medical Research Programs: http://cdmrp.army.mil/arp/default. shtml.

[30] However, individuals with autism are entitled to a free and appropriate public education under the Individuals with Disabilities Education Act (IDEA, P.L. 101-476, as amended), and public school systems provide services for children with autism from ages 6 to 21. Currently, 300,000 children with autism receive services under IDEA, and more than 6,000 individuals with autism participate in their vocational rehabilitation programs.

[31] Office of Autism Research Coordination, Interagency Autism Coordinating Committee, *2009 Autism Spectrum Disorder Research Portfolio Analysis Report*, June 2011, http://iacc.hhs. gov/portfolio-analysis/2009/ 2009_portfolio_analysis.pdf.

[32] Interagency Autism Coordinating Committee, *2011 Strategic Plan for Autism Spectrum Disorder Research*, January 2011, http://www.iacc.hhs.gov/strategic-plan/2011/IACC_ 2011_Strategic_Plan.pdf.

[33] U.S. Government Accountability Office, *Federal Autism Activities: Funding for Research has Increased, but Agencies Need to Resolve surveillance Challenges*, 06-700, July 2006, p. 12, http://www.gao.gov/new.items /d06700.pdf.

INDEX

E

F

G

H

I

Q

R

S

T

U

V

W

Y